Normalizing the Sports Journalism Niche

COMMUNICATION, SPORT, AND SOCIETY

Lawrence A. Wenner, Andrew C. Billings, and Marie Hardin
General Editor

Vol. 12

Nicholas R. Buzzelli

Normalizing the Sports Journalism Niche

Coexisting in a Modern News Landscape

PETER LANG

New York · Berlin · Bruxelles · Chennai · Lausanne · Oxford

Library of Congress Cataloging-in-Publication Data

Names: Buzzelli, Nicholas R., author.
Title: Normalizing the sports journalism niche : coexisting in a modern
news landscape / Nicholas R. Buzzelli.
Description: New York : Peter Lang, 2025. | Series: Communication, sport,
and society, 2576–7232 ; 12 | Includes bibliographical references and
index.
Identifiers: LCCN 2024036192 (print) | LCCN 2024036193 (ebook) |
ISBN 9781636678306 (paperback) | ISBN 9781636678290 (hardback) |
ISBN 9781636678368 (ebook) | ISBN 9781636678375 (epub)
Subjects: LCSH: Sports journalism. | Mass media and sports. | Digital
media.
Classification: LCC PN4784.S6 B89 2025 (print) | LCC PN4784.S6 (ebook) |
DDC 070.4/49796–dc23/eng/20240812
LC record available at https://lccn.loc.gov/2024036192
LC ebook record available at https://lccn.loc.gov/2024036193
DOI 10.3726/b22284

Bibliographic information published by the Deutsche Nationalbibliothek.
The German National Library lists this publication in the German
National Bibliography; detailed bibliographic data is available
on the Internet at http://dnb.d-nb.de.

Cover design by Peter Lang Group AG

ISSN 2576-7232 (print)
ISBN 9781636678306 (paperback)
ISBN 9781636678290 (hardback)
ISBN 9781636678368 (ebook)
ISBN 9781636678375 (epub)
DOI 10.3726/b22284

© 2025 Peter Lang Group AG, Lausanne
Published by Peter Lang Publishing Inc., New York, USA
info@peterlang.com—www.peterlang.com

Dedicated to my parents, grandparents, and Ashlyn and Emrie

CONTENTS

List of Abbreviations ix

Acknowledgments xi

Introduction: Assessing the Current State of Sports Journalism 1

Chapter One: Bypassing The Media Middleman: Team-Run Media's Challenge to Traditional Sports News 25

Chapter Two: Normalizing The New Wave: The Athletic's Impact on Sports Media Standards 49

Chapter Three: The One-Man Journalistic Band: Substack's Emergence from Startup to Sports Media Lifeline 83

Chapter Four: The Virtual Sports Bar: S.B. Nation Communities as Sports Media's Corporate Blogosphere 117

Chapter Five: Reimagining the Future of Digital Sports
                     Journalism   147

            Appendix A   171

            Appendix B   177

            Index   181

LIST OF ABBREVIATIONS

A.L.	American League
A.P.S.E.	Associated Press Sports Editors
CFB	College football
COVID-19	Coronavirus Disease 2019
D.O.I.	Diffusion of Innovation
L.S.U.	Louisiana State University
M.L.B	Major League Baseball
M.L.S.	Major League Soccer
N.A.B.J.	National Association of Black Journalists
N.B.A.	National Basketball Association
N.C.A.A.	National Collegiate Athletic Association
N.G.T.	Niche Gratification Theory
N.F.C.	National Football Conference
N.F.L.	National Football League
N.H.L.	National Hockey League
N.W.S.L.	National Women's Soccer League
SB Nation	Sports Blog Nation
S.E.C.	Southeastern Conference
S.I.D.	Sports Information Director

T.I.D.E.S. The Institute for Diversity and Ethics in Sport
U&G   Uses and Gratifications Theory
W.N.B.A. Women's National Basketball Association

ACKNOWLEDGMENTS

I extend gratitude to everyone whose support and feedback has been instrumental in the completion of this book. This would not have been made possible without their individual guidance. Foremost, my sincere thanks go to Dr. Andrew Billings, who has also been a source of inspiration—both personally and professionally. I consider myself fortunate to have studied under his guidance. In addition, I extend my appreciation to Dr. Reid Vance, Dr. Sean Sadri, Dr. Cory Armstrong, Dr. Patrick Ferrucci, Dr. John Vincent, and Dr. Marie Hardin, all of whom provided valuable mentorship during this process.

Special thanks also goes to my UA crew—Patrick, Edwin, Nate, Sean, Bumsoo, and J.C. Their feedback contributed to the overall quality of this book. Finally, my deepest appreciation goes to my family. Their support and encouragement has shaped the person I have become.

INTRODUCTION: ASSESSING THE CURRENT STATE OF SPORTS JOURNALISM

Tim Kawakami was the first to leave. Marcus Thompson II followed the next day. One week later, Anthony Slater made the jump. Three months after that, Andrew Baggarly was on board. In a short span, San Jose's *Mercury News* lost its core group of sportswriting talent to The Athletic, leaving Bud Geracie in a bind. Geracie, the executive sports editor of the Bay Area News Group, realized early on that Kawakami was his up-and-coming competitor's catalyst, the one chess piece needed to propel the battle forward for local sports readers. Once they had Kawakami, he reasoned that the rest of the dominoes would fall in place. When they finally did, he thought his newspaper could not compete with an upstart sports media conglomerate offering perceived job security, higher pay, and greater flexibility in terms of writing style (Gordon, 2018; Quinn, 2018).

It began in the fall of 2016 when Kawakami—a sports columnist who had written for *The Mercury News* since 2000—was approached by media entrepreneurs Alex Mather and Adam Hansmann to lead the Bay Area website of The Athletic, a new subscription-based sports news network (Lindsay, 2017). The Silicon Valley tech duo, who previously worked on the subscription-based fitness app Strava, knew their media market well (Peralta, 2019). After reading his columns on the Golden State Warriors' obscure rise from N.B.A.

Western Conference basement dweller to dominant basketball dynasty, it became apparent that Kawakami was critical to attracting Bay Area sports readers away from local newspapers and toward their innovative media brainchild. The bold move worked. After signing on as The Athletic's Bay Area vertical editor-in-chief, Kawakami assembled his all-star lineup of sportswriters, poaching first from his former employer and then from the other leading newspaper in town, the *San Francisco Chronicle* (Biasotti, 2017).

Geracie knew he could not keep his venerable sports staff forever because of the unstable nature of print journalism, one in which staff cuts have become increasingly common post-pandemic (Flynn & Fischer, 2023; Hare, 2020). It was only a matter of time, he thought, until his established sportswriters would jump from the instability of newspapers toward the perceived safety net that digital media was presumed to cast. However, this transitional period occurred at an accelerated pace. The veteran newspaperman who had been with *The Mercury News* since the late 1980s—beginning as an Oakland Athletics beat writer before transitioning to columnist and, later, sports editor—tried to combat The Athletic's advances whenever the poaching appeared imminent. However, there was no fight because of the substantial pay raises that Mather and Hansmann offered, sometimes double a reporter's original salary (Strauss, 2020). At that point, Geracie advised his reporters to leave if they had any doubt, citing the opportunity to make up to six figures in localized sports journalism as enough proof (Mullin, 2018).

The Athletic's structure is different than when the startup began poaching reporting talent from newspaper sports departments after its initial launch. In early 2022, the New York Times Company acquired The Athletic for a reported $550 million and began bundling The Athletic's content with its standard news subscription (Hirsch et al., 2022). Like most journalistic entities, The Athletic had suffered financial setbacks that led to layoffs (one of the most notable being Indianapolis Colts beat writer Bob Kravitz, who began an Indiana sports-based Substack newsletter after being furloughed; Kravitz, 2023). In July 2023, *The New York Times* announced that it was disbanding its sports department of 35 reporters and editors in favor of using content produced by The Athletic for its print and digital sports coverage (Robertson & Koblin, 2023). Additionally, The Athletic went through an editorial reorganization process during this time, in which its focus shifted to more on league-wide stories than local beat writing (Glasspiegel, 2023). Despite this, The Athletic has still made a significant ripple in sports journalism (as discussed in Chapter Two), notably in the form of increased competition with legacy media.

For some print sportswriters and editors, general disdain began when Mather, in October 2017, told *The New York Times* (the organization that he and his business partner would later sell to) that he aimed to let every local newspaper "continuously bleed" until his online-only entity was the last one standing (Draper, 2017, para. 2). After the comment went public, Dan Steinberg, the digital sports editor for *WashingtonPost.com*, tweeted a screenshot of the quote with the caption, "Rooting for The Athletic to succeed. But cmon with this [sic]" (Steinberg, 2017). Echoing Steinberg's sentiments, *Santa Rosa Press Democrat* sports columnist Phil Barber shared his thoughts by posting, "I love my local Athletic Bay Area colleagues and wish them well, but the predatory quotes in this article are gross" (Barber, 2017).

Despite its bold nature, Mather's 2017 quote may align with the perceived competitive nature of local sports journalism. Although it has been noted that The Athletic's conglomerate of hyperlocal city and sport-specific sites could serve as a "test for the digital-subscription model in journalism" (Boudway, 2019, para. 7), Gordon (2018) contends that The Athletic was cracking the "kneecaps [of its] competitors by [...] forcing them to fill the empty position, if they do at all, with a less experienced and less-well-sourced journalist" (para. 10).

Despite losing Kawakami, Thompson II, Slater, and Baggarly to The Athletic, Geracie's sports news operation weathered the storm. The cycle of sports reporters who write reputable content on deadline has continued, with a share of the Bay Area sports audience still sifting through the pages of *The Mercury News* each morning to read if the Giants won their previous game, who the 49ers' projected starting quarterback will be, and which local high school athletes have the potential to play Division I ball (of note, the paper's most recently reported print circulation figures, released March 2023, are 93,000 daily and 145,000 for the Sunday edition; "Print solutions: Daily newspapers," 2023).

It is important to note that this is not the first academic book focused on how digital technology affects the traditional practices of routinized sports journalism (see *Disrupting Sports Journalism*, McEnnis, 2022; *Sports Journalism: The State of Play*, Bradshaw & Minogue, 2020; and *The Digital World of Sport: The impact of emerging media on sports news, information, and journalism*, Duncan, 2020). However, unlike the aforementioned scholarly books, this work takes the position of competition versus coexistence in sports journalism through the lens of gatekeeping, niche gratification, diffusion of innovations, and boundary work to provide insight into the editorial perspectives of those producing written sports content. As will be detailed through qualitative in-depth interviews, writers in each specific subset of written sports journalism saw value in catering content to different audience perspectives. Thus, this book answers two central research questions: (1) How do writers from four digital-only sports news sites (e.g., team-run media, The Athletic, Substack, and S.B. Nation blogs) position themselves within the current context of sports journalism competition?; (2) Based on changing sports journalism norms, how do sportswriters perceive the future of written sports journalism?

Technology's Impact on Journalism

Sportswriting has transformed immensely since Henry Chadwick became the first full-time sportswriter in the 1850s (Washburn & Lamb, 2020). For one, using bylines in the sports section, which gave coverage "authority and originality," did not appear frequently until the 1920s (Carvalho, 2004, p. 48). Similarly, quoting athletes and coaches as sources did not begin until the 1930s as a response to radio sports broadcasting (Bryant & Holt, 2006). More recently, the highly descriptive play-by-play story, an industry standard before mass broadcasting, has been replaced with more analytical-based game recaps that break down the Xs and O's of specific moments attributed to swaying a game's overall outcome (Parnass, 2015). Innovation may be a buzzword (Green, 2013), yet journalism constantly changes with technology and it can sometimes be difficult for a news organization to keep pace (Manafy, 2017).

Villi et al. (2020) note that a newspaper's likely adoption of technology depends on its overall size and status in the community, with some newspapers being aware of the need to innovate yet struggling to do so promptly. Likewise, Kim (2010) contends that technological advancements in news dissemination can sometimes allow mid-sized news organizations to gain market share since they are more likely to experiment with new platforms than larger, more established outlets. This aligns with Doyle (2014), which finds that a practical response to the "gradual erosion in levels of print readership and print advertising" is for an organization to emphasize "multiplatform publishing" so it can remain relevant in the eyes of the audience and advertisers (p. 16).

Unlike the past, when local media was the only source of information for a specific town or geographic region, modern news consumers have many options for staying informed. Although subscription-based organizations remain a strong option for local news, convincing the public that journalism comes with a price tag can still be challenging (Lever, 2016). It has been reasoned that print journalism would be in a better financial position now if it had not committed "media's fatal flaw" in the late 1990s by giving away digital content for free (Littau, 2019, para. 1). In retrospect, Chyi and Tenenboim (2019) maintain that the news industry, when faced with a metaphorical fork in the road at the beginning of the twenty-first century, should have invested more resources into strengthening the print product—where the most significant advertising revenue is still generated—rather than emphasizing digital.

Online advertising sales are no longer the most stable way for a news outlet to sustain itself since Facebook and Google "take up the lion's share of digital advertising dollars" ("Paying for news," 2017, para. 1). As Bamberger et al. (2020) note, it is "easier to double down on subscriptions than compete against the digital giants for advertising dollars" (para. 3), which can mean that a winning media business approach must make the value of a subscription apparent to convert occasional readers into paying news consumers. Though they have consistently been able to adapt and survive in past instances of technological change, O'Sullivan et al. (2017) maintain that newspapers' primary focus should shift from technological developments to investing more in their "most precious resource"—journalists (p. 92).

Sports Journalism Norms and Routines

To understand the likely impact that online-only sports news sources have on the marketplace of competing journalistic institutions, it is essential first to understand the norms and routines of sports journalism, a subset of news rooted in the spread of information related to an athlete, team, or sports-based issue (Stoffer et al., 2010). As Chotiner (2014) maintains, there are two distinct types of sports journalism content: serious reporting (i.e., issue stories, human-interest profiles, etc.) and entertainment-based stories (i.e., game coverage). From the viewpoint of a news traditionalist, sports journalism has long struggled to maintain a legitimate professional identity within the newsroom since the reporting of sports news may not typically possess a critical perspective (Rowe, 2007). Whereas the standard for defining what constitutes legitimate journalism is often linked to one's adherence to ethical and moral values, those within sports journalism are not always able to meet these basic principles since stories woven around athletics can sometimes lack hard-hitting "social or political importance" (Oates & Pauly, 2007, p. 332).

Understanding why a general sportswriter may neglect to pen a potentially critical piece—which can aid in the perception that sports journalism represents a newsroom's "toy department"—has been an area of focus for sports media scholars (Boyle, 2006; Forde & Wilson, 2018; Lowes, 1999). Research demonstrates that a journalist's age and experience level may influence his or her adherence to ethics, with those assigned to major professional sports beats (i.e., M.L.B., N.B.A., N.F.L., N.H.L.) more likely to act ethically than reporters covering prep sports (Hardin et al., 2009). Weedon and Wilson (2020), similarly, argue that older sports editors are more likely to avoid controversial and social issue-based story topics than their younger counterparts. This is why Boyle (2017) contends that sportswriters must focus more on hard sports news—infused with the type of integrity that reporters "associate with their self-image"—than soft stories that lack "rigor and credibility" (p. 493). In other previous sports-related journalism studies, scholars have advocated for greater ethical engagement (Hardin, 2005), more investigative sports reports (Rowe, 2007), and increased social and political reporting within a sporting context (Forde & Wilson, 2018). Ramon-Vegas and Rojas-Torrijos (2018) argue that a new ethics code for sports journalism is needed, focusing more on public-service reporting than entertainment-based sports journalism.

However, sports journalism's growing emphasis on the intersection of sport and society has helped to pivot the profession away from the "fun and frivolity" that it was previously synonymous with (Rowe, 2007, p. 384) and more toward a vital watchdog function of the press (Reinardy & Wanta, 2015). A possible reason for this transition is that sporting events are no longer isolated. Instead, sport—and its subsequent media coverage—is an integral part of modern society, providing a platform for debating financial, social, and partisan issues in a public forum setting (Hardin et al., 2009). As illustrated by athlete activism spurred by the Black Lives Matter (B.L.M.) movement of 2020, sport provides a podium that changes the "conversation around racism" (Barlow & Trish, 2018, para. 1). Thus, the "just a game" mentality is no longer as applicable since contemporary sports journalists must find a balance between covering the actual game and also reporting on topics that have little to no concern on a contest's outcome (Schmidt, 2018, p. 2).

Changes to Sports Journalism Access

There was a time, before the Internet, when a sports organization relied on local newspaper coverage for promotion and publicity. Whether the content was a profile focused on a specific athlete, a recap of the previous game, or just a box score buried within the newsprint pages, sports teams needed journalists to spread the word about their sports product. Journalists, similarly, needed team access to cultivate readers in what Fry (2011) calls a "tacit bargain" (para. 9). This traditional relationship, McChesney (1989) notes, was mutually beneficial, with each party gaining something from the other. However, since official team websites (which first gained traction in professional sports in the late 1990s; Sreenivasan, 1998) effectively allow sports organizations to bypass the media middleman, the connection between these two independent entities is no longer symbiotic. Recent strategies employed by the media relations departments of collegiate athletic departments and professional teams, such as in-house content production and limited source access to external reporters, suggest this relationship is now more one-sided, with the scales tipping in favor of the team. Though print and online sportswriters still need to negotiate access to interview athletes and coaches, teams no longer rely as heavily on mainstream press for coverage. The increased competition created by team media, defined as a sports organization's hiring of journalistic talent to produce content for its website (Mirer, 2022), "threatens the legitimacy of journalists and their work practices," as Suggs (2016) writes (p. 261).

Moritz (2019), on the other hand, maintains that fluctuating levels of source access represent just "another one of the fundamental shifts happening in sports journalism" (para. 1). Additional journalism research has uncovered that the availability of source access tends to vary based on one's beat. For example, although a high school (via owned media like a website and social media) can disseminate information about its athletic programs, local news remains a prominent way for these teams to garner publicity (Shaul, 2015). It is possible that reporters, particularly those working for a local newspaper or television station, may have more frequent access to high school athletes and coaches because fewer journalists are covering these teams, and the coverage tends to be less critical.

On the contrary, those covering major collegiate and professional sports teams have been hit harder in this perceived battle for access (of note, some U.S. sports leagues have more lenient media policies than others, though; Eskenazi, 2016). For instance, in the pre-COVID-19 era, Moritz (2019) writes that Major League Baseball (M.L.B.) writers typically had the most interview time with players and managers since team clubhouses were open before and after each regular season game. Reporters on the professional basketball and hockey beats also generally received ample access to team personnel before the pandemic, albeit for a much shorter duration, via the traditional gameday media scrum. Those covering a National Football League (N.F.L.) team, though, have been forced to navigate highly structured routines (both before and after COVID-19) to interview sources, one in which some players elect to only speak in a moderated press conference format (Deitsch, 2017).

Aside from U.S.-based sports, it has been noted that journalists covering the top level of English soccer typically receive infrequent media access for interviews since some clubs may believe there is nothing to gain from granting reporters interviews on matchdays (Borden, 2015; Coombs & Osborne, 2012; Curtis, 2019). Bailey (2014) writes that this approach not only hinders the journalist's ability to perform their job but also places fans at a disadvantage since they cannot consume facts from an impartial source.

Conjoined Lenses for Deciphering Media Migration

Gatekeeping

Before gauging how those who write for various sports news outlets perceive the concept of beat competition and coexistence, it is essential first to understand media gatekeeping, which equates to the specific factors that decide which information gets mass disseminated for public consumption (Donsbach, 2004; Harcup & O'Neill, 2017). Stemming from Lewin's (1947) analysis of the sociological decisions that impact the type of food being served at the family dinner table, mass media gatekeeping suggests that the background of those who play a role in editorial decisions (and sometimes their organization's specific political stance) determine the type of information that seeps into the public sphere (Shoemaker & Vos, 2009). As Shoemaker (1991) asserts, gatekeeping translates to news personnel transforming the almost infinite number of messages in the world into select information that reaches an individual on any given day.

The idea that a news organization's editorial direction is shaped by its gatekeepers' experiences, attitudes, and ideology stems from the seminal research of White (1950), who was the first to apply Lewin's (1947) idea of gatekeeping to a journalistic context. White's (1950) analysis, in turn, paved the way for Shoemaker and Reese (1996) to argue that gatekeeping is better explained as a five-step function at both the micro and macro levels, with the first level focusing on the individual attitudes of the gatekeeper (e.g., one's background, past experiences, and beliefs) that influence the overall decision-making process. Shoemaker and Reese (1996) note that the dubbed second and third levels of gatekeeping revolve around media routines (i.e., newsroom culture) and an outlet's organizational influences and pressures (e.g., hierarchical structure, ownership, overall mission), respectively. Conversely, the fourth level constitutes the factors beyond the media producer's control (e.g., advertising, competition, government control), and the fifth level equates solely to media ideology.

Niche Gratification Theory

When scholars first studied print and broadcast mass media from an academic perspective in the 1950s, 1960s, and 1970s, most research focused on the effect of mass-disseminated news content on the consuming public. Thus, this type of media effects research aimed to determine whether mediated messages influenced the thoughts and attitudes of the target audience. However, while most research during this era concerned the media's influence on the public, few communication frameworks were woven around the idea that individuals seek media to fulfill specific needs. This underlying concept, thus, evolved into Katz et al.'s (1973) uses and gratifications (U&G) approach. In turn, uses and gratifications laid the foundation for Dimmick's (2003) niche gratification theory (N.G.T.) to explain how new and established media compete for news consumers, advertising revenue, and share of a specific media market.

In this regard, there is a relationship between niche gratification theory and uses and gratifications since the former both stems from and is informed by the latter. Similar to uses and gratifications, which is the idea that psychological reasons guide and motivate people to turn to media for personal satisfaction, niche gratification theory assumes that media—whether digital-only or legacy-based—serve different consumer needs. However, niche gratification theory does not examine the personal gratifications that impact an individual's media usage (e.g., escape, heightened perception of self/identity, information seeking). Instead, it best explains economic competition among media entities that vie for the same attention and/or disposable income of audience members. Under this guise, it can be assumed that people only have so much time and money to spend on entertainment and news. Consequently, all similar media types compete for an audience, whether online-only, print, or broadcast.

Likewise, another principle of niche gratification theory is the basic concept that the public uses new media, specifically Internet-based options, to satisfy particular needs that legacy outlets cannot meet. Besides being a direct offshoot of uses and gratifications, niche gratification theory does not share much with its theoretical forefather since it is rooted in the economic ecology of media—and not guided by psychological motivations of choice. The relationship, thus, can be considered symbiotic since niche gratification theory is somewhat dependent on U&G (a theoretical concept that can stand on its own if needed).

Whereas the seminal uses and gratifications approach by Katz et al. (1973) has been a common framework of media research for over 50 years, niche gratification theory is more than 20 years old, which means that it is still relatively new in terms of being a theoretical framework of media competition. Therefore, by applying the above theoretical concepts to the study of the overcrowded sports media marketplace, this book expands each approach and determines how different sports news sources have competed against or coexisted with other sports journalism outlets in the digital era.

Diffusion of Innovations

Concerned with the rate at which those within a specified social system adopt and implement new technology, Rogers' (1962) concept of diffusion of innovations (D.O.I.) helps explain why (and how) a further advancement is likely to become mainstream. According to Rogers (2003), the four main elements that influence an innovation's widespread adoption are the innovation itself (i.e., its perceived usefulness), the specific channel in which this information is communicated, the length of time after an innovation's first appearance, and certain factors (e.g., availability of technology, speed of communication, etc.) available to the social system. In this regard, the diffusion process only occurs once the usefulness of a specific innovation is fully communicated to members of a particular social system. Rogers (2003), therefore, notes that a specified social system can be broken into five separate groups: innovators (those who desire to be the first to try an innovation), early adopters (the leaders who embrace change), the early majority (those likely to adopt new ideas quicker than the average individual), late majority (people who will only adopt an innovation after it has gone mainstream), and laggards (the traditionalists who are the last to embrace change into their lives).

Innovators and early adopters (the two groups of pioneers in this process) are typically those most open to the risks of embracing an advancement before its mainstream acceptance. This is because they often realize the perceived societal utility an innovation can bring (Robinson, 2009). The early and late majority, who lay the foundation for an innovation's mainstream integration, often constitute the general public since they typically adopt the innovation after it is no longer considered a risk. Laggards, conversely, are cautious and tend only to adopt the technology when forced (for instance, those who only adopted smartphone technology when it was required for mobile ordering during the COVID-19 pandemic; Goldberg & Oreg, 2007; Maze, 2023). A social system's overall speed of adoption can sometimes be influenced by access to existing technology, like the Internet, which allows ideas to spread quicker because there is no traditional constraint of geography (McGrath, 2019).

In relation to journalism, certain newsrooms have adopted technology to aid in the reporting and distribution process of news based on perceived effectiveness. For instance, the paywall (something that is now an industry standard) was first implemented in local news in 1995, when San Jose's *Mercury News* charged readers $5 per month for access (*The Mercury News* later switched to free online content three years later because online readership dropped 90 percent after the paywall's implementation; West, 2009). The paywall then went national in 1996 when adopted by *The Wall Street Journal*, which decided to charge for content since it was targeted to businesses rather than individual news consumers. This approach, it was thought, gave the newspaper a reason to "go against the grain and go behind a paywall" (Hoffmann, 2022, para. 5). Similarly, journalistic innovations such as computer-assisted reporting and data journalism have become commonplace in most newsrooms (Léchenet, 2014).

Aside from the public-service function of journalism, Nelson (2021) demonstrates that digital journalists sometimes adapt their role to suit the needs of the intended or imagined audience. Therefore, a digital journalist's likelihood of innovation adoption is often predicated on his or her perception of the targeted reader base (Bossio & Nelson, 2021; Roberts, 2021). This means it is likely for all news outlets to respond to technology at different rates based on the perceived wants of the news consumer interacting with the news product. Regarding sportswriting, diffusion of innovations sheds light on technology's impact on the job's norms and routines. Whereas the effects of technology in journalism can be viewed as unfavorable because the once-traditional ways of news production have been disrupted, it has been beneficial because of the spurred movement of adoption for relevancy (Broersma & Singer, 2021; Deuze, 2008).

Innovators and early adopters exist in each subset of sportswriting examined (in-house media, The Athletic, Substack, and S.B. Nation) because they all have been influenced by reporting and dissemination innovations. Newspaper sports departments, for instance, had early adopters who saw potential value in emphasizing web-based and in-depth feature content to keep pace with other dissemination arms of sports news. As interviewee Shannon Ryan (formerly of the *Chicago Tribune* who now heads The Athletic's W.N.B.A. coverage) said, technology has forced reporters to look past media relations-cultivated press materials (e.g., stat sheet, rosters, scouting reports, etc.) by emphasizing "beyond the box score-type stuff." Despite short attention spans, she said, people will "still sit there and take the time to read" a good story.

Further, as will be discussed in the ensuing chapters, team-run media in the N.F.L. has also benefitted from innovators and early adopters who saw value in a sports team being able to publish journalistic information on its website. Mather and Hansmann, The Athletic's founders, can also be classified as innovators; their original approach to long-form sports journalism was one of the first forays into paywalled city and sports verticals. Substack and S.B. Nation have both been propelled by the adopters who saw value in entrepreneurial and blog-based sportswriting tailored to niche sporting perspectives. All interviewees, however, have valuable insight into the concept of sportswriting innovations based on their careers in this changing field (either as innovators or by being around journalistic innovations).

Journalistic Boundary Work

Although the concept of boundary work correlates to the main processes through which social phenomena are either accepted or rejected in a distinct social system., it is appropriate to apply to journalism because the industry's inherent elements (e.g., a news product, organization, norms, and routines, etc.) are constructed over time and continually evolve due to technological and attitudinal shifts in news dissemination (Carlson, 2019). Originating in sociology, boundary work—when applied to journalism—is especially important to understand in the current era of instant information since fluctuating technological, political, and social norms pose questions regarding what the current boundaries of reporting should be compared to past limitations.

While journalism has the norms of "personnel" (the news staff), "material artifacts" (the equipment needed to produce content), and "institutional commitments" (objectivity, accuracy, etc.), Carlson (2019) maintains that it should not blind the public to the inherent shifts in the profession that ultimately challenge how news decisions are made (p. 2). It is virtually impossible to clearly define who a journalist is (or what constitutes journalism) since there is not one standard used, nor is there a singular career path that all reporters must follow (Carlson, 2007; Perreault & Ferrucci, 2020). Journalistic boundaries, however, can be used to negotiate discourse that generates "symbolic contests in which different actors vie for control to apply or remove" the label of journalism and/or journalistic content (Carlson, 2015, p. 2).

In other words, boundary work enables journalists to identify what information to include or exclude from a piece of content. As Ferrucci and Vos (2017) state, the criteria that an individual who can be considered a journalist must meet is jointly dependent on who is thought to "produce legitimate knowledge" (p. 872). Prior academic research on boundary work within a journalistic context has examined how news professionals distinguish between legitimate journalism and entertainment-based reporting (Bishop, 1999) and how individual journalists differentiate themselves from unethical practices, like pack journalism (Frank, 2003)—defined as collaborative reporting that leads to cookie cutter-like content (Coddington, 2013). Further studies have shed light on the boundaries between hard news with a critical perspective and its soft, fluff journalism counterpart (Sjovaag, 2015) and the line between a news outlet's editorial and business arm (Coddington, 2015).

In sports journalism, reporters who make a living writing about teams and athletes negotiate their boundaries by aligning themselves more with traditional journalistic tenants than boosterism sports reporting—an argument critics use to reinforce the "toy department" moniker (Hardin et al., 2009). In this regard, sports reporters maintain that their work should be included in the discussion of legitimate journalism since sports routinely intersect with social issues. The specific boundaries that define a distinct profession, Gieryn (1983) posits, are defined by societal jurisdictions. However, because the boundaries are not fixed, new media entities can challenge their existence, threatening journalism's professional status (Carlson, 2015). This serves as the foundation for the work of Mirer (2017), who investigates the boundary that in-house sports reporters employed by a team must navigate to be recognized by the public and news peers as legitimate sports journalists.

Because this book focuses on both newer forms of professionalized (e.g., The Athletic, team-run media) sports media and hobbyist (e.g., Substack newsletters and the S.B. Nation network of fan blogging sites) forms of sportswriting, it is essential to understand Zelizer's (1993) work on journalists as interpretive communities. This seminal piece sheds light on how technology enables mass media to function less like an organized profession and more akin to a community of interconnected disseminators who all determine the public agenda. From a sociological perspective, journalism has long been classified as a profession with its standardized norms and routines (Schudson, 1978, 1982), which ultimately helped differentiate the work of professionalized sportswriters from those who wrote as hobbyists. In a way, the professionalization of journalism meant that those with a specific skill set were more qualified to act as news gatekeepers than the average person who did not possess journalistic experience (Tuchman, 1978). Zelizer (1993) notes that this standard effectively safeguarded the journalist's societal role. However, because one does not need the specific "trappings of professionalism" (p. 222) seen in other fields (i.e., medicine, law, etc.) since journalism lacks training formality, it functions as communal learning, where the trade is an experience learned through networking. Regarding Substack and S.B. Nation, this illustrates that the definition of a media gatekeeper or opinion leader is fluid depending on perspective, which reinforces the inclusion of these two subsets of sportswriting.

Interview Methodology

To determine how the shifting digital-first sports journalism landscape has affected the job function, routines, and norms of those working within various subsets of sportswriting, a series of semi-structured qualitative interviews with digital sports editors/writers, team-employed reporters, and bloggers were conducted from September 2019 to November 2023, a timeframe of change in sports journalism. Interviewees from these areas of written sports journalism (team-run media, The Athletic, Substack, and S.B. Nation blogs) were targeted because their job norms have been impacted, at least to a slight degree, by the expanding sports news marketplace. Semi-structured interviewing was used because it enables reflection, comprehension, and explanation around a specific theme to occur in a manner that organically elucidates the lived experiences of respondents (Tracy, 2013). This allowed interviewees to shed light on perceived issues, trends, and implications regarding competition versus coexistence in the current climate of written sports content.

Sampling. To accurately gauge the current perceived state of sports journalism, interviewees consisted of U.S.-based sportswriters (newspaper editor/

journalists, team-employed reporters, sportswriters from The Athletic, entrepreneurial sports newsletter personnel, and S.B. Nation site managers) who covered various sports teams/topics. These interviewees aligned with the book's purpose: to shed firsthand knowledge on how sports journalism has innovated because of technology and to understand the impact of perceived competition in both the professional and hobbyist sectors of sportswriting. In sum, each interviewee helped shape this book's content and direction.

To select potential interviewees from the newspaper, digital-only, and team-run media realm, individuals affiliated with these subsets of sports journalism whose contact information was readily available on their online bio page were sent an inquiry cold email. This initial contact stated the purpose of the research, the role of the interviewee, and how participation could benefit future understanding of sports journalism. Potential interviewees who agreed to be interviewed were then forwarded a consent form outlining the general interview procedure (inherent purpose, risks, etc.) and asked to schedule a phone interview time slot with the researcher. Snowball sampling was also used to cast a wider net of interviewees (i.e., interviewees were asked to recommend potential colleagues for participation). This was done by ending each interview with "Is there anyone you'd recommend who would have valuable insight on this topic?" This sampling tactic also ensured that sportswriters whose email addresses were not publicly listed could be included in the initial sample (interviewees from snowball sampling were also sent the same initial inquiry email). Of the 100 total interviewees, 80 were found via cold emailing—with the remaining 20 coming from snowball sampling.

Throughout data collection, 100 individual interviews were conducted. The breakdown is as follows: newspapers = 30; team-run media = 17; The Athletic = 21; Substack = 11; S.B. Nation = 17; miscellaneous = 4 (the miscellaneous interviewees were those whose positions did not fit one of the areas above). Of the 100 interviewees, 15 percent ($n = 15$) were women. This percentage closely aligns with newspaper sports journalism gendered demographics, in which The Institute for Diversity and Ethics in Sport (T.I.D.E.S.) reported that 16.7 percent of newspaper sportswriters in 2021 (the last time the report was published) were women (Lapchick, 2021a). It is important to note that official gender diversity reports among those affiliated with in-house media for a major professional sports team, The Athletic, Substack, and S.B. Nation do not exist. Although it can be presumed that some women work in these specific forms of sports media, there is no way to ascertain how many. All but one (Lindsay Gibbs of *Power Plays*, a Substack newsletter focused on sexism in sport) of the roughly 50 potential interviewees targeted from Substack and S.B. Nation were men. At the time of interview data collection, it was surprising that not more women had their own sports-centric Substack. This is because the barriers traditionally that have plagued sports journalism (i.e., workplace harassment, lack of editorial commitment to women's sports, etc.; Aykroyd, 2021) are absent. After all, the entrepreneurial aspect of Substack means there are no formal hiring practices.

Whereas anyone can create fan posts for an S.B. Nation fan community in the comments section, they still need to go through the hiring process with a site manager (even though it is only part-time, stipend-paid employment) to become a writer or editor. Therefore, a barrier of entry for women in non-full-time roles at S.B. Nation may still be apparent. None of the 35 paid S.B. Nation writers/site managers targeted as potential interviewees were women.

The average length of the 100 total interviews was approximately 29 minutes, with the longest lasting more than 75 minutes and the shortest being slightly less than 12 minutes. The average interview length for the different subsets of sports journalism examined are as follows: newspapers = 26.2 minutes, team-run media = 36.5 minutes, The Athletic = 26.4 minutes, Substack writers = 28.1 minutes, S.B. Nation = 28.2 minutes, and miscellaneous sports media professionals = 42 minutes. It is important to note that the miscellaneous interviewees consisted of Daniel Libit, a writer for *Sportico* who is also co-founder of the investigative college sports website *The Intercollegiate*, former *Sports Illustrated* national college football writer Ross Dellenger, Jon Solomon, editorial director of the Sports & Society Program for The Aspen Institute, and Megan Flood—an ESPN associate producer. Of note, although 100 total interviews were conducted, the perspectives of only half the interview sample appear in this book since more information was gathered than ultimately needed. For example, the newspaper interviewees, though not constituting a standalone chapter, were used to help construct the framework of the overall findings and are quoted at various points throughout the book (a complete listing of all sportswriters/editors interviewed is included in Appendix A).

Data Collection and Analysis

Before the interview phase commenced, a protocol of semi-structured interview questions was prepared and subsequently approved by the researcher's home Institutional Review Board (I.R.B.). Although each interview was guided more like a conversation than a back-and-forth question-and-answer session, sample questions ranged from, "What are some of the most notable changes regarding the newsgathering/dissemination process that you've noticed since entering sports journalism?" and "Do you believe that hometown newspapers, online-only sports websites, and blogging can coexist?" to "Do you view your work as catering to a specific sporting niche?" and "How can your specific subset of sports journalism position itself remain relevant among readers in the digital age?"

Each interview (conducted via telephone) was transcribed using Otter.ai. This speech-to-text program provides interview transcriptions for a nominal monthly fee and checks for comment accuracy/context. Each transcript was then analyzed using emergent thematic analysis, in which a code sheet was created to align with varying overarching themes from each subdivision of sports media represented. Once three to four themes were established for each chapter, transcripts were re-read to form a holistic understanding. Relevant quotations were then highlighted using Glaser's (1965) constant comparative method. This form of qualitative analysis revealed interview commonalities regarding competition versus coexistence.

Overview of the Book

This research sheds light on the concept of perceived competition in the evolving nature of sports journalism, as seen by those affiliated with various subsets of sportswriting. The findings have value from a professional application standpoint since each explains how digitally-minded sports journalists use the niche to mutually coexist with other sports news outlets in the digital information marketplace. Further, since this body of scholarship is rooted in journalistic norms and processes, it can serve as a foundation for other sports journalism-centric qualitative studies aimed at understanding the role of the niche.

Chapter One explores the rise of the in-house sports team reporter, from the industry pioneers who transitioned from newspaper to team employee to the sportswriters who did not previously work in local journalism before being hired by a sports team's editorial arm. This chapter also examines the notion that internal sportswriters use preferential source access that outside media is not afforded because of their standing. Finally, it discusses how internal sportswriters can leverage their unique position to tell stories in ways not previously possible through traditional modes of dissemination.

Chapter Two analyzes The Athletic's impact on the business and editorial perspectives of modern sports journalism through interviews with both writers and editors. This chapter details how *The New York Times'* purchase of The Athletic has shifted certain business ideals of sports journalism. Additionally, it sheds light on how The Athletic's paywall approach has been perceived to help normalize the notion that quality sportswriting has an associated fee.

Chapter Three centers on Substack, the upstart newsletter publishing platform that entrepreneurial-minded writers gravitate toward because of its ease of use and customizability. As this chapter reveals, there are three types of individuals who manage niche newsletters situated on sports journalism topics—those who rely on the platform's paywall implementation for total time income, those who disseminate their content for free yet hope to monetize it eventually, and those who host their sports-centric writings on the platform for the cathartic release it provides. This chapter also tackles the likelihood, or lack thereof, that anyone—regardless of the prominence of their byline—can use Substack's paywall feature to make sportswriting a full-time venture.

Chapter Four provides insight into the corporate blogosphere approach of S.B. Nation, the networked "for fans, by fans" Vox Media subsidiary that maintains individual fan communities. Through interviews with individual S.B. Nation writers and site managers/editors (each blog brands its job titles differently), this chapter discusses the 20+ year history of S.B. Nation before examining the perceived benefits and drawbacks (as seen by interviewees) of the communal blog model.

Chapter Five, the final section of this book, analyzes a possible direction of the future of sports journalism by recapping the significant implications and perspectives shared by each group of interviewees. Lastly, this chapter examines both the short and long-term prospects of written sports content, as seen by those with a relevant stake in its future. Because of each interviewee's professional insight, the topics outlined in this section may have value to those currently working in sportswriting and those who aspire to do so because of each interviewee's professional insight.

Although the norms and routines associated with sports journalism are constantly evolving, meaning the specific information about each platform presented in this book is likely to have changed (at least to some degree) since its initial writing, the inherent idea of competition or coexistence within the realm of written sports journalism is ever-present. Regardless of whether newspapers, team-run media, The Athletic, Substack, and S.B. Nation exist in the future, the concepts covered in this book show there is value in understanding what journalists believe can be done, from an editorial perspective, to allow multiple outlets covering the same beat to coexist harmoniously.

References

Aykroyd, L. (2021, April 9). *Facing the challenges of 2021: Women's sports journalists worldwide speak out.* Global Sport Matters. https://globalsportmatters.com/business/2021/04/09/womens-sports-journalists-worldwide-speak-out-stereotypes-opportunities/

Bailey, R. (2014, February 10). *Why the Premier League needs to have better player access.* Bleacher Report. http://www.bleacherreport.com/articles/1954279-why-the-premier-league-needs-to-have-better-player-access

Bamberger, S., Farag, H., Green, A., Rastogi, V., Stern, S., & Zuckerman, N. (2020, February 24). *In media, subscriptions matter most.* Boston Consulting Group. http://www.bcg.com/publications/2020/tmt-value-creators-media-subscriptions-matter-most

Barber, P. (2017, October 23). *I love my local Athletic Bay Area colleagues and wish them well, but the predatory quotes in this article are gross.* [Tweet]. Twitter. https://twitter.com/Skinny_Post/status/922497304283643904

Barlow, G., & Trish, B. (2018, October 16). *How athletes are changing the conversation around racism.* The Washington Post. https://www.washingtonpost.com/outlook/2018/10/16/how-athletes-are-changing-conversation-around-racism/

Biasotti, T. (2017, October 11). Fast-growing startup aims to "replace the sports page." *Columbia Journalism Review.* http://www.cjr.org/business_of_news/the-athletic-sports-news.php

Bishop, R. (1999). From behind the walls: Boundary work by news organizations in their coverage of Princess Diana's death. *Journal of Communication Inquiry, 23*(1), 90–112.

Borden, S. (2015, August 4). *English club shuts out journalists with new kind of defense.* The New York Times. http://www.nytimes.com/2015/08/05/sports/soccer/english-soccer-club-sets-up-tight-defense-but-this-one-repels-journalists.html

Bossio, D., & Nelson, J. L. (2021). Reconsidering innovation: Situating and evaluating change in journalism. *Journalism Studies, 22*(11),1377–1381.

Boudway, I. (2019, August 20). *The sports news site haters love to dunk on keeps signing up subscribers.* Bloomberg Businessweek. https://www.bloomberg.com/news/features/2019-08-20/an-upstart-sports-news-serviceis-thriving-amid-media-layoffs

Boyle, R. (2006). *Sports journalism: Context and issues.* Sage.

Boyle, R. (2017). Sports journalism: Changing journalism practice and digital media. *Digital Journalism, 5*(1), 493–495.

Bradshaw, T., & Minogue, D. (2020). *Sports journalism: The state of play.* Routledge.

Broersma, M., & Singer, J. B. (2021). Caught between innovation and tradition: Young journalists as normative change agents in the journalistic field. *Journalism Practice, 15*(6), 821–838.

Bryant, J., & Holt, A. (2006). A historical overview of sports and media in the United States. In A. A. Raney & J. Bryant (Eds.), *Handbook of sports and media* (pp. 22–45). Routledge.

Carlson, M. (2007). Blogs and journalistic authority: The role of blogs in U.S. Election Day 2004 coverage. *Journalism Studies*, 8(1), 264–279.

Carlson, M. (2015). Introduction: The many boundaries of journalism. In M. Carlson & S. C. Lewis (Eds.), *Boundaries of journalism: Professionalism, practices, and participation* (pp. 1–18). Routledge.

Carlson, M. (2019). Boundary work. In T. P. Vos & F. Hanusch (Eds.), *The international encyclopedia of journalism studies*. Wiley-Blackwell.

Carvalho, J. (2004). *Journal's* sports innovations evolve slowly over time. *Newspaper Research Journal*, 35(4), 40–51.

Chotiner, I. (2014, June 1). *There are two kinds of "sports journalism." Only one of them is really journalism.* New Republic. http://newrepublic.com/article/117964/nba-finals-preview-greg-popovich-and-sports-journalism

Chyi, H. I., & Tenenboim, O. (2019). From analog dollars to digital dimes: A look into the performance of U.S. newspapers. *Journalism Practice*, 13(8), 798–819.

Coddington, M. (2013). Defending judgment and context in "original reporting": Journalists' construction of newswork in a networked age. *Journalism*, 15(1), 678–695.

Coddington, M. (2015). The wall becomes a curtain: Revisiting journalism's news-business boundary. In M. Carlson & S. C. Lewis (Eds.), *Boundaries of journalism: Professionalism, practices, and participation* (pp. 67–82). Routledge.

Coombs, D. S., & Osborne, A. (2012). Sports journalists and England's Barclays Premier League: A case study examining reporters' takes on modern football. *International Journal of Sport Communication*, 5(3), 412–425.

Curtis, B. (2019, May 29). *U.K. sportswriting's access crisis.* The Ringer. http://www.theringer.com/sports/2019/5/29/18643311/uk-sportswriting-embargo-access-champions-league-independent

Deitsch, R. (2017, January 19). Media circus: The strangest restrictions N.F.L. teams impose on reporters. *Sports Illustrated.* http://www.si.com/media/2017/01/19/media-circus-nfl-teams-reporters-restrictions

Deuze, M. (2008). Understanding journalism as newswork: How it changes, and how it remains the same. *Westminster Papers in Communication and Culture*, 5(2), 4–23.

Dimmick, J. (2003). *Media competition and coexistence: The theory of the niche.* Lawrence Erlbaum.

Donsbach, W. (2004). Psychology of news decisions: Factors behind journalists' professional behavior. *Journalism*, 5(2), 131–157.

Doyle, G. (2014). Re-invention and survival: Newspapers in the era of digital multiplatform delivery. *Journal of Media Business Studies*, 10(4), 1–20.

Draper, K. (2017, October 23). *Why The Athletic wants to pillage newspapers.* The New York Times. http://www.nytimes.com/2017/10/23/sports/the-athletic-newspapers.html

Duncan, S. (2020). *The digital world of sport: The impact of emerging media on sports news, information and journalism.* Anthem Press.

Eskenazi, G. (2016, March 29). How access to athletes has changed over time for sportswriters. *Columbia Journalism Review.* http://www.cjr.org/first_person/cronyism.php

Ferrucci, P., & Vos, T. P. (2017). Who's in, who's out? Constructing the identity of digital journalists. *Digital Journalism*, 5(1), 868–883.

Flynn, K., & Fischer, S. (2023, January 24). *Washington Post cuts 20 newsroom jobs and shuts down its gaming section.* Axios. http://www.axios.com/2023/01/24/washington-post-layoffs-bezos-visit.

Forde, S., & Wilson, B. (2018). Radical sports journalism?: Reflections on "alternative" approaches to covering sport-related social issues. *Sociology of Sport Journal, 35*(1), 66–76.

Frank, R. (2003). "These crowded circumstances": When pack journalists bash pack journalism. *Journalism, 4*(1), 441–458.

Fry, J. (2011, September 15). *Rules of the game change as sports journalists compete against teams they cover.* Poynter. http://www.poynter.org/reporting-editing/2011/rules-of-the-game-change-as-sports-journalists-compete-against-teams-they-cover/

Gieryn, T. F. (1983). Boundary work and the demarcation of science from non-science: Strains and interests in professional ideologies of scientists. *American Sociological Review, 48*(1), 781–795.

Glaser, B. G. (1965). The constant comparative method of qualitative analysis. *Social Problems, 12*(4), 436–445.

Glasspiegel, R. (2023, June 12). *New York Times "reorganizes" The Athletic with layoffs, coverage changes.* New York Post. https://nypost.com/2023/06/12/new-york-times-reorganizes-the-athletic-with-layoffs/

Goldenberg, J., & Oreg, S. (2007). Laggards in disguise: Resistance to adopt and the leapfrogging effect. *Technological Forecasting and Social Change, 74*(8), 1272–1281.

Gordon, A. (2018, September 6). The sports pages' new clothes. *Slate.* http://www.slate.com/culture/2018/09/the-athletic-is-poaching-from-local-sports-pages-and-reading-like-them-too.html

Green, E. (2013, June 20). *Innovation: The history of a buzzword.* The Atlantic. https://www.theatlantic.com/business/archive/2013/06/innovation-the-history-of-a-buzzword/277067/

Harcup, T., & O'Neill, D. (2017). What is news? News values revisited (again). *Journalism Studies, 18*(12), 1470–1488.

Hardin, M. (2005). Survey finds boosterism, freebies remain problem for newspaper sports departments. *Newspaper Research Journal, 26*(1), 66–73.

Hardin, M., Zhong, B., & Whiteside, E. (2009). Sports coverage: "Toy department" or public service journalism? The relationship between reporters' ethics and attitudes towards the profession. *International Journal of Sports Communication, 2*(1), 319–339.

Hare, K. (2020, April 26). *Here are the newsroom layoffs, furloughs and closures that happened during the coronavirus pandemic.* Poynter. https://www.poynter.org/business-work/2022/here-are-the-newsroom-layoffs-furloughs-and-closures-caused-by-the-coronavirus/

Hirsch, L., Draper, K., & Rosman, K. (2022, January 6). New York Times Co. to buy The Athletic for $550 million in cash. The New York Times. https://www.nytimes.com/2022/01/06/business/new-york-times-the-athletic.html

Hoffmann, J. (2022, September 20). *It's time to pay the meter.* The History of the Web. https://thehistoryoftheweb.com/its-time-to-pay-the-meter/.

Katz, E., Blumler, J. G., & Gurevitch, M. (1973). Uses and gratifications research. *Public Opinion Quarterly, 37*(4), 509–523.

Kim, B. K. (2010). When and how middle-status newspapers innovate: The role of status and market identity in adoption of digital media. http://www.haas.berkeley.edu/wp-content/uploads/KimBo.pdf

Kravitz, B. (2023, July 20). I'm back. *Musings of an Old Sportswriter*. https://bobkravitz.substack.com/p/im-back

Lapchick, R. (2021a, September 22). *Sports media remains overwhelmingly white and male, study finds*. ESPN. https://www.espn.com/espn/story/_/id/32254145/sports-media-remains-overwhelmingly-white-male-study-finds

Léchenet, A. (2014). *Global database investigations: The role of the computer-assisted reporter*. Reuters Institute for the Study of Journalism. https://reutersinstitute.politics.ox.ac.uk/sites/default/files/research/files/Global%2520Database%2520Investigations%2520-%2520The%2520role%2520of%2520the%2520computer-assisted%2520reporter.pdf

Lever, R. (2016, August 11). *Newspapers rethink paywalls as digital efforts sputter*. Dawn. https://www.dawn.com/news/1276924/newspapers-rethink-paywalls-as-digital-efforts-sputter

Lewin, K. (1947). Frontiers in group dynamics II: Channels of group life; social planning and action research. *Human Relations, 1*(2), 143–153.

Lindsay, R. (2017, December 6). Taking their game online. *Oakland Magazine*. http://www.oaklandmagazine.com/December-2017/Taking-Their-Game-Online/

Littau, J. (2019, January 30). Media's fatal flaw: Ignoring the mistakes of newspapers. *Wired*. http://www.wired.com/story/medias-fatal-flaw-ignoring-the-mistakes-of-newspapers/

Lowes, M. D. (1999). *Inside the sports pages: Work routines, professional ideologies, and the manufacture of sports news*. University of Toronto Press.

Manafy, M. (2017, October 11). Media teams strive to adapt, but struggle to keep pace with digital. *Digital Content Next*. https://digitalcontentnext.org/blog/2017/10/11/media-teams-strive-adapt-struggle-keep-pace-digital-challenges/

Maze, J. (2023, September 23). *Mobile ordering takes off thanks to COVID*. Restaurant Business. https://www.restaurantbusinessonline.com/technology/mobile-ordering-takes-thanks-covid

McChesney, R. (1989). Media made sport: A history of sports coverage. In L. A. Wenner (Ed.), *Media, sports, and society* (pp. 49–69). Sage.

McEnnis, S. (2022). *Disrupting sports journalism*. Routledge.

McGrath, R. (2019, September 25). The pace of technology adoption is speeding up. *Harvard Business Review*. https://hbr.org/2013/11/the-pace-of-technology-adoption-is-speeding-up.

Mirer, M. (2017). "I did what I do" versus "I cover football." *Journalism Practice, 12*(3), 251–267.

Mirer, M. (2022). Just how they drew it up: How in-house reporters fit themselves into the sports media system. *Communication & Sport, 10*(3), 438–455.

Moritz, B. (2019, June 12). *Access in sports journalism (part 3): What's changing in the digital age*. Sports Media Guy. http://www.sportsmediaguy.com/blog/2019/6/12/access-in-sports-journalism-part-3-whats-changing-in-the-digital-age

Mullin, B. (2018, June 4). Sports site The Athletic expands aggressively, betting on subscriptions. *The Wall Street Journal*. https://www.wsj.com/articles/sports-website-the-athletic-expands-aggressively-1528110000?shareToken=st39465ba48bba4fd89ad35dd3288baacd&ref=article_email_share

Nelson, J. L. (2021). *Imagined audiences: How journalists perceive and pursue the public.* Oxford University Press.

Oates, T. P., & Pauly, J. (2007). Sports journalism as moral and ethical discourse. *Journal of Mass Media Ethics, 22*(4), 332–347.

O'Sullivan, J., Fortunati, L., Taipale, S., & Barnhurst, K. (2017). Innovators and innovated: Newspapers and the postdigital future beyond the "death of print." *The Information Society, 33*(2), 86–95.

Parnass, A. (2015, November 24). The changing beat. *The Cauldron.* http://www.the-cauldron.com/beat-witing-in-the-1st-century-833948012147

"Paying for news: Why people subscribe and what it says about the future of journalism." (2017, May 2). *American Press Institute.* http://www.americanpressinstitute.org/publications/reports/survey-research/paying-for-news/single-page/

Peralta, K. (2019). Pardon the disruption. *Notre Dame Magazine.* http://www.magazine.nd.edu/stories/pardon-the-disruption/

Perreault, G., & Ferrucci, P. (2020). What is digital journalism? Defining the practice and role of the digital journalist. *Digital Journalism, 8*(10), 1298–1316.

"Print solutions: Daily newspapers." (2023, March). *Bay Area News Group.* https://www.bayareanewsgroup.com/print-solutions/daily-newspapers

Quinn, A. (2018, September 12). Does The Athletic have a poaching problem? No, it's the nature of journalism. *The Gonzaga Bulletin.* https://www.gonzagabulletin.com/sports/does-the-athletic-have-a-poaching-problem-no-its-the-nature-of-journalism/article_cc30e4dc-b704-11e8-9034-4b0f7a3dfb2f.html

Ramon-Vegas, X., & Rojas-Torrijos, J.-L. (2018). Accountable sports journalism: Building up a platform and a new specialised code in the field. *Ethical Space: The International Journal of Communication Ethics, 15*(1/2), 15–28.

Roberts, J. (2021). Empathy cultivation through (pro)social media: A counter to compassion fatigue. *Journalism and Media, 2*(4), 819–829.

Robinson, L. (2009). *A summary of diffusion of innovations.* Changeology. https://www.enablingchange.com.au/Summary_Diffusion_Theory.pdf

Robertson, K., & Koblin, J. (2023, July 10). *The New York Times to disband its sports department.* The New York Times. https://www.nytimes.com/2023/07/10/business/media/the-new-york-times-sports-department.html

Reinardy, S., & Wanta, W. (2015). *The essentials of sports reporting and writing.* Routledge.

Rogers, E. M. (1962). *Diffusion of innovations.* Free Press.

Rogers, E. M. (2003). *Diffusion of innovations* (5th ed.). Free Press.

Rowe, D. (2007). Sports journalism: Still the "toy department" of the news media?. *Journalism, 8*(4), 385–405.

Schmidt, H. H. (2018). Sport reporting in the era of activism: Examining the intersection of sport media and social activism. *International Journal of Sport Communication, 11*(1), 2–17.

Schudson, M. (1978). *Discovering the news.* Basic Books.

Schudson, M. (1982). The politics of narrative form. The emergence of news conventions in print and television. *Daedalus, 3*(4), 97–112.

Shaul, M. (2015). *Sports information and sports media in high schools* [Unpublished master's thesis]. John Carroll University.

Shoemaker, P. J. (1991). *Gatekeeping: Communication concepts.* Sage.

Shoemaker, P. J., & Reese, S. D. (1996). *Mediating the message: Theories of influences on mass media content.* Longman.

Shoemaker, P. J., & Vos, T. (2009). *Gatekeeping theory.* Routledge.

Sjovaag, H. (2015). Hard news/soft news: The hierarchy of genres and the boundaries of the profession. In M. Carlson & S. C. Lewis (Eds.), *Boundaries of journalism: Professionalism, practices, and participation* (pp. 101–117). Routledge.

Sreenivasan, S. (1998, April 14). Baseball and the Internet are in the same ballpark. *Gainesville, Sun,* 6.

Steinberg, D. (2017, October 23). *Rooting for The Athletic to succeed. But cmon with this* [Tweet]. Twitter. https://twitter.com/dcsportsbog/status/922464835362852864

Stofer, K. T., Schaffer, J. R., & Rosenthal, B. A. (2010). *Sports journalism: An introduction to reporting and writing.* Rowman & Littlefield.

Strauss, B. (2020, March 4). *Sportswriting's future may depend on the Athletic, which is either reassuring or terrifying.* The Washington Post. http://www.washingtonpost.com/sports/2020/03/03/the-athletic-sports-media-future/

Suggs, D. W. (2016). Tensions in the press box: Understanding relationships among sports media and source organizations. *Communication & Sport, 4*(3), 261–281.

Tracy, S. J. (2013). *Qualitative research methods: Collecting evidence, crafting analysis, communicating impact.* Wiley-Blackwell.

Tuchman, G. (1978). Professionalism as an agent of legitimation. *Journal of Communication, 28*(2), 106–113.

Villi, M., Gronlund, M., Linden, C. G., Lehtisaari, K., Mierzejewska, B., Picard, R. G., & Roepnak, A. (2020). "They're a little bit squeezed in the middle": Strategic challenges for innovation in U.S. Metropolitan newspaper organisations. *Journal of Media Business Studies, 17*(1), 33–50.

Washburn, P. S., & Lamb, C. (2020). *Sports journalism: A history of glory, fame, and technology.* University of Nebraska Press.

Weedon, G., Wilson, B., Yoon, L., & Lawson, S. (2018). Where's all the "good" sports journalism? Sports media research, the sociology of sport, and the question of quality sports reporting. *International Review for the Sociology of Sport, 53*(6), 639–667.

West, J. (2009, November 3). *MediaNews to build the great paywall of Chico.* N.B.C. Bay Area. https://www.nbcbayarea.com/news/local/medianews-to-build-the-great-paywall-of-chico-jw/1882001/

White, D. M. (1950). The "gate keeper": A case study in the selection of news. *Journalism Quarterly, 27*(1), 383–390.

Zelizer, B. (1993). Journalists as interpretive communities. *Critical Studies in Mass Communication, 10*(1), 219–237.

BYPASSING THE MEDIA MIDDLEMAN: TEAM-RUN MEDIA'S CHALLENGE TO TRADITIONAL SPORTS NEWS

Geoff Hobson was unaware that he was ushering in a new era of sports journalism when he first crossed over from pro football newspaper reporter to Cincinnati Bengals team employee in 2000. Hobson, a veteran beat writer who worked for newspapers in Binghamton, NY, and Portland, ME, before coming to the *Cincinnati Enquirer* in 1990, had always wanted to transition to the "other side" (i.e., internal media). Until then, though, the only open door was to pivot to sports public relations, a move that most journalists committed to the craft's ideology of objective storytelling have traditionally been unwilling to make, except during "industry chaos" (Putterman, 2017, para. 17). Hobson, however, benefitted from the innovative media vision of Bengals' owner and president Mike Brown, son of team founder and former stadium namesake Paul Brown. During his tenure on the *Enquirer's* Bengals beat, Hobson formed what he described as a "good relationship" with those in the team's front office. This made him "clearly the best choice for bringing breaking news and insightful angles to Bengals.com readers," as Mike Brown said in a 2000 news release posted to the team's official website ("Bengals.com lands top writer," 2000, para. 6). In short, Brown wanted Hobson to continue writing articles on the Bengals, albeit for the team's newly launched website instead of for the respected nameplate of the *Enquirer*, now Cincinnati's lone daily newspaper (Suess, 2019).

Hobson did not understand why Brown wanted a print media veteran with little understanding of online news dissemination for this newly created role. Further, he enjoyed the editorial flexibility of being an outside media member. Hobson did not want to surrender his creative control by simply rewriting press releases or framing his journalism within the boundary of traditional media relations. The puzzlement was there when he asked Brown why the organization wanted him for this new experiment in team-managed news reporting. When he heard the straightforward answer, though, it all made sense. The Bengals wanted someone with an established local following whom fans could trust (and Hobson fit the bill).

In the two-plus decades that have passed, Hobson has been branded as a sports media pioneer because his first day on the job, April 15, 2000, was the day the team's website officially launched ("Bengals.com lands top writer," 2000; Hobson, 2015). He was not the first ex-print journalist to get poached by an N.F.L. team. The Jacksonville Jaguars implemented the practice in 1995 when Pittsburgh sportswriter Vic Ketchman was hired to head the franchise's official newspaper, *Jacksonville Inside Report*, in a joint venture with the *Florida Times-Union* (Stellino, 2011). However, Hobson's hiring prompted other sports organizations to see the value of having a reporting staff for team website content (Mirer et al., 2018).

Like Hobson, Michael Eisen was a tenured N.F.L. newspaper reporter, covering the New York Giants for various metro publications since the 1986 season, who also shifted to the team side in the early 2000s. After being switched to the *Newark Star-Ledger's* Rutgers football beat in 1999, Eisen yearned to get back to the N.F.L. because the overall lack of access to players and coaches in the collegiate ranks at the time contradicted the relationship-building practices he was accustomed to in the professional game. Wondering if Eisen was interested in filling his role as the *Enquirer's* Bengals writer, Hobson phoned his friend, asking if he wanted his name put in the ring with the editorial board. Desperate to get back to a full-time N.F.L. beat, Eisen strongly considered moving from the large metropolis of the New York City region to the midsize media market of Cincinnati. However, the more he thought about it, the clearer the realization. It was a lightbulb moment that occurred in the shower, Eisen admitted, but it just made sense; if Hobson could secure a job writing for the Bengals' official website, why couldn't he do the same for Giants.com?

So, using Hobson as his "inspiration," Eisen contacted Giants' co-owner John Mara to pitch the internal media idea initially conceived by the Bengals.

Naturally, Mara, who holds a law degree from Fordham University (Lattman, 2008), was deliberate in his negotiation, ensuring all intricate details of the job were ironed out before drafting a contract. Although Eisen's official pitch meeting occurred in May 2000, one month after Hobson's byline began appearing on Bengals.com, he was not officially hired until three months later, covering a Rutgers football game in Piscataway on a Saturday night for the *Star-Ledger* before making the 70-mile drive down I-95 to Philadelphia to work his first game for the Giants (a 1 p.m. game against the Eagles) the following day.

Much like Brown gave Hobson editorial freedom, encouraging him to cover the team precisely the same way he had while working for the local newspaper, Mara did not instill any parameters for Eisen to follow. From Eisen's perspective, team-run media was such a new advancement in 2000 that no one knew its full potential. Essentially, he "made it up as [he] went along" by carrying the thorough and accurate reporting from the newspaper to the team-controlled sphere.

Over two decades have passed since Hobson and Eisen first leaped from newspaper beat writers to online reporters for two of the N.F.L.'s early media adopters. During that time, both witnessed changes regarding how major professional sports organizations harness the power of media to communicate with their public. From an increased emphasis on quick-hitting multimedia content and social media posts to more analytical-based pieces instead of the conventional game recap, the role of the internal sports media reporter— interviewees noted—has shifted slightly as information consumption habits of the target audience have evolved. However, despite changing trends, the one constant of in-house media is that those who spent most of their career in newspaper journalism before working for the team still perceive themselves as legitimate journalists, even though their professional identity is no longer associated with independent media (Mirer et al., 2018).

Interestingly enough, however, fluctuations regarding how team-employed writers view their professional identity typically depend on one's background and/or the branding of their specific job title. For example, only those with previous careers in newspaper sports journalism are typically considered "team writers" or "senior writers." Others are categorized as "digital media managers" or "content managers." This distinct job branding, in turn, reflects variation in professional identity and how those in team-run media perceive themselves—as either a legitimized sportswriter, public relations professional, or a hybrid of both.

Hobson and Eisen may have inevitably paved the way for other former newspaper sportswriters to transition from legacy to new media. However, as two of the first in-house N.F.L. writers who have both been on the job since before most of today's N.F.L. rookies were born, their experiences as industry veterans differ from those who have been in similar roles for a shorter period. Virtually every sports team sees value in distributing content and controlling its message (Sherwood et al., 2016). Not every organization operates in-house media similarly and/or requires reporters to abide by the same editorial structure to communicate directly with the target audience (Fry, 2011).

Through qualitative interviews with those in the field, it is revealed that each team/sports league handles its internal media differently. The N.F.L. and N.B.A. allow each team to negotiate the role of internal media on its own. Conversely, reporters covering the M.L.B. as internal beat writers are "not direct team employees" but rather working as a "subsidiary of the league" (Mirer, 2019, p. 76). For instance, M.L.B. Advance Media, branded as the "interactive media and Internet arm of Major League Baseball" (Weaver, 2010, p. 9), employs 30 individual beat writers, according to Anthony DiComo, who covers the New York Mets for M.L.B.com. Despite this general inconsistency regarding structure, interviews with in-house sportswriters (N.F.L. = 10, N.B.A. = 4, M.L.B. = 2) and one N.F.L. social media specialist (Jill Beckman of the Tampa Bay Buccaneers) revealed three main themes: (1) there is a general learning curve associated with transitioning from external to internal media, (2) relationship building with sources is more accessible, but team reporters do not receive preferential access, and (3) there is intrinsic value, from a publicity and promotion standpoint, in a team employing its content creators.

As will be explained further, the concept of journalistic boundary work, which focuses on the standards and norms that define one's role as a reporter, provides the basis for this chapter (Carlson, 2015). It is no secret that sports journalism, as a whole, is a profession in flux, one where conventional routines constantly change because newer forms of technology afford media gatekeepers innovative ways to distribute information to the consuming public. Because of this, sportswriters in both the print and digital spheres must continually renegotiate their role and the work they produce, depending on whether the overall goal is to compete against or coexist with other journalistic outlets covering the same teams.

Pivoting Toward a New Era: "It's a completely different job and a completely different mindset"

The journalistic job routines and norms of those working for team-employed media can be the same as those tasked with covering a sports organization for outside news organizations. This is because both are predicated on the journalistic fundamentals of writing, reporting, and interviewing on deadline (Stofer et al., 2010). Therefore, it may seem as if the transition from one facet of sports media (legacy) to another (digital) can be seamless for most newspaper sportswriters since they still do what they have always done (write about sports), albeit for the team's official website. For some, the transition was an adjustment because of the inherent editorial differences between internal and external media. Independent sports journalism has traditionally been very scoop (or breaking news) driven, although not as much emphasis is now placed on what Moritz and Mirer (2021) define as the "scoop scoreboard." Most professional teams, however, are more hesitant to take the traditionalist approach since it often means tackling negative news about the organization. In other words, ex-newspaper reporters who transitioned to team media agree that one of the most notable challenges to job acclimation was learning what stories were permissible to publicize and which topics were forbidden. The ability of an outside media member to break news related to the local N.B.A. or N.F.L. team may have diminished due to the rise of ESPN Insiders like Adam Schefter (N.F.L.) and Adrian Wojnarowski (N.B.A.), both of whom have massive social media followings and connections to players' agents (Draper, 2014; Greene, 2017; Maese, 2014).

However, chasing the latest scoop is often the furthest thing from the mind of a team-employed journalist because of the nature of working alongside an organization's public relations arm. In most cases, in-house reporters made it clear that they can only report on breaking news subjects (e.g., injury reports, roster transactions, and coaching hires/firings) after the team has issued an official statement to outside media on the particular matter. This is because, most interviewees said, teams only want verified information circulating in the public sphere. So, instead of attributing material to an outside source, internal media must pump the brakes on hard news, waiting for P.R. to put out the press release before writing the accompanying online article.

For a journalist like Jim Wyatt, who spent the first half of his professional career in legacy sports journalism, the adjustment from one end of the media spectrum to the other required him to shake the proverbial breaking news mentality that came with being a former newspaper journalist. Wyatt, a senior writer/editor for TennesseeTitans.com, experienced the different editorial strategies between internal and external media firsthand when he left *The Tennessean*, Nashville's Gannett-owned daily newspaper, to cover the team for its official website in 2015 ("Titans reporter Jim Wyatt Leaving Tennessean," 2015). The University of Tennessee journalism graduate had written about the Titans for the newspaper since their relocation from Memphis to Nashville in 1999. He described himself as the de facto "guy" on the beat, the reporter whom other local media members wanted to emulate for his hard-nosed approach to reporting.

During his 16-year tenure covering the Titans for *The Tennessean*, Wyatt broke news, wrote recap and feature stories, and gave readers everything they needed to know about the A.F.C. South team. From his perspective, he did what all reporters should do: "own the beat" so readers can receive information from the local journalist and not from national sources like ESPN and the N.F.L. Network. Wyatt admitted that his job as lead Titans reporter for Nashville's only daily print publication took its toll. He was so tethered to his phone that major breaking stories often interrupted family time. Then again, the constant grind to be the best in his media market was the part of the job that Wyatt loved most.

So, going from a standard 24/7 journalistic routine for the newspaper, where he was constantly "chasing breaking news," to a more relaxed media environment essentially meant pivoting toward an entirely new era, even though the overall basis of writing about sports was the same. Being a team employee made Wyatt aware of the organization's inner workings. However, just because he had access to privileged information did not mean he always had the head coach and/or general manager's blessing to go after hard news. As he put it:

> When you're working for the team, you're trying to find a more optimistic look at things [...] As a journalist, I still know that people want objective writing and don't want sunshine and rainbows all the time. So, I try to have balance, and I still try to put things in perspective, and still try to tell it like it is, even though I know that you can't cross a line, you can't follow up on the negative. (J. Wyatt, personal communication, January 27, 2021)

Like Wyatt, Arizona Cardinals' senior writer Darren Urban was forced to navigate similar murky waters when "the team came calling" in 2007. During the hiring process, Urban, who had covered the Cardinals for the *East Valley Tribune* (AZ) since the 2000 season, clearly understood the job's editorial limitations yet still wanted to treat it like a standard sports beat. For the initial interview with the media relations department, Urban went in with a series of hypothetical scenarios, asking his higher-ups how they would react if he covered each instance of player news. Unsure if the title of in-house beat writer was suitable for someone who had been in the newspaper business for the previous 15 years, Urban bluntly told team officials that they could easily hire multiple younger reporters for what it would cost to sway him to the team-run side. The Cardinals, though, wanted an individual with institutional knowledge of the team, someone with an established following to cover the beat from a newspaper perspective.

Despite the aforementioned editorial strategy negotiation, Urban acknowledged that a lot of "learning on the fly" occurred during his transition. For one, coming from a standard newsroom meant he did not receive the type of editing he was accustomed to from the Cardinals' staff. On top of that, his former paper had yet to shift to the immediacy of online news in 2007, meaning he was not pressured to get his newspaper copy finished and posted right after a game. The most noticeable learning curve, however, was straddling the line between publishing the type of content that fans needed to know while also being aware of the editorial wants of players, coaches, and the front office.

For instance, if Urban witnessed a player sustain an injury during practice as a newspaper reporter, he was free to include a blurb about it in his daily notebook published in print. As a team-employed journalist, the same type of freedom was not there. After seeing a player injure his leg during a drill in his first season as an in-house writer, Urban's journalistic instinct took over, and he included the observation in a write-up. Head coach Ken Wisenhunt, however, was not pleased that he "slapped a headline" on the injury, proving—firsthand—the subtle nuances associated with switching media sides. Urban said there had been benefits to the job, though, instances in which he was able to break a big story based on his status as the team reporter without fear of having someone review his content before it got posted (the few times this practice was implemented, he said, was coverage about team ownership).

As evidenced by the above comments from both Wyatt and Urban, reporters who left traditional media to write for a sports team's official website were often discouraged from tackling specific aspects of news because of the continual boundary renegotiations that occur (interviewees, though, did not specify if they have ever given a news tip for a potentially damaging story to external media member). Although Mirer (2019) finds that reporters who move from internal to external media reject the notion that they are leaving the tenets of journalism behind, some team-employed writers have noted that they tried to legitimize their work by negotiating editorial boundaries during the initial hiring process.

Having worked in team media for two different N.F.L. organizations after a 12-year stint as a newspaper sportswriter for the *Florida Times-Union*, Jacksonville Jaguars' senior writer John Oehser said the overall adjustment from legacy to team media typically depends on "what the team wants from you." The first N.F.L. franchise that Oehser worked for (the Indianapolis Colts) took a by-the-book approach, while the Jaguars, he said, are more open to traditional sports journalism norms. Oehser, who was on the Jaguars beat for the local newspaper before being hired by the Colts before the 2001 season, said he was the N.F.L.'s fifth ex-newspaper reporter to pivot to a team's official website. Despite having future hall-of-famer Peyton Manning in this third year running the offense, the Colts had not—as Oehser described, "penetrated their market very well yet,"—which gave team P.R. representative Craig Kelly an idea. Searching for a talented young journalist to hire, Kelly was recommended to interview Oehser by then-ESPN national football writer Len Pasquarelli. Once Oehser realized the Colts' offer was more than he was earning at the *Times-Union*, the move made sense (of note, most interviewees did not specify if being a team employee is a more financially lucrative sportswriting position than working for a newspaper).

Oehser said the Colts, and former general manager and team president Bill Polian in particular, were hesitant to give him the flexibility he was used to in external news because of the widespread fear that media, regardless of position or lean, represented the enemy. He was discouraged from analyzing or providing his take on team-related matters. Instead, he was forced to be "very vanilla" by solely reporting what Manning and the coaching staff said in each press conference leading up to a Sunday game. Going from a mindset focused on being the authoritarian provider of information on an N.F.L. beat when he was with the *Times-Union* to someone who had to take a "by-the-book" approach meant the job switch was somewhat of a learning curve. However, acclimation was relatively easy since he had the core writing and reporting skills needed in any journalistic job. In other words, team media at the time was "far less advanced" than what he "was normally doing for the newspaper." The adjustment, therefore, was just concerned with him getting comfortable not being able to touch exciting and controversial angles. As Oehser admitted, a team allowing a "former newspaper writer inside their building was, five years before this, something that would have never happened [. . .] But he [Polian] knew the times were changing. It was sort of a necessary evil."

When he returned to Jacksonville in 2011 after his nearly eight-season stint with Colts.com, this time to serve as the Jaguars' senior in-house writer, Oehser experienced greater control and editorial freedom. He said the Jaguars were among the first organizations to encourage writer opinion and analysis (while still avoiding critical news or hot takes) because, as a small market team, the front office realized that it "had to engage the fan as much as possible on as many fronts." In this sense, the transparency was a trickle-down effect that began at the top of the hierarchical chain of command with ownership before moving to the individualized media philosophy of the communications staff. Oehser said the relationship between internal media and a sports organization's front office would never be a "completely comfortable marriage" since some front office executives likely believe journalists' only concern is prying for information. However, the link between football operations and in-house media is expected to be built on mutual understanding, a concept that old-school football minds may only sometimes like, but one that comes with perceived value.

Whereas today's sports organizations are fully aware of the importance of utilizing varying web and social media channels to cater content to a specific perspective (Williams et al., 2014), there may always be a distinct separation in terms of the boundary between those on the business, sport, and media sides. Most in-house interviewees who previously worked in print sports journalism discussed the importance of upfront boundary negotiation. The journalistic professional identity that these interviewees had in common was closely tied to their ability to provide beat-style coverage on a specific team. As a result, the avoidance of breaking news topics often came as a learning experience, something that Mirer (2019) notes is expected since in-house media serve as a close relative to native advertising, with the team-produced content typically framed with an underlying marketing purpose (Mirer, 2019).

While Wyatt, Urban, and Oehser viewed themselves as legitimate journalists, the role of an internal media member differs from an external sportswriter's because most teams are resistant to chasing breaking news. Thus, even though a former legacy reporter who now works for team-run media may still uphold the tenets of accurate and credible reporting on deadline, there is an apparent difference because of the connection to the team being covered (Mirer, 2019). Though the interviewees mentioned above transitioned from newspaper sports journalism to team-run media, Myles Simmons went from being a team-employed reporter to a newspaper sportswriter. Simmons began his sports media career as a senior writer/team insider for the Los Angeles Rams in 2014 before joining the *Las Vegas Review-Journal* to serve as the Raiders beat reporter (when the team first moved to Las Vegas) in August 2019. Simmons was only in that position for one N.F.L. season before an opportunity to serve as a senior writer/editor for the Carolina Panthers (his same title with the Rams) opened. Eight months later, Simmons said he was headhunted for an opportunity to write for Pro Football Talk, Mike Florio's N.F.L. news site that became a legitimized NBC Sports property in 2009.

The transition from in-house media to newspaper journalism was a minor adjustment, Simmons admitted, since he mostly had flexibility with the Rams to cover the team how a newspaper reporter would (albeit without critical pieces advocating for a coaching change). He noted the switch was more apparent (going from the *Review-Journal* to the Carolina Panthers) because of that team's emphasis on longer-form editorial projects instead of daily coverage. Simmons noted, "It was a totally different editorial philosophy because the approach I took to the Rams was not the one that would work for the Panthers. It depends on the organization to say what works and what doesn't."

Although the above interviewees all had external media experience, whether as a beat writer for a local newspaper or online-only news site, before being hired by an N.F.L. organization, Briana McDonald's career path demonstrates that professional journalistic experience is not a prerequisite for one to produce content for a team's official website. McDonald, the San Francisco 49ers digital media coordinator, began contributing written content for the team as an intern studying broadcast journalism and sports administration at the University of Miami before being hired as a full-time content creator (producing written, audio, and video content) in June 2022. Because she went straight from a college classroom to a full-time position with the 49ers without having first worked for external sports media, McDonald said that the job function of team-run media differs slightly from the standard journalistic routines learned in college; however, because her position acts as an extension of the marketing department, McDonald mentioned that her content typically comes "from a marketing aspect" since she and her colleagues are "more so selling the team." This professional mindset, she said, does impact the editorial direction of her 49ers content (as others mentioned) since her department will not ignore negative news surrounding the team. However, a philosophy rooted in marketing is to find a "workaround" in those situations.

Despite fluctuations regarding one's perceived professional identity (whether it is more aligned with journalism, marketing/P.R., or a hybrid), the main item to emphasize is that the differing approaches are all perception-based, meaning that where an interviewee situates him or herself on this spectrum may not indeed be where the professional boundaries align. It is one thing for an in-house senior writer or digital media coordinator to view him or herself as a journalist or marketing professional who happens to write news content for a professional sports team's website. However, it is another way for the media profession, as a whole, to classify this person (and his or her role) as a legitimate journalist because of the shared agreement that journalism must be objective, timely, practice autonomy (i.e., coverage free from conflict of interest), and fulfill a public service (Deuze, 2005; Weedon et al., 2018). Based on these points, it is likely that an in-house sports reporter would not truly fit the mold of a genuine journalist because an individual in this role cannot separate him or herself from the built-in conflict of interest that comes with covering one's employer.

Maintaining Face: "I don't want to constantly flaunt access that [other media members] don't have"

Although relationship building has typically enabled sportswriters to become familiar with the athletes and coaches they cover, how journalists get close to sources has been drastically altered in the digital age (Strauss, 2020). Because a sports team may try to limit negative news about its brand, access to the major beats in the professional and collegiate ranks is often significantly less than it once was (McCollough, 2018). It is now commonplace for a traditional sports journalist to only receive interviews with players, coaches, and team personnel during specified media availability time slots, meaning that the all-crucial "one-on-one" is rare—especially in the post-COVID-19 journalism landscape. Therefore, relationship building is much more complicated than in years past since sportswriters cannot put in the time required to get to know an athlete or member of the coaching staff on a personal level (Politi, 2020).

In-house media brings a unique perspective regarding source building and access. Although it could be assumed that team-employed writers have an easier time constructing source relationships and getting preferential access because of their position within the organization, interviewees noted that this is not always the case. Most team-employed writers agree that familiarizing oneself with sources is much easier—chiefly because of the ability to "bump" into these individuals in the building; however, they rarely receive extra access not given to outside media members. This is because a team's media relations department typically wants to ensure everyone is on an equal playing field regarding access by not displaying direct or subtle favoritism toward coworkers in the same role.

Although he generally agreed that someone in his position is likely to form a close working relationship with members of the team, Portland Trail Blazers digital reporter Casey Holdahl said his ability to craft exciting stories is a byproduct of being around the organization since 2007, enabling players to become familiar with him. Holdahl viewed the key to relationship building as being professional and not taking advantage of unique situations because of his status.

He travels with the team on chartered flights. Holdahl, though, does not greet each player as he walks into the cabin, hoping to grab a few minutes of that individual's time for an upcoming story. He may ride the team bus, but the Portland native does not pick players' brains regarding the keys to winning an upcoming game. Holdahl sometimes sees coaches in the practice facility, the bowels of the Monda Center, or other private areas where outside media are not permitted. However, he rarely uses those accidental run-ins as opportunities to get quotes. For him, it is all about doing his job as a journalist in the time allotted to every other reporter during regular media availability.

Because his job norms and routines are similar to outside media, Holdahl said it is not uncommon for a Portland player to confuse him for a writer covering the team for *The Oregonian*, *Portland Tribune*, or any other legacy organization. To them, he is not a team-employed journalist. Instead, he is a sportswriter who is always around, familiarizing himself with those on his beat. Holdahl also noted that it is most likely easier to form these relationships with sources because he is not required to be as critical of the Trailblazers organization as a newspaper sportswriter (for instance, Holdahl said that he does not have to ask players and the head coach tough, probing questions after a blowout loss). He noted, "It's still a relationship business, and if you burn guys or if they feel like you don't conduct yourself responsibly, they're going to remember that, and they're going to act accordingly, regardless of who you work for."

When Minnesota Vikings staff writer Lindsey Young was a featured columnist for *Vikings Territory*, an external blog branded as the place for "friends to gather and discuss all things Minnesota Vikings" ("About Vikings Territory," n.d.), she was able to forge contacts with players, building a friendly rapport that allowed her to tell impactful stories. However, Young admitted that relationship building after transitioning to the team was more accessible because of the day-to-day aspect of interacting with sources at various times in the team facility. Being able to gauge the "behind the scenes" occurrences of all things Vikings enabled Young to do much more of the type of content that she had only dipped her toes in as a blogger.

While access for internal media is highly dependent on the individualized stances of a team's public relations department and the media philosophies of the coach and general manager, working for the team has enabled Young to know Vikings players and coaching personnel on a more personal basis—as long as the standardized process of requesting interviews through media relations is followed. While some in-house sportswriters, like Hobson and Eisen, said they are typically permitted to schedule interviews with players independently, Young must generally go through media relations, a protocol that her external media peers must also follow. There are some instances, such as grabbing a player for a quick sound bite after exiting the field during a training camp practice, where Young can arrange interviews on her own. For the most part, though, the Vikings' media relations staff expects her to follow the route of outside media and gather quotes during the scheduled media availability sessions or weekly press conferences.

The relationship building that Young mentioned is on a case-by-case basis, in which some players find it easier to let their guard down and open up on a more personal level. Because all team members have their daily work requirements (Young included), there is not ample opportunity for personal interaction outside the predetermined media availability time slots. However, being a familiar face in the team facility (especially in the cafeteria line) can make a player feel more comfortable with Young because of her status as a team-employed reporter. While the interview access may be similar between an internal and external media member, the ability of a team writer to be strategically inserted into positions that build rapport likely provides a competitive edge.

When an in-house writer works for a team website that is traditionally more critical than its peers in the same sports league, however, the ease in relationship building and maintenance with sources can sometimes act as a double edge sword, something former Dallas Cowboys' internal staff writer David Helman experienced. Because of the Cowboys' prominent status as "America's team," in which Helman noted that a large portion of the website traffic comes from fans living in various parts of the country, the organization gave him and the official website's two other writers leeway to run the editorial process more like a traditional media organization than the standard in-house operation. From Helman's perspective, the ability to "get away with saying and writing a lot of the things" that other in-house reporters could never do speaks to the forward-thinking of both the entire Dallas Cowboys organization and team owner Jerry Jones, whom Helman said understands the value of building journalistic trust with the fanbase. The concept is straightforward yet innovative enough to counter the practices in place for most other in-house interviewees; if fans can trust the information from the team-employed reporters, they will be more likely to digest content from the sports organization's official website.

Unlike the total autonomous freedom enjoyed by outside media covering a team commonly designated as one of the most valuable sports team brands (Badenhausen, 2020), there were still limitations, like specific topics off limits for the in-house writers. However, compared to the average team journalist, he had more freedom to run the beat however he saw fit. As Helman, who left the team in 2022 to serve as FOX Sports' Cowboys writer and podcaster, said, "If I felt like all I was doing was being a mouthpiece for the organization, I don't think I would have lasted [in that job]."

Despite the opportunity for relationship building that came with working in the same building as players that he covered daily, Helman noted that taking a more conventional and critical journalistic stance sometimes rubbed sources the wrong way. As he put it, some players and coaches had difficulty understanding why a team employee would openly criticize their colleagues in a work environment. To this degree, Helman saw it as a fine line that he walked in building trustful relationships with sources, while doing his journalistic duty, by publishing objective and impartial Cowboys content. Helman admitted that he had probably "done something to aggravate somebody in every part of the power structure." However, the overwhelming feedback he received from fans on his critical content while working for the team had been positive. Helman said fans appreciated that he did not hold back, toe the company line, or push a positive agenda because he was an employee.

This flexibility represents a team-run media stance that is generally uncommon in the industry since most other organizations, Helman noted, shy away from being brutally honest each week. The downside is that Helman and the other staff writers were treated as outside media, only receiving interview time during press conferences. The only exception, he said, is that media relations would sometimes "throw us a bone" by giving the team-employed reporters first access to an interview if a player signed a contract extension and the team wanted to be the first to report the news.

As mentioned, in-house writers must still go through media relations for interview time and access. Hobson and Eisen, the N.F.L. in-house reporters who have each worked for their respective teams (the Bengals and Giants) for over two decades, are the only interviewees who noted that they are free to coordinate interviews on their terms (i.e., they do not need media relations clearance). Hobson, the Bengals' only in-house beat writer who has been covering the team in some capacity since 1990, has experienced changes to the access he has received (both as an internal and external media member) during the previous three decades. When he began writing for the Bengals team website, access to players and coaches was "as much as you wanted it to be." It was an adjustment for sources at first, he said, because he went from scrutinizing them while working for the local paper to all of a sudden being on their side.

Because he has been in his role for so long, Hobson can cultivate sources independently instead of going through traditional channels, thus reinforcing the importance of having his relationships to get interviews outside the team. The Zoom interviews that were the byproduct of the COVID-19 pandemic threw a wrench into the equation, though, meaning that Hobson was not afforded increased access because everyone was forced to work remotely.

Eisen, similarly, can skip the traditional media relations route to secure interviews with sources on the Giants beat. Being around the team, as both a newspaper reporter and in-house journalist since 1986, means that he has seniority over most other team employees, allowing him access that no one else is generally afforded. One of his favorite activities, Eisen noted, is to frequent the Giants' locker room when outside media is not permitted to strengthen the interpersonal relationships that enable him to perform his job function. Before the COVID-19 pandemic, which began to affect in-person interviews in March 2020, Eisen had the freedom to coordinate player interviews roughly "98 percent of the time," he estimated. If he wanted to talk with someone in particular during that time, he would "grab him." Some players were better at sticking to these informal interviews than others (most notably former Giants quarterback Eli Manning, who was constantly on time, and receiver Odell Beckham, Jr., who rarely showed up). However, the remote working environment initially caused by the coronavirus pandemic had been a curveball in

Eisen's ability to set up a quick one-on-one, forcing him to fall back on media relations to assist with interview scheduling.

The general sentiment expressed by in-house writers regarding the inability (for most) to schedule interviews themselves is a boundary that may inadvertently help these individuals still cling to some semblance of external media norms. Although the position of an internal reporter is one created by the sports organization for its benefit, in-house reporters with a prior background in professional journalism said they feel like any external sportswriter since they generally receive the same type of access. As Mirer (2019) notes, this aids in constructing and maintaining credibility and enables team-employed writers to further separate their professional identity from public relations.

Brand Promotion Through Journalistic Content: "We're always thinking about how we can help tell *our* story"

Since the rise of the Internet as a news dissemination platform, professional and major collegiate sports organizations have pondered the value of giving outside sportswriters and reporters access to sources for feature and game coverage (Morrissey, 2016). Unlike the past, when mainstream media and hometown sports teams relied on each other equally, the current relationship between both entities is more one-sided since in-house reporting essentially allows a team to go straight to the fanbase (Claxton, 2020). This notion of forgoing traditional press in favor of curating individually tailored content first prompted former Dallas Mavericks' owner Mark Cuban to question the role of external sports media in a 2011 post published on his aptly named *Blog Maverick* site.

Cuban, over a decade ago, believed that outside media coverage was no longer a necessity since his then-N.B.A. franchise had "finally reached a point" where it could "communicate any factual information [...] as effectively as any big sports website" (Cuban, 2011, para. 1). Since the interests of the two parties were "no longer aligned," the billionaire likened the role of traditional sports reporters more to paparazzi than factual news disseminators (para. 1). It was not that Cuban—the lively sports executive who made his fortune in software before purchasing the Mavericks in 2000—wanted to banish all external journalists from the home locker room of American Airlines Center, the team's home venue. As he wrote, it was essential to credential newspaper and television sports journalists since a segment of his fanbase at the time relied on legacy media for Mavericks news. He also respected the publicity that unpaid Internet reporters and fan bloggers provided since those who tackle the craft as a "labor of love" generally back up what they say with "well thought out and in-depth analysis" (para. 7).

However, the bane of external media, Cuban wrote, was the paid Internet sportswriters who were more concerned with clickbait than legitimized journalistic activity. These individuals, he believed, were only fixated on transaction rumors and negative headlines, the type of publicity that did not benefit the team's brand image. This prompted Cuban, who realized that he possessed the power to reach the same online audience that these writers target, to wonder if his media department could compete "with information that does a better job of selling the Mavs" (para. 16). Nearly a decade-and-a-half has passed since Cuban gave his take on team media. Regardless of one's stance related to its perceived benefit, or lack thereof, his view on using in-house reporters to do the work of an external media member reflects the intrinsic value of a sports organization controlling its own media message.

Based on the themes outlined earlier in this chapter, the professional role and identity of an external beat writer and internal journalist may be similar since both entities typically receive the same source access (except in the case of Hobson and Eisen). However, as some interviewees noted, not all team-employed media members try to mimic an external journalist's job function and editorial output. Some, like former Atlanta Falcons digital managing editor Matthew Tabeek, viewed written and digital content posted to the team's official website as a vehicle that can extend the brand's reach to those who would have otherwise never turned to traditional news sources. Tabeek, who worked for the Falcons from 2017 to 2021 before joining Front Office Sports as a senior managing editor, said engaging and unique in-house web content could potentially turn young people in both the Atlanta area and nationwide into Falcons' fans (of note, Tabeek was interviewed in January 2021, two months before leaving the team). Whereas the fandom and media consumption habits of older individuals are often difficult to sway, Tabeek admitted that Millennials and members of Generation Z are the most impressionable, meaning that a solid digital and social media strategy had the potential to transform a passive Falcon fan into a loyal consumer of the brand.

However, it was more than just the recaps and feature stories. If he and his team could pay "attention to what pops" and correlate their content to what people talk about online, they could potentially have boosted ticket and revenue sales by further promoting the Falcons' brand online. From this standpoint, a successful digital-first team media strategy should not solely focus on emulating the same old beat concept that has defined the profession since the "golden age" of sports and sportswriting in the 1920s (Bohn, 2009). Instead, the function of today's internal media goes hand-in-hand with the basic principles and goals of a team's marketing department; it all comes back to promoting the brand and determining "how we can help tell our story." As Tabeek saw it:

> We [were] constantly discussing knowing our audience, what platforms reach differ-
> ent audience segments, and why each has value. And, so, it's more than just a matter
> of competing with newspapers. It's competing with newspapers, but also winning over
> all those different segments of the audience and making sure that we're checking
> those bucket lists and making sure that we're putting out great content. (M. Tabeek,
> personal communication, February 1, 2021)

Using in-house media to zone in on audience trends by strengthening the brand of a relatively young professional sports franchise in a city in which one team still reigns supreme is something New Orleans Pelicans' writer Jim Eichenhofer grapples with daily. Although the Pelicans, who have been a staple in the city's sporting scene since 2008, are not New Orleans' first N.B.A. team (the Crescent City hosted the New Orleans Jazz from 1974 to 1979), a portion of sports fans in the region grew up during a time in which the Saints were the only team in town. Thus, those in their late 40s and early 50s were forced to gravitate toward other N.B.A. teams during their adolescent years. Eichenhofer is in a unique situation. He is tasked with using his reporting chops for N.B.A.com to not only sell the team to an older generation but also appealing content to teenagers and twenty-somethings who are interested in the digital engagement aspect of team media.

In this regard, media has a niche to fill, and Eichenhofer said the overall goal of the franchise is to build a presence in the New Orleans market, whether from his reporting or from the cooperative working relationships he has with outside media. When reporters have worked in print journalism for much of their professional careers, they most likely understand the importance of being on good terms with media peers. The added publicity reporters from NewOrleans.com and The Athletic provide also helps reinforce the Pelicans' brand. Whereas his take on media competition may be different if he was asked that question in 2007, when the news was not nearly as immediate, and there was more of an "adversarial-type relationship" between journalists,

Eichenhofer said any press that his team can receive, whether from internal or external media, helps in the long-run.

Although the internal media model of the M.L.B. differs from the N.B.A. and N.F.L., the goal of using centralized news content to cultivate a budding audience, especially in a sport like baseball that predominantly skews toward an older demographic (Jacoby, 2016), remains the same. For Anthony DiComo, an M.L.B. Advance Media reporter assigned to cover the New York Mets for Major League Baseball's website, the obvious benefit of the online-only model is not having to "fill in a news hole every day," meaning that aside from game coverage he can spend more time working on more extended features and special projects that can gain more traction in both the web and social media spheres. DiComo, who has been in his current position since 2010, said extending a baseball team's reach in today's digital-first era boils down to telling the reader not only "what happened" in a sport in which "the games are still king" but also "why it matters."

Perhaps the often forgotten benefit of the league-run electronic model, DiComo mentioned, is the notion that M.L.B.com can be construed as the authoritative source on all baseball news that has occurred in the past two decades since all articles dating back to 2001 can be found archived on the web. Similar to *The New York Times'* long associated stance as the "newspaper of record," DiComo sees centralized league media as filling a void left by cut-backs and layoffs at legacy media outlets, most of whom he said are "not always able to cover what's right in front of them." Thus, having a reporter employed by the league who can travel to each of an assigned team's road games is an apparent advantage that helps to fortify the importance of internal media, whether the oversight is from an individual team or the league itself.

Comparable to Eichenhofer's take that external media does not represent competition to team-employed journalists, most interviewees noted that they do not go after the same type of content, or fan, that is the main target of the local newspaper. Sure, the argument has always been that there are only so many fans of a specific team in a particular media market, meaning that two or more news entities are bound to compete for readers. Content overlap is likely to exist to some degree. However, because internal beat writers typically do not emphasize breaking or critical news, the common belief is that they can focus on their work without worrying about another reporter stealing their story topic.

For Seattle Seahawks digital media reporter John Boyle, the internal and external media story is no longer centered on competing journalists vying for the same audience. Instead, like sports content consumption in the digital age, competition between legacy and new media has evolved as Internet options have multiplied based on the specific niche populations they seek to serve. Even if there are only a finite number of readers in a professional sports market, Boyle believes that only some look for the same type of content. This view ultimately reinforces his professional identity as an internal media member. As Boyle asserted, "You're always competing to get people to your site. But what I do is different from what the *Seattle Times* does. And that is different from what The Athletic does. All those things can coexist well, going after different readers." In this manner, because of the differentiation of audience, Boyle sees his work as helping the Seahawks tell their individual stories and increase the brand impression. At the same time, external media has the same impact, albeit in a slightly altered form.

The above emphasis on sports teams using their internal beat writer to act as an extension of the marketing department coincides with the notion that all forms of online and mobile-based marketing can influence public perception toward a sports brand (Baena, 2014). Before the Internet allowed a sports team to disseminate content, brand publicity only came from legacy media coverage, whether it focused on game recaps, feature stories, or a combination of both. Since the rise of in-house team media operations, the capacity to market oneself to the masses has been transformed since "brand content reflects efforts by more institutional actors to take advantage of these same tools to go around journalists and directly reach audiences" (Mirer et al., 2018, p. 489). As previously mentioned, boundary work in journalism is a process by which an institution achieves or loses rank based on commonly held norms of those in the profession. Those who said their function is slightly different from the role of legacy reporters reinforce how sports journalism norms evolve as sports organizations uncover more effective communication techniques to target fans.

However, it is essential to note that written articles are not the only form of content professional sports organizations use to position themselves within a specified target market. As evident by Jill Beckman, the Tampa Bay Buccaneers social media specialist who was the only social media-centric interviewee, content marketing derived from an in-house staff allows a sports organization to humanize its athletes in a manner that a newspaper sportswriter could not achieve because of access restrictions. Beckman mentioned that part of expanding the Buccaneers' social reach (from less than 250,000 Instagram followers when she was hired in 2018 to roughly 1.4 million in

November 2023) can be attributed to both team success and "knowing how to show the personality of some of our players so they can be relatable to the fans" (to illustrate this, Beckman pointed to the Buccaneers' former social media show, *Tommy and Gronky*, in which Tom Brady and Rob Gronkowski discussed relevant topics while sitting in lawn chairs outside the team's practice facility). Whereas some N.F.L. in-house reporters noted that they must still work within the constraints of traditional media access, Beckman—a graduate of Penn State's Bellisario College of Communications—said that social media affords more flexibility in terms of "speaking directly to the fans."

Based on the notion that team-run media can be used further to promote a professional sports team from a marketing perspective, it can be inferred that this specific subset of sports media is not one marked by a stiff direct competitor but rather one that is complementary to newspaper beat reporting (and other types of daily written sports coverage, for that matter) since it caters to a specific type of sports fan—those who want news about their favorite team viewed through the lens of the team itself. Each internal media interviewee mentioned that boundary work must be negotiated within team-run media because it constantly changes. The role of in-house media extends beyond basic principles of journalism since its basis is more closely aligned with the goals of a team's marketing department, despite some interviewees perceiving their role as still being journalistic. This notion helps to illustrate internal content creation's role in shaping a team-specific narrative, fostering brand identity, and adapting to the evolving norms of digital sports media. In conclusion, the landscape of sports team media has undergone a significant transformation in the digital age, challenging traditional relationships between teams and external sportswriters. In-house sportswriting may highlight a shift toward teams utilizing internal reporting and publicity; if anything, though, it is likely viewed as a two-pronged approach bundled with external coverage since in-house sports reporting has evolved beyond mere replication of newspaper beat reporting to encompass a variety of specific perspectives based on one's career backgrounds before transitioning to the team.

References

"About Vikings Territory." (n.d.). *Vikings Territory.* http://www.vikingsterritory.com/about

Badenhausen, K. (2020, July 31). The world's most valuable sports teams 2020. *Forbes.* http://www.forbes.com/sites/kurtbadenhausen/2020/07/31/the-worlds-most-valuable-sports-teams-2020/?sh=113a433d3c74

Baena, V. (2014). Online and mobile marketing strategies as drivers of brand love in sports teams: Findings from Real Madrid. *International Journal of Sports Marketing and Sponsorships*, 17(3), 202–218.

"Bengals.com lands top writer." (2000, April 5). *Cincinnati Bengals*. https://www.bengals.com/news/bengals-com-lands-top-writer-734337#:~:text=Geoff%20Hobson%2C%20widely%20regarded%20as,head%20writer%20for%20Bengals.com

Bohn, M. K. (2009). *Heroes and ballyhoo: How the Golden Age of the 1920s transformed American sports*. Potomac Books.

Carlson, M. (2015). Introduction: The many boundaries of journalism. In M. Carlson & S. C. Lewis (Eds.), *Boundaries of journalism: Professionalism, practices, and participation* (pp. 1–18). Routledge.

Claxton, D. (2020, August 3). Sports teams take control of their media. *Business of Sport*. http://businessofsport.net/2020/08/03/sports-media/

Cuban, M. (2011, April 4). *What's the role of media for sports teams?* Blog Maverick. http://blogmaverick.com/2011/04/04/whats-the-role-of-media-for-sports-teams/

Deuze, M. (2005). What is journalism? Professional identity and ideology of journalists reconsidered. *Journalism*, 6(4), 442–464.

Draper, K. (2014, December 16). *Basketball's biggest reporter is waging war on ESPN—And he'll do anything to win*. The New Republic. https://newrepublic.com/article/120572/adrian-wojnarowski-how-basketballs-reporting-machine-gets-his-scoops

Fry, J. (2011, September 15). *Rules of the game change as sports journalists compete against teams they cover*. Poynter. http://www.poynter.org/reporting-editing/2011/rules-of-the-game-change-as-sports-journalists-compete-against-teams-they-cover/

Greene, N. (2017, June 30). *There is no shelter from the Woj bombs*. Slate. http://www.slate.com/culture/2017/06/adrian-wojnarowski-and-espn-a-match-made-in-hype-heaven.html

Hobson, G. (2015, July 22). Hobson's choice: Fame and fortune. *Cincinnati Bengals*. https://www.bengals.com/news/hobson-s-choice-fame-and-fortune-15509664

Jacoby, S. (2016, August 18). Baseball and its aging fans. *The Wall Street Journal*. https://www.wsj.com/articles/baseball-and-its-aging-fans-1471534364.

Lattman, P. (2008, February 5). Law blog Lawyer of the Day: John K. Mara, Esq. *The Wall Street Journal*. http://www.wsj.com/articles/BL-LB-5261

Maese, R. (2014, September 2). Adam Schefter is an N.F.L. reporting machine. *The Washington Post*. http://www.washingtonpost.com/spors/redskins/adam-schefter-is-nfl-reporting-machine/2014/09/02/93e009f2-32cc-11e4-9f4d-24103cb8b742_story.html

McCollough, J. B. (2018, October 9). Sports journalists battle for relevancy. *NiemanReports*. https://niemanreports.org/articles/sports-journalists-battle-for-relevancy/

Mirer, M. (2019). Playing the right way: In-house sports reporters and media ethics as boundary work. *Journal of Media Ethics*, 34(2), 73–86.

Mirer, M., Duncan, M. A., & Wagner, M. W. (2018). Taking it from the team: Assessments of bias and credibility in team-operated sports media. *Newspaper Research Journal*, 39(4), 481–495.

Moritz, B., & Mirer, M. (2021). The end of the scoop scoreboard: Boundary work and breaking news in sports journalism. In R. Domenghetti (Ed.) *Insights on reporting sports in the digital age*. (1st ed., pp. 130–147). Routledge.

Morrissey, R. (2016, December 21). The disconnect between pro sports teams and the media is growing. *Chicago Sun-Times*. http://www.chicago.suntimes.com/2016/12/21/18351670/the-disconnect-between-pro-sports-teams-and-the-media-is-growing.

Politi, S. (2020, July 6). Sports are back (for now). Sportswriters? We're still on the sidelines. *NJ.com*. http://www.nj.com/yankees/2020/07/sports-are-back-sportswriters-were-still-on-the-sidelines-politi.html.

Putterman, A. (2017, August 24). *Saying bye to sportswriting: Ex-reporters explain why they're leaving the profession amid industry chaos*. Awful Announcing. https://awfulannouncing.com/online-outlets/saying-good-bye-sportswriting-industry-chaos-reporters-leaving.html

Sherwood, M., Nicholson, M., & Majoribanks, T. (2016). Controlling the message and the medium: The impact of sports organizations' digital and social channels on media access. *Digital Journalism*, 5(5), 513–531.

Stellino, V. (2011, January 19). *Vic Ketchman resigning as editor of Jaguars.com*. Jacksonville.com. http://www.jacksonville.com/sports/football/jaguars/2011-01-19/story/vic-ketchman-resigning-editor-jaguarscom?page=1

Stofer, K. T., Schaffer, J. R., & Rosenthal, B. A. (2010). *Sports journalism: An introduction to reporting and writing*. Rowman & Littlefield.

Strauss, B. (2020, May 14). Amid layoffs and furloughs, sportswriters wonder what will be left of a storied profession. *The Washington Post*. http://www.washingtonpost.com/sports/2020/05/14/amid-layoffs-furloughs-sportswriters-wonder-what-will-be-left-once-storied-profession/

Suess, J. (2019, April 9). *Our history: Enquirer has adapted over its long history since 1841*. Cincinnati.com. http://www.cincinnati.com/story/news/2019/04/09/our-history-enquirer-adapted-over-long-history-since-1841/3414049002/

"Titans reporter Jim Wyatt Leaving Tennessean." (2015, July 20). *The Tennessean*. https://www.tennessean.com/story/sports/nfl/titans/2015/07/20/titans-reporter-jim-wyatt-leaving-tennessean/30435039/

Weaver, R. J. (2010). Online fantasy sports litigation and the need for a Federal Right of Publicity Statute. *Duke Law & Technology Review*, 9(1), 1–25.

Weedon, G., Wilson, B., Yoon, L., & Lawson, S. (2018). Where's all the "good" sports journalism? Sports media research, the sociology of sport, and the question of quality sports reporting. *International Review for the Sociology of Sport*, 53(6), 639–667.

Williams, J., Chinn, S. J., & Suleiman, J. (2014). The value of Twitter for sports fans. *Journal of Direct, Data and Digital Marketing Practice*, 16(1), 36–50.

· 2 ·

NORMALIZING THE NEW WAVE: THE ATHLETIC'S IMPACT ON SPORTS MEDIA STANDARDS

In today's journalistic ecosystem, one marked by a proliferation of online outlets covering virtually every media market and news topic, it is difficult to visit a major news website without running into a paywall, a method of hiding content for anyone who does not pay a subscription fee (Hill, 2020). There was a time when the business model of news organizations (including both newspaper websites and entities that solely existed in the online sphere) was exclusively rooted in advertising revenue, allowing readers to consume information free of charge (Benson, 2019). However, based on the current climate of news, revenue rates are tapering off, staff layoffs are abundant, and the ad-based model—as O'Brien et al. (2020) write—is "severely challenged" (p. 643). Therefore, implementing a paywall can sometimes be viewed as a survival tactic in a free-market news economy, with the public needing quality journalism and those who produce this work needing paid for their services (Williams & Stroud, 2021).

This notion that subscription revenue alone may be able to sustain a journalistic entity was the guiding principle behind the innovative sports media vision of entrepreneurs Alex Mather and Adam Hansmann. Although neither possessed a newspaper sports journalism background, they were ardent supporters of their hometown teams (with Mather being from Philadelphia and

Hansmann growing up in Cincinnati; Peralta, 2019). Both believed other passionate sports fans would rather pay for a news subscription focused on sports coverage than bundling sports with politics, arts, and local news (Biasotti, 2017). The original goal for their sports media platform, aptly named The Athletic, was to cater to a segment of fans who desired substantive, quality reporting in an advertising-free environment (Bilton, 2016). It is important to note, however, that The Athletic has since introduced advertising on its website and app as part of *The New York Times'* 2022 acquisition, despite the displeasure of some readers (Perpich, 2022; Jones, 2022).

When it officially launched in early 2016, The Athletic's strategy was a gamble on multiple fronts. For one, it emphasized hiring established newspaper sportswriters with substantial social media followings instead of cultivating young (and relatively unknown) journalistic talent (Gordon, 2018). Secondly, its editorial style focused on an area of coverage rarely accentuated by other news outlets in the digital age—feature and enterprise-based sports reporting. Perhaps The Athletic's most brazen strategy, though, was its implementation of the hard paywall, hiding all content behind the subscriber curtain in a pioneering approach that Mather and Hansmann, in a 2018 introductory post, called "the future of sports journalism" (Mather & Hansmann, 2018, para. 5).

In the years since, The Athletic has grown from a small San Francisco startup in only a handful of media markets to a legitimate national sports news network under the *New York Times'* umbrella, with verticals covering every professional, international, and major collegiate sports team (Fischer, 2021; Fischer, 2022). The Athletic's expansive growth in sportswriters poached, number of teams covered, and total subscriber base does not mean it was always profitable before the *Times'* acquisition. Toonkel (2021) reports that The Athletic operated at a deficit ($95 million spent, with only $73 million in revenue) between 2019 and 2020. This inability to yield a consistent revenue gain prompted it to seek a potential buyer as early as March 2021, when Mather and Hansmann tried to negotiate a possible marriage with digital news publisher Axios (Berr, 2021). However, when that ultimately fell through, The Athletic eyed *The New York Times* as its next possible parent in June 2021 (that initial merger was unsuccessful since both parties could not agree on a price; Patel, 2021). Seven months later, though, in January 2022, it was announced that a new round of negotiations ended with The New York Times Company's purchase of The Athletic for $550 million in cash (Toonkel, 2022). According to the reporting of Hirsch et al. (2022), the deal between the two media entities was part of *The Times'* larger plan to increase its digital subscription total to 10 million by 2025. Of note, *The New York Times* had 7.6 million digital-only subscribers at the time of the January 2022 purchase, yet hit the coveted 10 million mark one month later, prompting the goal to be raised to 15 million total subscribers by the end of 2027 (Owen, 2022; Tracy, 2022).

As explained by Kafka (2022), this "marriage of convenience" (para. 3) benefitted both sides since it effectively gave the other what it was previously lacking. The New York Times Company wanted a way to increase a digital subscription rate that fell stagnant after former President Donald Trump left office in early 2021 (a move that marked the end of the colloquially dubbed "Trump bump" of subscriptions; Debre, 2021, para. 2). The Athletic's 1.2 million subscribers were viewed as a likely way to bundle what those individuals already paid for (sports news) with *The New York Times'* national and international hard news coverage. Further, with the merger, The Times Company received a new business venture that had virtually little overlap with its existing core editorial product (although it does still employ a few sportswriters, *The New York Times* focuses its coverage on the business side of sports, opting to run content from The Athletic for daily sports reporting, as interviewee Jenny Vrentas said). The Athletic, meanwhile, was still able to exist as a standalone entity with a larger marketing engine for promotional purposes (of note, founders Mather and Hansmann stayed on as co-presidents after the merger since The Times Company operated The Athletic separately from its main editorial output). From David Perpich's perspective—*The New York Times* executive who led acquisition efforts of The Athletic and now serves as its publisher—purchasing Mather and Hansmann's sports news network made sense since it was easier for his employer to acquire The Athletic instead of "trying to replicate what they're doing" (Hirsch et al., 2022, para. 19).

For Vrentas, a *New York Times* sportswriter bumped from the sports to the business desk, the move was unexpected and brought up concerns about the future of the newspaper's sports coverage. The former *Sports Illustrated* reporter, whose first day at the *Times* (January 4, 2022) was less than one week before the acquisition was publicly announced, said the internal message was to continue the editorial operation as usual. She said, "I was told, 'The two entities [*The New York Times'* sports department and The Athletic] are complementary. They can coexist.' That was true for the first 18 months. And then there was another shock when they announced they were disbanding the [sports] department." Though content from The Athletic is now published online and in the *Times'* printed product, Vrentas noted that The Athletic's reporters are not treated the same as all *New York Times* journalists regarding salary minimums and benefits under the *Times'* guild contract. Not treating sportswriters from The Athletic the same as other *Times* journalists, she said, "sends a message about how you view sports journalism," adding that "there's a lot about this decision that has been unfair to workers on both sides."

In a sense of irony, the acquisition contradicts a 2017 quote by Mather, in a *New York Times* profile, in which he described The Athletic's ultimate expansion goals as wanting to "wait every local paper out and let them continuously bleed until we are the last ones standing" (Draper, 2017, para. 2). This move, however, speaks to the larger context of media consolidation in the digital age. This is because the goal of some new media startups that lack mainstream appeal may be to survive long enough to be bought by a traditional media company, and then cash in on potential earnings.

The following chapter examines how The Athletic and its unconventional editorial and business approach to sportswriting have, in many ways, altered how the public perceived subscription-based sports media before the 2022 merger. Semi-structured interviews with 21 current and former reporters and editors for The Athletic, each representing a variety of sports beats, reveal that consumer sustainability of this journalistic venture may undoubtedly influence future evolution and innovation in mainstream sports media. Interviewees ranged from those who primarily covered college football/basketball ($n = 7$), M.L.B. ($n = 5$), the N.F.L. ($n = 4$), the N.B.A. ($n = 2$), the N.H.L. ($n = 1$), and those who serve as individual sport vertical editors ($n = 2$; of note, all interviews, except Vrentas, took place before The New York Times Company's acquisition). Using Glaser's (1965) emergent thematic analysis, the three emergent themes from these interviews are that The Athletic has impacted sports media regarding editorial content and focus, organizational structure, and the eventual normalization of the journalistic paywall.

From a theoretical perspective, Dimmick's (2003) niche gratification theory (N.G.T.) sheds light on news competition and why the public dedicates time and money to media. Because it predicts that Internet-based media will replace legacy news if it satisfies the exact needs more successfully, N.G.T. serves as a suitable framework. Because it stands out from the competition by tweaking the once standardized formulaic approach to sportswriting, The Athletic is likely to coexist with other forms of sports media since "there is the presence of some ecological difference between them" (Gaskins & Jerit, 2012, p. 193).

Before diving into The Athletic's perceived impact on the sports media sphere, as seen by those working for this industry giant, it is essential first to understand the attitudes of legacy media reporters who opted to leave the cozy confines of newspapers, magazines, and established national sports websites to join an online startup predicated on the paywall. Despite co-founder Mather's brash "continuously bleed" comment detailed above (Draper, 2017, para. 2), leaping toward an unproven outlet in its infancy was still a risk, even for established sportswriters who believed in the company's mantra of making the public "fall in love with the sports page again" (Mather & Hansmann, 2018, para. 9).

Laying the Groundwork: "If somebody needed to be talked into it, they probably weren't coming"

Stewart Mandel knew the sports journalism industry hit a low point in 2017, when the president of his then-employer, FOX Sports, eliminated written web content in favor of sports "hot takes" delivered via video format (e.g., roundtable discussion, trade rumors, opinions on player performance, etc.). Mandel, who made a name for himself during a 12-year run as a national college football reporter for *Sports Illustrated*, was aware FOX Sports was planning an eventual and exclusive editorial pivot to video roughly six months prior. When the announcement was made official, it still came as a "demoralizing moment" for someone known for his unique ability to write quality college football content. With little room for job advancement at traditional and established media corporations, Mandel realized that his future in the business likely hinged on his ability to become his own boss, so he planned to launch his own college football-centric news website.

It started as a simple what-if, with Mandel—a graduate of Northwestern University's prestigious Medill School of Journalism—bouncing ideas off Daniel Uthman, a former *U.S.A. Today* senior editor of college sports coverage. With a 20-plus-year background in journalism at that point, Mandel believed that he had a "good sense" of the type of content readers wanted. He knew it was vital to monetizing fans' growing fascination with "voraciously reading news stories about their favorite teams" on smartphone applications. He also saw the best reporters, many of whom were laid off and considering a career switch to the marketing or public relations sector. Soon, Mandel said, discussion of a partnered college football vertical with Uthman began to include recruiting former *Sports Illustrated* and *ESPN The Magazine* reporter Bruce Feldman, a national college football insider.

However, he was not the only forward-thinking media entrepreneur to conceive the idea for a new sports media startup. In early 2017, Mandel was made aware of The Athletic by his former *Sports Illustrated* boss, Paul Fichtenbaum. Living near the startup's home base in the San Francisco Bay Area, Mandel had Fichtenbaum, who was hired to advise the editorial operation of a sports news network that had only launched a year prior (Feder, 2016), connect him with co-founders, Mather and Hansmann. Looking back, Mandel pointed out that he never envisioned a subscription-based sports website, with all content hidden behind a paywall, being sustainable since the public had become accustomed to receiving sports news for free.

Hearing Mather and Hansmann's vision caused him to reconsider his previous thought, realizing that *this* was the alternative sports media option he wanted to create. Simply put, The Athletic was headed in a direction that no one else had yet paved, and Mandel knew he wanted a part of the action. If then-FOX Sports president Jamie Horowitz wished to terminate the publication of written articles, Mandel wanted to terminate his employment with FOX Sports. So, he joined The Athletic as editor-in-chief of its college football coverage and was given an eight-week timeframe to recruit the talent needed to build his all-star cast of six national reporters pocketed throughout the country.

His first hire was Max Olson of ESPN.com. Next, Mandel grabbed Feldman and former Notre Dame reporter Matt Fortuna, who was then a freelancer after leaving ESPN in December 2016 (Winn, 2017). Later, Chris Vannini and Chantel Jennings were on board. Finally, he secured *U.S.A. Today's* Nicole Auerbach, the newspaper's general assignment college basketball writer (in August 2024, after seven years with The Athletic, Auerbach left to join NBC Sports as a college football and basketball insider). Whereas many viewed it as a risk to impetuously shift toward a company built around the concept of a paywall that, Mandel said, only had 25,000 paying subscribers spread across four U.S. media markets at the time, his team saw The Athletic as an opportunity in the otherwise bleak media sphere. Like most early hires, Auerbach shared The Athletic's vision of providing readers with in-depth sports journalism that newspapers could not produce. Unlike the others, though, most of whom were laid off from mainstream sports media positions at the time, she had the most to lose by giving up her cushy national newspaper gig to transition to the upstart organization.

Auerbach viewed her primary beat at *U.S.A. Today* (college basketball) becoming a "one month a year sport" because most readers only pay attention to it during the March N.C.A.A. Tournament period. Consequently, she wanted to transition to a national college football beat that would garner year-round interest. With this in mind, Uthman—her editor at *U.S.A. Today* who is now The Athletic's senior managing editor for talent development—connected Auerbach with Mandel and, eventually, a new job opportunity. The offer was appealing, Auerbach admitted, because it effectively ensured that she would receive the flexibility needed to tackle long-form topics on a more prominent sport with national appeal. However, since The Athletic did not have an established reputation then, Auerbach wanted to confirm she would still be recognized as a legitimate reporter if she left a national newspaper brand behind. So, while at the Atlantic Coast Conference (A.C.C.) football media days in July 2017, the then-28-year-old bluntly asked head coaches, sports information personnel, and athletic directors how her access would change if she transitioned to the new organization.

In short, she was reassured that it would not be altered. Each person Auerbach asked confirmed that access was less about her specific job affiliation and more about the trust she had established within the framework of college athletics. Once Auerbach was met with this comfort, she fully embraced The Athletic, gravitating toward it based on the notion that her journalistic work could be valued more than "zero cents." Besides, Auerbach thought that if she worked for The Athletic for two or three years and it had not taken off, she could easily transition back to legacy media, this time with more contacts in college football. So, in August 2017, she made the jump, writing for The Athletic until 2024. Soon, others followed. Eventually, as The Athletic grew in subscriber size, market presence, and reporter recognition it was viewed as less of a risk and more as a career advancement. This was because notable names like ESPN.com senior college basketball writer Dana O'Neil, baseball reporters Jayson Stark and Jim Bowden, and longtime *Sports Illustrated* college basketball columnist Seth Davis joined the ranks (Glasspiegel, 2017; Grathoff, 2017; McCarthy, 2017).

During its first two years of existence, Mandel noted that The Athletic did not anticipate becoming a national player in sports media. Instead, the goal was to focus on in-depth sports reporting in an advertisement-free environment (Biasotti, 2017). Mandel knew The Athletic would be influential within its first five years. He also knew the business and editorial model would succeed since it focused on an angle rarely emphasized in traditional sports journalism. However, it had never occurred to him that a startup could hit the coveted one-million subscriber mark, much less in the same amount of time it typically takes to graduate with a bachelor's degree.

In the early days of his tenure, the business side would show the editorial operation projected subscriber numbers that were the target. Being a realist, Mandel would laud the optimistic goal yet never believe it would be achieved. However, he said that each milestone reached occurred quicker than projected, allowing the company to go from a tiny San Francisco office when he first came aboard, in which Mather and Hansmann rented desk space to an individual who did not even work for The Athletic, to a national sports news network. Mandel said the market expansion was inevitable. It accelerated as soon as Mather and Hansmann saw that they "had a model they could easily replicate, city by city, that was proven to work."

Coalescing Resources: "I have a built-in advantage that local outlets can't match"

While sports journalism has changed over the previous two decades, mainly in the form of increased competition and altered consumption habits (Duncan, 2020), one constant remains—sports fans' steadfast support for the various teams that constitute their circle of fandom (Klugman, 2017). No matter the mode, method, or form, some individuals gravitate toward sport as an outlet for entertainment and as a socializing agent. Sports fandom, in this regard, is often shaped by one's environment while growing up, in this case, his or her hometown, or the attitudes of family (i.e., parents/grandparents, siblings, close friends, etc.; Absten, 2011; James, 2001; Serazio, 2013). For instance, if a person was raised in the south suburbs of Chicago, he or she may have been forced to choose the White Sox over the Cubs at an early age based on geographic affiliation. Moreover, a young sports fan whose parents attended the University of Pittsburgh may develop a rooting interest in the Panthers' athletic programs because of the familial connection, even if he or she was raised outside western Pennsylvania.

However, some sports fans today do not spend their entire lives in the same geographic region. Because of educational and employment opportunities, though, some people move around during various stages of life, meaning it is possible to develop an affinity toward specific teams based on the different cities that one has called home. Thus, modern culture, coupled with mass broadcasting, has given rise to the displaced sports fan, a term that

Collins et al. (2016) maintain is "reserved for people who moved away from the city they grew up in yet still support the team associated with that city" (p. 656). Displaced fans often navigate sports media offerings (e.g., reading the hometown newspaper online or turning to a sports blog) to stay current on the franchises no longer in their specified media market (Harrison, 2020; Singh, 2019).

The problem, however, lies in the notion that those who favor select teams spread through the U.S. and/or the world are often forced to turn to an amalgamation of news disseminators to stay current. For instance, an individual who grew up in Cincinnati as a Reds fan, attended the University of Michigan, and now lives in Atlanta would either have to subscribe to local newspapers from three different media markets or seek content from multiple sports-centric websites if he or she wanted to stay up-to-date. In theory, shopping for sports content can work if an individual has the time and is okay with paying for excess information (e.g., political news, arts and entertainment, obituaries, etc.) packaged in a newspaper bundle. However, easing the consumption process for today's displaced sports fans by providing a subscription platform marketed as a one-stop-shop is how The Athletic has positioned itself in the sports media marketplace.

For Brendan Marks, The Athletic's Duke and University of North Carolina at Chapel Hill men's basketball reporter, this strategy effectively targets only the most passionate consumers of the sport who want and are willing to pay for insightful and in-depth information on a variety of different sports leagues or teams. The Athletic essentially provides information that cannot be found for free elsewhere. Whereas legacy media outlets and other forms of online-only news dissemination are designed to focus solely on teams in one specific sports market, The Athletic, he said, has the resources to cater to fans in most U.S., Canadian, and European markets.

Thus, it is possible that what The Athletic is to sports journalism in the current media ecosystem is similar to what Netflix did for subscription home entertainment in the past two decades (first with its mail-order DVD network and later with normalizing Internet-streamed content). The Athletic is in a similar position, carving its niche in the sports media sphere in regard to editorial focus on long-form content. Interviewees said news consumers value The Athletic's product. However, the question is whether they value it enough to continue subscribing, especially considering that only 21 percent of U.S. adults paid for a news subscription in 2023, according to the *Reuters Digital News Report* (Newman, 2023).

To Marks, who previously wrote for the *Charlotte Observer's* sports section before joining The Athletic in late 2019, the geographic movement of a modern lifestyle gives his employer brand recognition. No matter where one moves, there is a good chance that a writer within The Athletic's network covers that area's teams. However, brand recognition does not mean he can attract readers based on The Athletic's name alone. Covering what can be argued as two of the most prestigious college basketball beats in Duke and North Carolina, Marks competes with every other journalist on the beat regarding breaking news and incremental updates. However, as he noted, his advantage over competitors comes in the form of The Athletic's multi-pronged attack of "deeply thought out and well researched and interviewed pieces" that readers have come to expect from the outlet, coupled with the breaking news articles that are a staple of the newspaper diet.

Moderate competition percolates in this regard, but Marks said no other news outlet in the country can compete with The Athletic on human-interest articles since no one else is "as spread out and as tapped in." From his perspective, context is critical, informing readers of breaking news and providing the analysis by conveying what an issue means. Marks mentioned that his company's main mantra is "write tomorrow's story today" by reporting something first and then telling the story with more context later. It is a top-down approach in which editors instill that there is no additional value in simply relaying information uttered in a press conference. In an era when fans can watch most professional and significant collegiate press conferences via YouTube, the redefined role of the beat reporter becomes explaining why something matters and how it came to fruition.

Whereas The Athletic can focus on the same storylines as the hometown newspapers that its city verticals overlap, its reporters instead tweak the standard coverage routine slightly by emphasizing more feature-based reporting, something that the coalescing of resources from a national organization provides. Thus, The Athletic may cover the same sports and teams that already receive a bulk of mainstream media coverage from the other national players like ESPN, FOX Sports, NBC Sports, etc. However, approaching the job in a slightly different manner allows for coexistence, despite interviewees perceiving it to have a competitive advantage since the average consumer typically has 12 paid media and entertainment subscription offerings (O'Brien, 2022).

Marks said that perhaps the most fundamental reason The Athletic has grown its sports media market share is that writers can work on the type of collaborative projects employed by ESPN in "the old days." Having a network of writers who cover each team in a sport and are spread nationally means that fans are better served whenever a story impacts two teams. Reporters from The Athletic can work in tandem by sharing source contact information, interview quotes, etc., in a way that most organizations cannot because of regionality. Marks explained that this interconnected network functions as a "built-in advantage that local outlets can't match." When the overall goal is to create a singular fan experience and show consumers that their return on investment exceeds the marginal cost, simplifying the sports news-consuming process is critical. From Marks' perspective, combining resources to market The Athletic via its system of unified verticals (previously categorized by city but currently sorted by sport) makes it easier for fans to navigate the information cycle.

He mentioned how the verticals, or niche areas of sporting focus, are the primary ways that The Athletic catalogs its information to cater to fan preferences. Whereas the outlet previously employed what was known as the city-based mode, comparable to newspaper journalism in which local reporters cover all teams in a coverage area under the supervision of a regional editor, it switched to a strategy centered on sport-specific verticals in March 2021. This means that all sportswriters within a specified market, say those who cover the Philadelphia Eagles, Phillies, Flyers, and 76ers, are no longer under the jurisdiction of The Athletic's Philadelphia editor. Instead, the move puts reporters under the umbrella of an editor who focuses on their specific sport (e.g., an Eagles writer reports to an N.F.L. editor instead; a Flyers beat writer works directly with an N.H.L. editor, etc.). So, instead of having a regional editor manage all journalists covering a major professional or collegiate beat in their market, that person is now only responsible for a conglomeration of writers centered on one sport, like the N.B.A. or N.F.L. Instead of having to work with two separate editors, one who oversees their sport and another who supervises the hometown media market site, writers now communicate with a national editor on their particular sport-specific beat.

The work routine transition was an adjustment, editorial interviewees noted. However, most understood why the decision was implemented. For Dan Brown, one of The Athletic's former editors of its Bay Area vertical, the move meant that he would no longer work with the team that he was "pretty bonded" with since most of the writers, along with Brown, had worked together at the San Jose Mercury News before joining The Athletic. When the structure overhaul was first initiated, the city editors, like Brown, may have been a little resistant to change because it meant assimilating to a new staff. However, from a purely editorial perspective, he said, the new system is beneficial on all ends. Instead of working with writers who cover virtually every sport, Brown is now able to focus solely on baseball coverage as one of the editors of The Athletic's M.L.B. vertical, overseeing the outlet's Milwaukee Brewers, Arizona Diamondbacks, Houston Astros, and Kansas City Royals beat writers.

What ultimately persuaded most editors to go for this altered organizational concept was the idea of having an off-season, meaning they would no longer be on call at all times. When Brown was one of the Bay Area Athletic editors, scheduling vacation time was challenging because at least one local sports team was always in season. When he was out on jury duty for two weeks after The Athletic switched to the sport-based vertical, Brown noted that the outlet's other baseball editors could substitute for him. Whereas his absence previously would have created a strain for the other Bay Area editors, requiring them to work "impossible hours," since the editorial staff was only four editors—Brown and Tim Kawakami among them—the new system proved more efficient.

Daniel Shirley also viewed the refined sport vertical editorial model as beneficial for the workflow of both the reporter and the editor. Shirley, who previously oversaw the Atlanta vertical's coverage before becoming one of The Athletic's senior college football editors, noted that the restructuring effort was all about cutting down communication channels on the writers' end. When he was in charge of The Athletic's Atlanta arm, Shirley, who formerly worked for the Macon Telegraph and S.E.C. Country, mentioned that the staff under his umbrella had to technically work with two editors—himself and the editor in charge of that person's sport. So, Tori McElhaney, his former Atlanta Falcons writer, not only pitched story ideas and sought feedback from Shirley but also had to touch base with an N.F.L. editor attached to her beat. As a result, journalists like McElhaney were sometimes unnecessarily burdened when it came time to properly communicate with each of their superiors.

Since he only oversees select college football writers now, Shirley noted that the process works better regarding channel flow since everyone only receives one message. That is not to say that he does not miss working with his former staff or that relationship building with his staff is easier now. Instead of being assigned the University of Georgia, the University of South Carolina, Clemson, and other southeastern-based beat writers—all of whom had always reported to a college football editor and were never attached to a city vertical—Shirley was given a college football staff of individuals who were previously linked to a city site. So, he was allocated a staff of nine beat writers whose work was formerly housed on a city vertical. Despite the restructuring, Shirley retained Atlanta-based senior columnist Jeff Schultz, even though he writes about all sports because the executives within the company did not want to dismantle the relationship those two developed.

These tight bonds that journalists create with their editorial supervisors are something that McElhaney saw as an advantage during her time with The Athletic. When McElhaney, a 2018 University of Georgia journalism graduate, was transitioning from The Athletic's Georgia Tech beat to the Atlanta Falcons, Shirley helped her navigate the basics of what stories worked well, which ones garnered positive audience feedback, and what the matrix numbers yielded regarding the total number of reads. Above all else, she noted that Shirley never edited her voice out of a story, which can be commonplace at other news organizations, she said. As a journalist, McElhaney (now a team-employed writer for the Falcons, yet was interviewed while she still worked for The Athletic) said The Athletic strived to maintain the integrity of each reporter's writing style.

McElhaney's take that her former editors from The Athletic were active in her growth as a journalist negates the perceptions expressed by some newspaper sports editors in Buzzelli et al. (2020). This qualitative research, which interviewed newspaper sports editors in media markets where The Athletic had a presence (many of whom had lost beat writers to the startup's poaching recruitment strategy), revealed that some individuals in charge of newspaper sports sections did not believe that their competing beat writers at The Athletic received as much journalistic oversight because writers were scattered throughout the country and, therefore, lacked a singular newsroom to interact with colleagues face-to-face. It is important to note that editors with this viewpoint were typically newspaper veterans who were adamant that young journalists thrive in a newsroom setting when other thorough reporters surround them.

However, not every editor Buzzelli et al. (2020) interviewed echoed this sentiment. Those who mentioned knowing a person on the editorial staff of The Athletic typically had faith in its editing oversight. Similarly, others stated that it was likely that The Athletic provided ample editorial oversight because small and midsize newspapers, even before the COVID-19 pandemic, were being stretched thin and forced to cut editors "faster than we're cutting reporters because we need the content" (p. 11). The only newspapers where sports editors tended to be confident that their sports department received as much, or more, editing and collaboration than The Athletic were those in larger media markets (e.g., Miami, San Jose, Pittsburgh, etc.). Despite the newspaper sports editors' critiques regarding The Athletic's structure and its editorial overhaul from the city to a sport-based vertical, McElhaney said that her relationship with The Athletic's former N.F.L. editor, Michael Sanserino, was positive since he also helped her "understand what readers are looking for" and how to focus a story more narrowly.

As previously mentioned, collaboration was one constant that interviewees continually referenced when asked about the strengths of working for a nationwide sports media network like The Athletic. Those employed by The Athletic noted that the organization's position as a giant in the industry based on market share and writer talent, coupled with its emphasis on collaboration in reporting projects and editorial feedback, has enabled it to thrive in terms of subscriber numbers and positive reader feedback. Collaboration, Schmidt (2019) writes, is a way for newsrooms to "do more with *more*" (para. 1). Therefore, from the N.G.T. perspective, it makes sense why The Athletic encourages cross-pollination among its staff to differentiate its work from that of the competition. As is a tenet of niche gratification theory, the public turns to Internet-based news applications to satisfy the type of needs that legacy media organizations cannot meet. Although multi-city newspaper chains exist (e.g., Gannett, Advance Publications, Tribune Publishing, etc.), most must actively share writer resources and/or facilitate collaboration to improve the overall sports content disseminated. Therefore, it is plausible that some news consumers gravitated toward The Athletic's tone and style to read in-depth journalism that other organizations did not produce.

Because of consistent layoffs and furloughs, it can be imperative for new employees in today's journalistic sphere to feel like their organization provides them with the tools needed to be successful. Based on news of The New York Times' acquisition of The Athletic in January 2022 (Fischer, 2022), the subscription business model of sports-only media that supports reputable journalistic talent may need to be refined. However, from an editorial standpoint, interviewees appreciated being able to work for a company that provides writing flexibility and network collaboration rarely seen in other avenues of sports media.

Decimating the Derivative: "The ability to break away from the daily gamer makes the job feel fresh and new"

Traditional modes of sports journalism have long been defined by the standardized routine of covering events on deadline, ensuring that readers are provided with the basic *who, what, when, where, why,* and *how* information presented in the style of an inverted pyramid (Broussard, 2019). Sports fans got used to the nuts-and-bolts coverage that provided them with everything needed to stay informed (Lowes, 1999). Most reporters would acknowledge that the process was sometimes repetitive. However, this routine was how traditional sports journalism operated for years and continued functioning in the digital age (Moritz, 2015). The push for greater audience engagement and pageviews has created a world where each news organization may try to publish as many articles on the beat per day as possible. Whereas what constituted news was more selective in the pre-Internet era, virtually any information that could garner a click is given a headline and a social media share button on the web (Frampton, 2015).

Citing too many pop-up advertisements in the digital sphere, Mather and Hansmann prioritized giving their reporters flexibility to cover sports stories that garner public interest (Biasotti, 2017). If local media members were going to cover the hometown team one way, The Athletic would take the inverse approach by covering stories that no one else was doing. Sure, The Athletic's sportswriters still tell readers who won or lost the previous matchup. However, interviewees mentioned that this information is typically summarized in a single tweet instead of a 500-word write-up. Therefore, The Athletic's primary emphasis is context, telling readers what happened, why, and what it means moving forward. It was an approach that was attractive to those who were stuck in the routinization of legacy sportswriting.

One of those reporters who was excited by this push for deep dive coverage that newspapers did not have the resources to meet was Andrew Baggarly, who resigned from his San Jose *Mercury News* post in December 2017 to spearhead The Athletic's San Francisco Giants coverage. Baggarly, a seasoned journalist who has covered every California-based Major League Baseball team, except the San Diego Padres, in some capacity since the 1998 season, said he grew frustrated with traditional media's practice of putting a headline on every piece of trivial information instead of actively trying to "curate the news." From his vantage point, the role of a journalist is to set the news agenda by informing readers of information on the beat that is essential to know. Thus, Baggarly grew puzzled with the *Mercury News* when he was told to put "the eighth most important thing of the day on the same level as the most important thing of the day" by assigning both a headline. However, as he learned, the online operation of a legacy news outlet is built upon feeding the machine with page views and overall clicks. When this occurs, the need-to-know news is not always amplified for public consumption.

That is why Baggarly found it refreshing to venture toward an organization like The Athletic, which he described as an inspiring place that enables him to tell "meaningful stories" rooted in conversations—not just interviews. Besides, he often receives the green light to pursue human-interest stories that he otherwise may not had the time to focus on had he stayed in newspaper journalism. The Athletic's editorial team, Baggarly said, pushes its writers to do "good work," even if an angle may not be popular. As long as it is compelling and can be reported well, he will get the go-ahead to be more creative in his approach, citing that there has not been a time during his tenure with The Athletic when he pitched a non-conventional story topic and was told "no." As Baggarly admitted, though, his experience of never having a proposed story idea rejected by an editor from The Athletic may be something that cannot be generalized to all reporters.

Because interviewees only emphasized the positive aspects of the job (while either not mentioning or purposely leaving out the drawbacks), it is possible that halo-effect bias came into play when asking individuals to comment on the editorial arm of their employer. The halo effect, whose theoretical foundation can be linked to cognitive dissonance theory, posits that individuals tend to select and interpret messages that support their attitudes (Kim, 2017). Thus, because someone who works for The Athletic may want to radiate a positive impression of the company to the public, interviewees may have opted to focus only on the benefits of working for this organization because they want to justify—to the interviewer—their decision to leave other sports media outlets to join The Athletic.

Baggarly, though, was not the only reporter attracted to The Athletic's editorial approach since it broke the traditional sports journalism mold. For Fluto Shinzawa, who was previously a *Boston Globe* reporter for 14 years, The Athletic represented a chance to revert from the formalized routine that he was tethered to in print journalism. There was a "churn," as he called it, in newspaper journalism, in which he was expected to check certain boxes regarding the type of content produced in his primary coverage area, the Boston Bruins.

Simply put, the mentality when he was with *The Globe* was to focus more on the nuts and bolts than the odd and exciting by writing one version of a story for the print product and then later updating it for online readers. When The Athletic's Boston editors called in March 2018, though, the opportunity to "launch something new" was appealing, especially considering there is no existing editorial formula that he is expected to follow. As he put it, Shinzawa has a blank canvas and gets to figure out what type of content can "get new people within the door," a view ultimately reinforcing the flexibility granted to a relatively new journalistic product compared to print.

Though the experiences of both Baggarly and Shinzawa illustrate a degree of the flexibility that The Athletic gives its writers, perhaps this free rein is most apparent in its editorial handling of M.L.B. coverage, a strategy in which reporters are effectively allowed to choose which games merit standard recaps. Unlike newspaper journalism, which typically has baseball beat reporters write a game story for each of a team's 162 regular season contests, those working for The Athletic noted that they are given autonomy to determine when to write a "gamer" in a sport largely still predicated on daily coverage.

One of those baseball reporters who can decide if he will write a game story on any given day is Chad Jennings, one of The Athletic's two Boston Red Sox beat writers. Jennings, who previously covered the Red Sox for the *Boston Herald* and the New York Yankees for Westchester County's *Journal News*, noted that close to two decades in newspaper journalism made him grow tired of the mundane editorial approach of publicizing *every* single game (especially when travel to 81 regular season away games made the job more challenging than it was rewarding). Thus, The Athletic's focus on long-form reporting rather than daily coverage represented an appealing alternative to Jennings' prior newspaper jobs. In his current role, he is sometimes encouraged to skip a game or press conference to work on a longer-form Red Sox-centric story if he believes it could generate more reader interest than a standard game recap.

Whereas he was not afforded this type of flexibility while a member of print sports journalism, Jennings said that breaking away from the daily gamer, notebook story, and/or Sunday column "makes the job feel fresh and new." Simply put, the strategy regarding which games to cover depends on team success. He noted that if the Red Sox are playing well, his editors value having a modified "straight gamer" (i.e., feature-style recap) that focuses on a unique or quirky observation and weaves a game's outcome around this angle. On the other hand, if the team is not playing well (e.g., out of the wild card/divisional race), the belief is that it is not worth writing the day-to-day updates since a fan can just read a box score and digest the critical takeaways. In those instances, when the Red Sox are on a losing skid, Jennings said his editors believe it is more beneficial for him to spend two to three days working on a player profile, anniversary feature, or anything that can make a "good story."

The above statement reflecting that The Athletic only publishes a Red Sox game story if the team is playing well aligns with the boosterism critique of sports media, which Hardin (2005) describes as members of the press being "fervent sports fans" (p. 67). Although journalistic ethics have long been perceived to be relaxed in the sports media sphere, leading sports departments to be dubbed the "toy department of the news media" (Rowe, 2007, p. 385), picking what games deserve a write-up based on team performance and/or win-loss outcome deviates from the traditional notion of sports journalistic objectivity, which Weedon and Wilson (2020) equate as "telling it like it is" (p. 1386).

Consequently, deciding not to cover each game, regardless of the outcome, because the team is not playing well gives the impression that The Athletic's editorial staff is telling its M.L.B. beat writers to display an implicit form of boosterism by not following the professional norm of informing the public of both the good and bad of a team's performance. This editorial strategy of picking when to write aligns with Boyle's (2006) take that "winning and success on the field of play remains the most important driver In shaping journalistic opinion and comment" (p. 125). Ultimately, this non-conventional journalistic tactic is more akin to what a reader would expect from a sports blog that cuts off reflected failure when a team struggles than a legitimate and credentialed national sports news network (Buzzelli, 2017).

Regardless of one's take on The Athletic's handling of baseball game coverage, Jennings said that deviating from the steady news diet of daily coverage is more accessible to navigate on a beat like the Red Sox, with two assigned reporters. Like the dual beat writer responsibility that Baggarly shares with Grant Brisbee on the San Francisco Giants beat, Jennings teams with Jen McCaffrey, who previously wrote for MassLive.com and the Cape Cod Times, for Red Sox coverage. When in-person interviews were more fluid in non-COVID-19 times, he and McCaffrey would be present for pregame clubhouse access to get quotes for more significant stories. After that, one person would head home while the other would stay at Fenway Park for the duration of the game, yet not necessarily pen a recap unless something "worth writing" occurred, like a pitcher throwing a no-hitter or a player launching multiple home runs in a single game. As he put it, "We kind of have the green light to call our editors and go, 'Look, we can write something tonight if you want, but I don't feel like there's something here that works out well.'"

Like Jennings, Audrey Snyder also mentioned that she has tried to determine the role of the game story in modern sports journalism, citing that a beat's editorial approach should effectively reach both the passionate and casual fans of a team. Snyder, The Athletic's Penn State football reporter who has been covering the team in some capacity since the 2012 season, said her readers are often so varied, from the "diehards in the weeds who want to know about the third-string defensive tackle" to the more passive fan who responds to novelty or logistics-based stories. Despite constantly questioning how many Penn State-centric articles to write per week, Snyder said she tries to reach both subsets of fans. This is done by emphasizing the standard game story a little less in favor of a game-based column supplemented by original reporting and bulleted instant analysis posted to the website before head coach James Franklin begins his postgame press conference.

For Snyder, a Penn State graduate, less emphasis on the traditional game story represents not only The Athletic's specified editorial stance but also a shift in reader preferences. She thinks like a fan by asking herself, "What does a college football fan in general want to know about this program?" or "What should the ultra-casual fan know about State College?" Occasionally catering to the average sports fan with no rooting interest in Penn State, she said, pays off whenever one of her non-football features (e.g., a profile on the German DJ whose song has become a Beaver Stadium pump-up tradition or a collection of vignettes on gameday traffic) appear on The New York Times homepage or in print.

This differentiation regarding each editorial strategy (newspapers vs. The Athletic) and the type of fans likely to gravitate toward competing news outlets supports the current niche approach to media. Most interviewees noted that local and national media covering the same beats represent a slight form of competition regarding readership; however, the different editorial approaches enable each to stand out in the crowded digital sports media marketplace. Based on its business model, former Athletic Chicago White Sox beat writer James Fegan (now a freelancer for the Chicago Sun-Times) noted the editorial output is rooted in "driving interest in subscriptions." At the same time, he said, most other media organizations are concerned with "creating as many reasons for you to click different things as possible."

The inherent emphasis on taking what was once a staple in newspaper journalism—the game story—and tweaking it based on team success aligns with the concept of niche gratification. Although Gaskins and Jerit (2012) note that overlapping populations serving the same niche will continue to compete until one drives the other out of existence, The Athletic's fresh take on traditional norms of written sports content sheds light on how it has been able to coexist with each sports news outlet that covers the same sport, teams, or athletes. Dimmick (2003) argues that the lack of overlap in necessary resources enables peaceful coexistence. Although this would seem to counter the comments that Mather, the co-founder, told *The New York Times* in an October 2017 profile when he said, "We will wait every local paper out and let them continuously bleed until we are the last ones standing" (Draper, 2017, para. 2), most interviewees suggested that media coexistence benefits all because it means more industry jobs.

A majority of interviewees likely shared this viewpoint because they know or have worked with reporters who represent other sports media segments. From The Athletic's perspective, having more jobs industry-wide may serve as a farm system for cultivating writer talent. Keeping competition intact may provide a platform for inexperienced writers to hone their skills while working smaller beats for smaller publications. Then, as the reporter's brand recognition increases, it is possible that The Athletic—if it genuinely perceives itself as the big leagues of sportswriting—may poach the then-established journalist. Above all else, it is likely that having other sports media outlets coexist, regardless of whether they compete with one another for readers, may ultimately serve as a lifeboat for displaced journalists if The Athletic somehow flounders from a financial standpoint. In other words, a stable sports journalism marketplace could represent other viable job options for The Athletic's reporters if they are laid off.

Like virtually every media organization, The Athletic was not immune to staff layoffs due to the COVID-19 sporting hiatus, axing eight percent of its total staff (46 employees) in a June 2020 round of cuts and forcing most writers to take a 10 percent pay cut for the remainder of that year (Draper, 2020). As Strauss (2020) posits, it is no secret that The Athletic provided a lifeline for legacy media sports journalists who were either let go or were in jeopardy of losing their jobs by their former newspapers. What needs to be clarified is what it would mean for the industry if The Athletic suddenly ceased to exist. If this were to occur, there would be an abundance of sportswriting talent on the market, but not enough industry-wide positions to keep everyone employed. As former *Sports Illustrated* editor-in-chief and current Seton Hall University sports media program head B.J. Schecter told

The Washington Post, a scenario of that magnitude "would be catastrophic" (Strauss, 2020, para. 8).

Information Innovation: "The landscape has changed in the last four years, and The Athletic has a lot to do with it"

In many ways, the Internet has effectively revolutionized how the public reads sports news. The standardized routine of turning to legacy media, which was once the only disseminator of pertinent news for public consumption, has been upended, for better or for worse, because of web-based applications (Martin, 2018). From the consumer's standpoint, there are obvious benefits to reading news online—among them being the ability to receive rapid updates in real-time from sources not bound to traditional geographic constraints. However, the apparent double-edged sword of Internet-based news media has been the tendency of select information-disseminating institutions (until the paywall normalization of 2011) to give news away for free to anyone armed with a smartphone or online connection (Chyi & Ng, 2020).

It is a blessing for the average sports fan who can receive updates on a favorite team or player in a few short clicks. For the media organization trying to survive amid an era of layoffs, furloughs, and widespread mergers, it represents industry disruption reminiscent of the business approach implemented in the early days of online news. In its simplest form, technology both transformed—and yet effectively destroyed—the profitability of journalism when the public bought into the guise that *all* news, no matter the outlet or lean, should be readily available without charge. Media experts point to it as a downfall when discussing the future viability of paid written content (Goodwin, 2020; Shafer, 2016).

A portion of the public still refuses to pay for a news subscription. According to Reuters Institute's 2023 *Digital News Report*, approximately 83 percent of those globally and 79 percent in the U.S. do not pay for a digital news subscription (Guaglione, 2023; Newman, 2023). The report also revealed that roughly half of U.S. non-digital news subscribers reported that nothing could influence them to pay for news, "with lack of interest or perceived value remaining fundamental obstacles" (Newman, 2023, para. 17). However, strides have been made (i.e., individualizing the news product) to reassert the narrative that good journalism costs money to produce (Kammer et al., 2015), with the COVID-19 pandemic reinforces the importance of quality journalism (Casero-Ripollés, 2021).

Because both verified and inaccurate information shape how the public responds to a situational health crisis, Ferreira and Borges (2020) maintain that people must have access to trustful and easily digestible information to stay adequately informed. From a newsroom perspective, this meant making "pandemic coverage a priority" (Natividad, 2020, para. 1), some of which was offered for free (thus fulfilling journalism's public-service role). At the same time, other COVID-19-related information was hidden behind legacy media paywalls (aligning with the news industry's need to be financially stable; Retta, 2021). Since 21 percent of Americans paid for a digital news subscription in 2023, according to Reuters *Digital News Report* (Newman, 2023), it can be construed that the desire to pay for factual reporting can translate to sports media. As Newman (2023) notes, paying for more than one subscription has become more common in the United States, with a large number of digital subscriptions "going to a few upmarket national brands," which reinforces "the *winner takes most* dynamics that are often associated with digital media" (to illustrate this further, the report cites *The New York Times* as a news industry bright spot because its products have over six million combined digital-only subscribers; para. 18).

In addition to Reuters' *Digital News Report*, interviewees also noted that The Athletic positioned itself at the forefront of this crusade to change how people view the value of news subscriptions by helping normalize paywall culture. Interviewees said Mather and Hansmann facilitated a viable path in the otherwise unstable sports media marketplace that other organizations can attempt to emulate based on perceived positive reader reaction toward the duo's once cutting-edge sports media business and editorial approaches. The Athletic may not have been the first media outlet to implement what is known in the industry as a "hard paywall" (i.e., a user must pay a subscription fee to read any content; Owens, 2020, para. 4). However, editors and writers from The Athletic maintained that it developed one of the first successful hard paywalls in sports media, which may have encouraged other sports media giants like *Sports Illustrated* (by placing its top writers and archives behind the "premium" content paywall; McCarthy, 2021) and ESPN (through the introduction of ESPN+) to follow suit (Feldman, 2020; Bleier, 2021).

For Joe Vardon, The Athletic's positioning from both an editorial and business perspective enabled it to become the "Netflix of sports," where readers can access a library of information on virtually every major sport and/or team.

Vardon said that unlike other movie and television entertainment streaming options available (e.g., Hulu, Max, Disney+, etc.), in which a viewer may subscribe for a short period to catch up on a favorite show and then promptly end the subscription, Netflix effectively retains its subscriber base. As he put it, the public knows that Netflix has quality content in its entertainment library, meaning that once an individual begins a plan, it is likely that he or she becomes a long-term subscriber. In contrast, in 2023 Netflix had a 1.6 percent churn rate—a metric used to measure the percentage of customers who end their subscriptions—which was the lowest of all major entertainment streaming platforms (Canal, 2023). So, in the comparison equating The Athletic to Netflix, it is plausible to believe that the former can retain its high volume of readers since they have come to expect quality sportswriting from the organization (for reference, The Athletic last publicly stated its renewal rate, claimed to be 90 percent, in 2018; Fischer, 2018).

Vardon, one of The Athletic's senior writers who covers the N.B.A., said his employer's strategy to hide all content behind the paywall, a move not always taken in media since it can be challenging to gain reader backing without allowing them to sample articles for free (Owens, 2020), "got everybody's attention" at first. After a while, though, the skepticism surrounding the business model subsided, leading Vardon (in July 2021) to note that The Athletic had reached its "critical mass point" and was "probably here to stay in some shape or form." Vardon said it is no coincidence that he runs into a lot more paywalls when clicking on the work of his media colleagues at other organizations, something he said did not occur as much "until The Athletic really blew up" in terms of subscribers and market share.

Like Vardon, Jeff Howe viewed The Athletic as helping to make the subscription model in sports media "more prevalent and desirable," even if he did not think that society was at the point where everyone saw value in paying for a news subscription. The former *Boston Herald* and New England Sports Net reporter who is a national N.F.L. reporter for The Athletic admitted that it will still take time to convince people to pay for information since everyone, except those within the Gen Z bracket, has been alive during a time in which online news was distributed for free. As someone born in the early 1980s, Howe noted many similarities between today's free versus paid news content debate and the peer-to-peer music download dispute of the 1990s. As he put it:

> I grew up with Napster, where you could just download free music. And it took me
> a while to get to the point where I was going to start paying for music on my phone,
> even though there was no way to get free music anymore. I was like, "Oh man, I'll

just listen to the radio. I'll exhaust the free SiriusXM subscription I got with my new truck." Then I was like, "I need to start spending money on this stuff. Like, grow up." I think that's kind of becoming the case with a lot of sports media. And you're seeing another side of it [with writers] who have taken the bigger model from The Athletic and just individualized it. (J. Howe, personal communication, April 15, 2021)

This individualization of The Athletic's paywall model Howe alluded to is another way that the organization has potentially influenced the future direction of sports media. It is an approach that benefits not only entrepreneurial sportswriters within a national network setting but also small, one-man journalism bands who disseminate niche sporting content through subscription-based platforms like Substack and Ghost (which are online newsletter platforms that enable an individual to earn revenue through paywall implementation of their writing; Tobitt, 2023). Of note, the next chapter will further explore this topic through interviews with sportswriters who ditched mainstream journalism in favor of newsletters, including those who use it as a primary source of income via the paywall and others who have full-time media jobs yet disseminate their writing on these platforms for personal gratification.

Aside from the paywall discussion, interviewees also said The Athletic set the foreseeable sports media agenda regarding routinization and increased sports media focus on long-form journalism. For as many setbacks as the sports media industry has faced in recent years, both regarding staff cuts and shifting reader habits, Scott Dochterman noted that The Athletic's most significant impact may be its emphasis on enterprise journalism. Writing for *The Gazette* (Cedar Rapids, IA) and Land of 10, a former Big Ten-centric news site, before pivoting to The Athletic in 2018 to cover University of Iowa football and men's basketball gave Dochterman a feel for the aggregation-based editorial models employed at other outlets. It was a practice, he said, that bred very little content differentiation since everyone produced work using the same press conference quotes. When the competition for his previous employers was so formulaic in its approach, opting to focus solely on "news of the day" instead of more impactful stories, his organization had little incentive to innovate.

Mather and Hansmann, though, wanted to differentiate their entity from run-of-the-mill content and, in doing so, prioritized the written word by allowing "sports media to revisit what's important." In this regard, Dochterman said, The Athletic's emphasis on investigative and enterprise journalism and the positive audience feedback that typically comes with this type of content may potentially persuade newspapers to shift gears away from aggregation and toward more original sports reporting. Although, aside from speculation, it is only known partially if the emergence of The Athletic has influenced other properties to once again devote more resources toward long-form work. Building off the seminal mass media research of McCombs and Shaw (1972), which posits that media sources inform the public of the salience of news topics based on the amount and depth of coverage, Dochterman's agenda-setting-related point is that other competing entities in sports journalism sphere may once again revisit impactful journalism since The Athletic found an audience willing to pay subscriber fees for this type of work.

Dochterman, one of three interviewees from The Athletic who pitched themselves to the company instead of being directly poached from a local newspaper, noted it is a quantity versus quality debate, with newspapers taking the former position and The Athletic occupying the latter. He said the agenda being set by new media would allow coexistence to thrive in the current climate, noting, "I think there's room for all of this. What we've done is carved a niche, a hole in the landscape, that allows us to provide more depth in reporting. And I hope other outlets follow suit because competition helps everybody."

The notion that The Athletic is driving an increased interest in long-form sports journalism, one that can be reverberated throughout the industry, is a sentiment also echoed by Bob Sturm, a Dallas-based sports radio host who previously served as one of the outlet's two Dallas Cowboys staff writers (of note, Sturm's interview occurred in 2021, before he was laid off in The Athletic's June 2023 reorganization). Sturm, whose approach was to cover the team from a more analytical, X's and O's point of view instead of traditional beat coverage, said The Athletic's presence ultimately "improves the playing field" for everyone in sports media. From the perspective of a journalism purist like Sturm, there was concern about the future viability of written sports content before The Athletic's launch, considering that most legacy outlets were "shells of their former selves," relying more on surface-level freelancers than substantive reporting.

However, The Athletic, Sturm argued, has altered how all organizations disseminate sports news since "the landscape has changed in the last four years" and The Athletic "has a lot to do with it." This is because, as Sturm said, those in sports media have been forced to improve their reporting, pay higher salaries to retain talent, and demand better journalism overall. The Athletic, in this regard, has become what he dubbed an "industry leader," pointing to the fact that both academic and mainstream press had documented its rapid rise as proof that it "achieved a certain level of excellence." Based on his two-decade-long tenure in sports radio, mainly as a host for 1310 The Ticket in Dallas, Sturm equated The Athletic's impact on sports journalism to a successful sports radio station in a large market. If there is a well-received station in a particular region, he noted, other broadcasts quickly realize that they must produce original material, as opposed to airing syndicated content, hire good talent, and engage with listeners to compete.

It may be cliché, he admitted, but the phrase, "rising tides raise all boats," fits digital sports media since journalistic heavyweights are needed to set the pace for everyone else. Sturm also noted that all Dallas and Fort Worth sports media entities have raised their game since The Athletic arrived in 2018. Like Dochterman, Sturm—whose Cowboys column previously appeared in *The Dallas Morning News*—pitched himself to The Athletic. When he was offered to join the organization, which was "significantly more than *The Morning News* ever paid," the newspaper somehow found the money to match The Athletic's salary. Sturm noted that this example illustrates how legacy media has little incentive to prioritize employee morale without competition.

> Nobody makes much money if there's an auction and only one person shows up. You need multiple bidders, and that's what feeds a healthy industry. And so, I think a lot of people, competitors, and employees of The Athletic should be very pleased that The Athletic is sort of anchoring this part [long-form written content] of the industry right now, one that honestly, five years ago, kind of looked dead and gone. But I think it has fueled the revival if you ask me. (B. Sturm, personal communication, April 14, 2021)

Regardless of what this renewed "revival" in written sports journalism may look like, either from a business or editorial perspective, it is likely that the demographics of those in the industry will continue to shift further away from the previously conceived population of middle-aged white men and more toward a diversified talent base. As interviewees noted, The Athletic is seen as a benefit to journalism because it opened more doors regarding job growth and enabled a more significant push for traditional media to evolve financially to retain its reporters. There is a problem related to the lack of racial and gender diversity in sports media (Fischer & Baker, 2020; Price et al., 2013; Whiteside, 2013). However, what often goes unnoticed is the notion that an increase in sports journalism positions may chip away at the homogeneous hierarchical power structure.

Though he was the only interviewee to mention this topic, Law Murray raised an interesting point when asked what The Athletic's influence on sports media may be. Murray, who is Black, said diversifying the talent pool was part of the agenda for a meeting in April 2021. However, Murray—the outlet's lone Los Angeles Clippers staff writer—noted that diversity is not just about being more encompassing regarding race, ethnicity, and/or gender. Instead, it equates to how potential reporters "go about what they do" and their previous careers.

Before he "committed to a career in sports media" by first writing for ClipperBlog and later serving as a statistician for N.F.L. Media and an N.B.A. editor at ESPN, Murray was a social entrepreneur corps member in both Philadelphia and Los Angeles for City Year, a nonprofit youth service organization aimed at curbing the school dropout rate. This background experience, Murray said, influenced how he approaches journalism since "[. . .] We cover people. It's important to look at the future [of sports media] based on what the world looks like and what the country looks like." The Athletic has been criticized in the past by those within the media for its apparent tendency to follow the status quo regarding substantial minority hiring (an April 2018 tweet by Gregory Lee, former president of the National Association of Black Journalists, revealed that The Athletic was 87.3 percent white at this time, with zero Black employees holding an editorial position; Lee, 2018).

However, as admitted by Taylor Patterson, The Athletic's communications director, when asked by the *New York Daily News* in 2018 about the company's hiring practices following Lee's tweet, "Diversity is a huge priority for us, and we have a lot of work to do on that front" (Phillips, 2018, para. 21). Consequently, being able to take potential writing talent whose view of sports media may be different than the mainstream—either because of race, gender, or never having been previously employed by legacy media—and giving them journalistic opportunity may be one of the keys to sustaining online written sports content. Agenda-setting may have been part of the discussion that was mentioned by interviewees regarding coaxing newspapers to once again focus on enterprise and in-depth journalism. However, despite not being emphasized nearly as much (aside from Murray), an important point is how The Athletic may be setting this industry's future agenda regarding non-conventional hires in a predominantly white and male-dominated field.

The collective focus on the three aforementioned main elements that interviewees from The Athletic shared (e.g., how its emergence has impacted sports media regarding editorial tactics, organizational structure, and the eventual normalization of the journalistic paywall) sheds light on both the uncertain nature and difficult predictability of the sports media field. Yet, from a more theoretical perspective, the findings elucidate how different sports media entities (The Athletic included) can coexist, though "uncomfortably at times" (McCollough, 2018, para. 12). Buzzelli et al. (2020) revealed that newspapers covering the same teams as The Athletic typically stick with their forte (daily coverage) instead of directly competing with it on human-interest and issue-based reporting. Thus, newspapers focus on what they believe they do best, and The Athletic has done the same, meaning there needs to be more ecological overlap between both approaches.

This theme of coexistence, though, is not just limited to The Athletic and its relationship with legacy media. As evident by the findings of the previous chapter, team-run media has also carved its editorial niche to remain relevant within the current state of sports media. As interviews from the prior chapter suggest, team-employed reporters focus on analysis, commentary, and quick-hitting news content more than the traditional journalistic approach of notebook-style coverage. Whereas The Athletic and newspaper sports sections target fans with disposable incomes, team-run media most likely caters to a more general interest or casual fan (or even younger consumers of sport without the financial means to purchase a new subscription). By revolving content on areas of coverage that are often neglected by legacy and new media and offering this information for free via the team's official website, internal beat writers have been able to stand out and, at the same time, coexist with the other entrants since each serves a slightly different editorial function for consumers of sports news.

Further, because the structure of The Athletic (a news network with reporters spread throughout most major U.S., Canadian, and European cities) is rooted in tackling both national and hyperlocal content, legacy hometown media can coexist with The Athletic since these outlets typically only emphasize sports news that occurs within the target coverage scope. Interviewees noted that gathering resources with other colleagues from The Athletic regarding longer, more in-depth enterprise projects enables them to benefit more than their legacy media counterparts. However, national newspaper chains like Gannett, Advance Publications, and Tribune Publishing exist, meaning newspapers can implement a similar resource-pooling approach to journalism.

The Athletic's most noticeable contribution to sports media, in a sentiment echoed by almost all interviewees, has been its push for paywall normalization. Virtually every editor/reporter interviewed noted that Mather and

Hansmann's strategy of placing all content behind the hard paywall and not letting non-subscribers view any articles for free (aside from a story's first two paragraphs that appear in preview mode) has helped persuade the public that quality journalism cost money to produce and, thus, is a worthy cause to support. Because of the unstable nature of news today, the paywall will likely be a constant variable in the future of written sports media. Therefore, with its push to base a new website's business operation on a nontraditional media revenue source, other organizations may follow suit if The Athletic (and its parent company, *The New York Times*) proves the financial benefits of employing the subscriber-only model.

References

Absten, S. L. (2011). *Factors that influence team identification: Sport fandom and the need for affiliation* [Unpublished master's thesis]. Western Kentucky University.

Benson, R. (2019). Paywalls and public knowledge: How can journalism provide quality news for everyone? *Journalism, 20*(1), 146–149.

Berr, J. (2021, March 28). Axios, "The Athletic" in preliminary merger talks. *Forbes.* https://www.forbes.com/sites/jonathanberr/2021/03/28/axios-the-athletic-in-preliminary-merger-talks/?sh=7c0af5fc18c6

Biasotti, T. (2017, October 11). The fast-growing startup aims to "replace the sports page." *Columbia Journalism Review.* http://www.cjr.org/business_of_news/the-athletic-sports-news.php

Bilton, R. (2016, May 25). *Chasing subscriptions over scale, The Athletic wants to turn local sports fandom into a sustainable business—starting in Chicago.* NiemanLab. http://www.niemanlab.org/2016/05/chasing-subscriptions-over-scale-the-athletic-wants-to-turn-local-spors-fandom-into-a-sustainable-business-starting-in-chicago/

Bleier, E. (2021, January 26). *"Sports Illustrated" ready to follow ESPN's lead with paywall.* InsideHook. http://www.insidehook.com/daily_brief/sports/sports-illustrated-following-espn-paywall

Boyle, R. (2006). *Sports journalism: Context and issues.* Sage.

Broussard, R. (2019). *A Field Theory Analysis of sports journalists' coverage of social justice protests in sports* [Unpublished doctoral dissertation]. University of Alabama.

Buzzelli, N. (2017). *The booster beat: College football framing of wins and losses by sportswriters and S.B. Nation Bloggers* [Unpublished master's thesis]. Kent State University.

Buzzelli, N. R., Gentile, P., Sadri, S. R., & Billings, A. C. (2020). "Cutting editors faster than were cutting reporters": Influences of The Athletic on sports journalism quality and standards. *Communication & Sport, 10*(3), 417–437.

Canal, A. (2023, December 16). *2023 was the year your streaming bill got (a lot) more expensive.* Yahoo! Finance. https://finance.yahoo.com/news/2023-was-the-year-your-streaming-bill-got-a-lot-more-expensive-165706892.html?guccounter=1&guce_referrer=aHR0cHM6Ly93d3cuZ29vZ2xlLmNvbS88&guce_referrer_sig=AQAAAGr66XJzVIVhM4lyJCuULqgN-GjoL75iApHBy7Hixa8KInIdrx0rgZKiC9VhkyCHlQjWh8mXrE7TGRoYoc2pbQdOlRUwNaaDKxymdzEK1FpgZOXIkBn6AubI8jyPS8HgmFNU_qg3yadgO_Ao6gjWQBLBr4QtxtWP2iUs9JtG6KO3#:~:text=Consumers%20cancel%20streaming%20plans%20as%20prices%20balloon&text=Lionsgate's%20Starz%20(LGF%2DA),churn%20rate%20at%20just%201.6%25

Casero-Ripollés, A. (2021). The impact of Covid-19 on journalism: A set of transformations in five domains. *Comunicação E Sociedade, 40*(1), 53–69.

Chyi, H. I., & Ng, Y. M. M. (2020). Still unwilling to pay: An empirical analysis of 50 U.S. newspapers' digital subscription results. *Digital Journalism, 8*(4), 526–547.

Collins, D. R., Heere, B., Shapiro, S., Ridinger, L., & Wear, H. (2016). The displaced fan: The importance of new media and community identification for maintaining team identity with your hometown team. *European Sport Management Quarterly, 16*(5), 655–674.

Debre, E. (2021, May 12). The media used Trump to sell subscriptions. Now what? *Slate.* https://slate.com/business/2021/05/media-fundraising-trump-bump-slump.html

Dimmick, J. (2003). *Media competition and coexistence: The theory of the niche.* Lawrence Erlbaum.

Draper, K. (2017, October 23). Why The Athletic wants to pillage newspapers. *The New York Times.* http://www.nytimes.com/2017/10/23/sports/the-athletic-newspapers.html

Draper, K. (2020, June 5). The Athletic lays off 8 percent of staff. *The New York Times.* http://www.nytimes.com/2020/06/05/sports/the-athletic-layoffs.html

Duncan, S. (2020). *The digital world of sport: The impact of emerging media on sports news, information and journalism.* Anthem Press.

Feder, R. (2016, January 25). The Athletic: New "thought-provoking" Chicago sports website debuts. *Robert Feder.* http://www.robertfeder.com/2016/01/25/the-athletic-new-chicago-sports-website-debuts/.

Feldman, J. (2020, October 22). *ESPN to move writers to ESPN+ while adding radio show telecasts.* Sportico. http://www.sportico.com/business/media/2020/espn-to-move-writers-behind-paywall-1234615310/?sub_action=logged_in

Ferreira, G. B., & Borges, S. (2020). Media and misinformation in times of COVID-19: How people informed themselves in the days following the Portuguese declaration of the state of emergency. *Journalism & Media, 1*(1), 108–121.

Fisher, S. (2018, October 30). *Exclusive: The Athletic raises $40 million in new funding.* Axios. https://www.axios.com/2018/10/30/the-athletic-40-million-series-c-round

Fischer, S. (2021, May 25). *Scoop: New York Times in talks to buy The Athletic.* Axios. http://www.axios.com/new-york-times-nytimes-acquisition-athletic-7f1dabf4-9315-4975-93f9-68e13c642a43.html

Fischer, S. (2022, January 6). *The New York Times to acquire The Athletic for $550 million in cash.* Axios. https://www.axios.com/new-york-times-athletic-deal-valuation-b13346c5-1bb0-4826-a00f-66214e133518.html

Fischer, S., & Baker, K. (2020, July 7). *Sports media's race reckoning.* Axios. http://www.axios. com/sports-media-race-reckoning-985b6ca2-acf3-4df6-8eeb-8b092ed8bcf8.html

Frampton, B. (2015, September 14). *Clickbait: The changing face of online journalism.* B.B.C. News. https://www.bbc.com/news/uk-wales-34213693

Gaskins, B., & Jerit, J. (2012). Internet news: Is it a replacement for traditional media outlets? *The International Journal of Press Politics, 17*(2), 190–213.

Glaser, B. G. (1965). The constant comparative method of qualitative analysis. *Social Problems, 12*(4), 436–445.

Glasspiegel, R. (2017, July 24). *Seth Davis explains why he joined The Athletic, believes in market for national college coverage.* Audioboom. https://audioboom.com/posts/6188223-seth-davis-explains-why-he-joined-the-athletic-believes-in-market-for-national-college-cover age?playlist_direction=forward

Goodwin, T. (2020, November 6). *Why making content on the Internet free was our biggest mistake ... and how to fix it.* What's New in Publishing. http://www.whatsnewinpublishing.com/ why-making-content-on-the-internet-free-was-our-biggest-mistake-and-how-to-fix-it

Gordon, A. (2018, September 6). The sports pages' new clothes. *Slate.* http://www.slate.com/ culture/2018/09/the-athletic-is-poaching-from-local-sports-pages-and-reading-like-them-too.html

Grathoff, P. (2017, April 26). *ESPN layoffs include Jayson Stark, Ed Werder, Dana O'Neil and some anchors.* The Kansas City Star. https://www.kansascity.com/sports/spt-columns-blogs/ for-petes-sake/article146846264.html

Guaglione, S. (2023, June 16). *As news subscriptions stall, the U.S. market is faring better than most.* Digiday. https://digiday.com/media/as-news-subscriptions-stall-the-u-s-market-is-far ing-better-than-most/#:~:text=The%20U.S.%20market%20is%20faring%20slightly%20 better%3A%2021%25%20of%20the,to%20stall%20in%20the%20U.S

Hardin, M. (2005). Survey finds boosterism, freebies remain problem for newspaper sports departments. *Newspaper Research Journal, 26*(1), 66–73.

Harrison, L. (2020, April 21). *Sports fan demographic data.* Acxiom. https://www.acxiom.com/ blog/learn-how-to-capture-displaced-sports-on-tv-fans/

Hill, M. (2020, December 7). Paywalls, newsletters, and the new echo chamber. *Wired.* http:// www.wired.com/story/paywalls-newsletters-and-the-new-echo-chamber/

Hirsch, L., Draper, K., & Rosman, K. (2022, January 6). *New York Times Co. to buy The Athletic for $550 million in cash.* The New York Times. https://www.nytimes.com/2022/01/06/busin ess/new-york-times-the-athletic.html

James, J. D. (2001). The role of cognitive development and socialization on the initial development of team loyalty. *Leisure Sciences, 23*(1), 231–261.

Jones, T. (2022, September 13). *The Athletic adds ads; readers are not pleased.* Poynter. https:// www.poynter.org/commentary/2022/the-athletic-advertisements-new-york-times-reader-response/

Kafka, P. (2022, January 6). Why The New York Times is buying the Athletic. *Vox.* https:// www.vox.com/recode/22870773/athletic-new-york-times-550-million-explained

Kammer, A., Boeck, M., Hansen, J. V., & Hauschildt, L. J. H. (2015). The free-to-fee transition: Audiences' attitudes toward paying for online news. *Journal of Media Business Studies*, 12(2), 107–120.

Kim, J. (2017). Elaborating the halo effect of S.C.C.T.: How and why performance history affects crisis responsibility and organizational reputation. *Journal of Public Relations Research*, 29(6), 277–294.

Klugman, M. (2017). The passionate, pathologized bodies of sports fans: How the digital turn might facilitate a new cultural history of modern spectator sports. *Journal of Sport History*, 44(2), 306–321.

Lee, G. [@nabjprez2011]. (2018, April 2). *A few weeks ago, I tweeted about the lack of diversity at three of @TheAthleticHQ sites* [Tweet]. Twitter. http://www.twitter.com/nabjprez2011/status/900842338598625280?ref

Lowes, M. D. (1999). *Inside the sports pages: Work routines, professional ideologies, and the manufacture of sports news*. University of Toronto Press.

Martin, N. (2018, November 30). How social media has changed how we consume news. *Forbes*. http://www.forbes.com/sites/nicolemartin1/2018/11/30/how-social-media-has-changed-how-we-consume-news/?sh=22393363c3a

Mather, A., & Hansmann, A. (2018, January 30). *Playing the long game*. The Athletic. http://www.theathletic.com/225963/2018/01/30/playing-the-long-game/

McCarthy, M. (2017, May 12). *Seth Davis laid off at Sports Illustrated, cracks joke on way out.* Sporting News. http://www.sportingnews.com/us/ncaa-basketball/news/seth-davis-laid-off-sports-illustrated-job-cbs-sports-college-basketball/1fy9i21umge5212y1sg0hgqlja

McCarthy, M. (2021, February 1). *Inside Sports Illustrated's paywall plan for "premium" content.* Front Office Sports. http://www.frontofficesports.com/si-metered-paywall-ryan-hunt-sports-illustrated-feb-2/

McCollough, J. B. (2018, October 9). *Sports journalists battle for relevancy.* NiemanReports. https://niemanreports.org/articles/sports-journalists-battle-for-relevancy/

McCombs, M. E., & Shaw, D. L. (1972). The agenda-setting function of mass media. *The Public Opinion Quarterly*, 36(2), 176–187.

Moritz, B. (2015). The story versus the stream: Digital media's influence on newspaper sports journalism. *International Journal of Sport Communication*, 8(1), 397–410.

Natividad, I. (2020, May 6). *COVID-19 and the media: The role of journalism in a global pandemic.* Berkeley News. https://news.berkeley.edu/2020/05/06/covid-19-and-the-media-the-role-of-journalism-in-a-global-pandemic/#:~:text=To%20inform%20the%20public%20during,accurate%20information%20to%20the%20public

Newman, N. (2023, June 14). *Overview and key findings of the 2023 Digital News Report.* Reuters Institute Digital News Report. https://reutersinstitute.politics.ox.ac.uk/digital-news-report/2023/dnr-executive-summary

O'Brien, S. (2022, June 2). *Consumers spend an average $133 more each month on subscriptions than they realize, study shows.* CNBC. https://www.cnbc.com/2022/06/02/consumers-spend-133-more-monthly-on-subscriptions-than-they-realize.html

O'Brien, D., Wellbrock, C. M., & Kleer, N. (2020). Content for free? Drivers of past payment, paying intent and willingness to pay for digital journalism—a systematic literature review. *Digital Journalism, 8*(5), 643–672.

Owen, L. H. (2022, February 2). *The New York Times hits 10 million digital subscriptions, three years ahead of its goal.* NiemanLab. https://www.niemanlab.org/2022/02/the-new-york-times-hits-10-million-digital-subscriptions-three-years-ahead-of-its-goal/

Owens, S. (2020, February 28). *Why local news outlets struggle with digital subscriptions.* What's New in Publishing. https://whatsnewinpublishing.com/why-local-news-outlets-struggle-with-digital-subscriptions/

Patel, S. (2021, June 17). *The New York Times and The Athletic end acquisition talks.* The Information. http://www.theinformation.com/articles/the-new-york-times-and-the-athletic-end-acquisition-talks

Peralta, K. (2019). Pardon the disruption. *Notre Dame Magazine.* http://www.magazine.nd.edu/stories/pardon-the-disruption/

Perpich, D. (2022, September 11). *Publisher's note: Introducing our new advertising experience.* The Athletic. https://theathletic.com/3580709/2022/09/11/publishers-note-introducing-our-new-advertising-experience/

Phillips, C. J. (2018, May 8). *Phillips. Why diversity must become sports journalism's most important priority.* New York Daily News. http://www.nydailynews.com/sports/more-sports/diversity-sports-journalism-priority-article-1.3977157

Price, J., Farrington, N., Kilvington, D., & Saeed, A. (2013). Black, white, and read all over: Institutional racism and the sports media. *International Journal of Sport & Society, 3*(1), 81–90.

Retta, M. (2021, March 9). What the pandemic means for paywalls. *Columbia Journalism Review.* http://www.cjr.org/covering_the_pandemic/what-the-pandemic-means-for-paywalls.php

Rowe, D. (2007). Sports journalism: Still the "toy department" of the news media?. *Journalism, 8*(4), 385–405.

Schmidt, C. (2019, May 20). *The power of journalism collaboration is also the power of inclusion—here's how to harness it.* NiemanLab. http://www.niemanlab.org/2019/05/the-power-of-journalism-collaboration-is-also-the-power-of-inclusion-heres-how-to-harness-it/

Serazio, M. (2013, January 29). *Just how much is sports fandom like religion.* The Atlantic. http://www.theatlantic.com/entertainment/archive/2013/01/just-how-much-is-sports-fandom-like-religion/272631/

Shafer, J. (2016, October 17). What if the newspaper industry made a colossal mistake? *POLITICO Magazine.* https://www.politico.com/magazine/story/2016/10/newspapers-digital-first-214363/

Singh, S. (2019, July 29). *The digital displacement of sports fandom.* VentureBeat. https://venturebeat.com/business/the-digital-displacement-of-sports-fandom/

Strauss, B. (2020, March 4). *Sportswriting's future may depend on the Athletic, which is either reassuring or terrifying.* The Washington Post. http://www.washingtonpost.com/sports/2020/03/03/the-athletic-sports-media-future/

Tobitt, C. (2023, May 2). How Substack has helped F.T. persuade readers to pay for email newsletters. *Press Gazette*. https://pressgazette.co.uk/newsletters/ft-newsletters-substack/

Toonkel, J. (2021, October 4). *The Athletic burned through $95 million between 2019 and 2020*. The Information. https://www.theinformation.com/articles/the-athletic-burned-through-95-million-between-2019-and-2020

Toonkel, J. (2022, January 6). *NYT to buy The Athletic for $550 million*. The Information. https://www.theinformation.com/articles/nyt-to-buy-the-athletic-for-550-million

Tracy, M. (2022, February 2). The Times hits its goal of 10 million subscriptions with the addition of The Athletic. *The New York Times*. https://www.nytimes.com/2022/02/02/business/media/nyt-earnings-q4-2021.html

Weedon, G., & Wilson, B. (2020). Textbook journalism? Objectivity, education, and the professionalization of sports reporting. *Journalism, 21*(10), 1375–1400.

Whiteside, E. (2013). Using a post-structural approach to theorize diversity in sports media organizations. In P. M. Pedersen's (Ed.) *Routledge handbook of sport communication*. Routledge.

Williams, K., & Stroud, S. R. (2021, February 15). *The ethics of news paywalls: Should we pay for news in our digital democracy?* The University of Texas at Austin Center for Media Engagement. http://www.mediaengagement.org/research/the-ethics-of-news-paywalls/

Winn, A. (2017, January 5). *Catching up with Matt Fortuna*. Her Loyal Sons. http://www.herloyalsons.com/blog/2017/01/05/catching-matt-fortuna/

· 3 ·

THE ONE-MAN JOURNALISTIC BAND: SUBSTACK'S EMERGENCE FROM STARTUP TO SPORTS MEDIA LIFELINE

A new business or editorial approach in journalism rarely blossoms unexpectedly. Instead, the novel ways of updating the mainstream press are often rooted in past media principles (Stober, 2004). Curated news updates delivered via social media are akin to the standard newspaper brief designed to inform the public on a preselected topic. The online paywall, furthermore, is simply the print news subscription model in modern form. Thus, it may be cliché to say *everything old is new again*, but media innovation has a history of looking toward the past for future inspiration (Drezner, 2021).

Perhaps nowhere is this notion of current media borrowing from previous information incarnations more apparent than the contemporary newsletter boom initiated by Substack. This online platform that provides independent writers the publishing, payment, and infrastructure needed to create their own journalistic startup (Allyn, 2020). Billed as a vehicle that current information-savvy entrepreneurs can use to escape "the turbulence of the media industry" (Shephard, 2021, para. 1), Substack effectively combines the news realm occupied by the blogosphere of the early-to-mid-2000s with the ability, if a writer chooses, to implement a subscription paywall. However, giving news consumers the ability to receive information in their email inboxes is not a novel approach to media (newsletter marketing can be traced back to the Internet's infancy; Davis, 2017). Similarly, hard-copy sports newsletters and other print publications catering to a niche sporting appeal existed before the current do-it-yourself era of online publication. For instance, Elinor Kaine Penna's *Lineback*, a weekly newsletter that aggregated N.F.L. betting lines from local newspapers, began printing in 1961 (of note, one of Penna's early slogans for *Lineback* was "America's oldest and only pro football newsletter"; Weiner, 2020, para. 20). What Substack made new again, however, is the belief that email newsletter journalism can be a sustainable media venture from either a business (i.e., income) or personal (i.e., self-gratification) standpoint.

Whether a sportswriter was furloughed, and wants to use the newsletter model as a source of income, or has a desire to write about sports for a cathartic release, Substack has transformed how writers perceive job opportunities in the sports media field (Strauss, 2020b). Like The Athletic, Substack lends itself to the unbundling nature of the current sports media ecosystem, in which readers can subscribe to only the sports information they value instead of purchasing an entire news bundle (Schrager, 2020). Unlike The Athletic, though, the focus is simplified, with individual Substack writers targeting a small but dedicated audience willing to pay for specialized content. As Baker (2020) sees it, "the rise of independent journalism has breathed new life into niche content" (para. 2).

Since its 2017 launch, Substack has shown that journalists keen on self-promotion can make a living as a one-man band. Jobs in the media industry may have dwindled, but opportunities for writers to become their boss have expanded. This created what Substack co-founder Hamish McKenzie (himself a former journalist for both Tesla corporate and tech blog PandoDaily) called, in a post published on the company's website, "early signs that we are witnessing the emergence of a new media economy" (McKenzie, 2020, para. 15). It may be possible that Substack, like The Athletic, represents an alternative for sportswriters either laid off by newspapers or those looking to diverge from standard news norms. Despite Substack's effect on how sports reporters disseminate content and the public's information consumption, the long-term viability of building a niche subscription newsletter from scratch is still unclear. Consequently, this chapter explores the motives guiding Substack sportswriters, gauging if they gravitated toward the platform under the guise of perceived editorial income, writing flexibility, or simply as a journalistic hobby that can fill the resume hole until the next corporate media job (Oremus, 2021).

As detailed below, interviewees noted that the platform provides a pivot from the standard media grind, albeit in a slightly different form, depending on the person's news background and employment experiences. Interviewees said Substack is appealing on multiple fronts, with the main draw being likened to the ability to write about niche content areas best described as passion projects. However, perhaps the most notable theme gauged from the perspectives of the 11 Substack interviewees is that the newsletter platform has enabled niche sports reporting to once again find a home, as seen by writers who fit into one of the three preselected categories of Substack writing motives (those who used their prior media following to create a financially stable Substack, those whose content is free while testing the viability of the subscription model, and those who have outside employment and write on Substack for personal gratification).

It is important to note that all Substack sportswriters interviewed for this research were men, a trend that mirrors industry demographics. It is not that women do not manage and/or write for Substack newsletters (some of the most notable niche newsletters on the platform, like Emily Atkin's climate change newsletter, *HEATED*, and *Common Sense*, the culture/politics newsletter by former *New York Times* op-ed writer Bari Weiss, are written by women). However, a limited number of women operate sports-specific Substack newsletters. One of those women is Lindsey Gibbs, an *Athletic* contributing writer who covers the University of Maryland women's basketball and the Washington Mystics of the Women's National Basketball Association (W.N.B.A.) for her *Power Plays* newsletter, which focuses on the intersection of gender inequalities in sports. Gibbs, one of the notable female Substackers, was contacted for an interview request but never responded. Those who advocate for greater female presence within Substack, most notably trans feminist writer Jude Ellison Sady Doyle, argue that the platform's agenda is aimed at "giving massive advances [...] to people who actively hate trans people and women [...]" (Ha, 2021, para. 4).

Rogers's (1962) concept of diffusion of innovations (D.O.I.), this chapter's underlying theoretical background, illustrates how Substack, a relatively young online publishing platform, was adopted as a legitimate way for former sportswriters to deliver their writing to the public (either behind or in front of a paywall). Diffusion of innovations serves as a suitable theoretical lens to examine Substack's inherent effect on how writers disseminate information and the method of consumption of today's sports media consumers. This is because D.O.I. sheds light on how new ideas spread and/or were adopted by a specific social system (Oelrichs, 2023). In the case of Substack, publishing technology has enabled subscription sports media to evolve to such a degree that the online paywall process is no longer limited to significant media power players, nor is traditional blogging seen as the only online writing-based form of cathartic release. Further, sportswriters using Substack believe that consumers—both free and paid—have adopted the platform for its ease of use, one that allows sports information to be delivered to a subscriber's email inbox instead of forcing him or her to search the Internet for preselected information.

As previously mentioned, the five stages of the diffusion process are innovators, early adopters, early majority, late majority, and laggards. Former professional sportswriters who turned to Substack as a profit-making tool after being furloughed by mainstream sports media constitute the innovators and early adopters since the perceived success of these newsletters encouraged others (chiefly interviewees categorized in this chapter's second section, most of whom can be classified as the early majority) to adopt the platform. Most did this by assessing if Substack could be a viable option to either make a livable wage through writing or be used to transition to a full-time sports media position elsewhere.

Lastly, though not all interviewees (quoted in this chapter's third theme) constitute the late majority, it was determined that having a Substack presence to enjoy sportswriting was the byproduct of adopting the platform after its usefulness for free sports information dissemination was proven. The late majority saw value in the viability of a paywall-free Substack only after it had been demonstrated that readership on the platform could be constructed and sustained by those who had the paywall in place. This coincides with Moore's (1999) assertion that a significant gap exists between the early adopters, who are most often a community's forward thinkers and opinion leaders, and the early majority, which constitutes a bulk of the population. In this manner, those who gravitated toward Substack early in its infancy benefitted the most by having a paywall function and cultivating an audience willing to fund the venture.

Despite Substack's rise from a novel newsletter platform in October 2017 to a legitimized media platform that, as of February 2024, claims to have over three million total paying subscribers (Fischer, 2024), uncertainties related to its long-term sustainability remain. Most notably, questions persist whether Substack can become the solo writing monetization mechanism that never materialized during the last "major Internet writer-driven movement"

(Perlberg, 2020, para. 5) of early-2000s blogging. This is notable considering that only 21 percent of U.S. news consumers pay for online news, according to Reuters' *Digital News Report* (Newman, 2023).

The constant shelling of various mediums behind a paywall can lead to what Faulconbridge (2019) describes as "subscriber fatigue," meaning that even those who do pay for at least one news subscription are opting for other freemium or bundled content instead of feeling the need to purchase separate subscriptions for news media (Faulconbridge, 2019, para. 6). Substack's perceived influence on information dissemination and consumption in sports journalism, as seen by those who use the newsletter platform for the three purposes above, is explored. Unlike this book's other interview-based chapters, in which the individualistic themes presented overlapped from interviewee to interviewee, this section is broken up by motives for Substack sports newsletter usage. Taking this somewhat different approach is warranted because interviewees, based on their specific reasons for publishing a sports-centric Substack newsletter, only gravitated toward the platform for one purpose in particular—whether that was to earn an immediate livable salary via Substack writing, use the platform as a stepping stone to total time income, or write purely for personal satisfaction, with no concept of revenue generation in place.

Financial Feasibility: "I don't think I could have made it a viable financial proposition if I didn't have a built-in reader base already"

To the media outsider, it may appear that the digitization of information has solely been a positive, taking what was once deemed an antiquated process (reading about the previous day's events the morning after) and transforming it to align with the instant update mentality of today's news consumer (Lee et al., 2017). For members of the mainstream press, though, technology inevitably puts journalism in a precarious position (Lareau, 2010). Despite the perceived benefits of online news from the public's perspective, web-based dissemination creates dissonance between journalism's dual role of fulfilling a public service while also being an independent business that needs financial stability to function. As more news organizations turn to layoffs and furloughs to counterbalance economic deficits created by shrinking advertising and subscription revenue, job assurance becomes more of a rarity than the rule (Ekdale et al., 2015; Glickhouse, 2020).

Thus, the most advantageous pivot to combat the woes of an industry that can no longer offer position stability is to look past the conventional corporate media structure and toward an approach in which a writer effectively sustains him or herself through a niche paid subscriber base. When first implemented in the realm of written sports content by Dejan Kovacevic (founder of the subscription-based D.K. Pittsburgh Sports website) in 2014, the tactic was "cutting edge" (Kalaf, 2018, para. 1). The concept went mainstream when mimicked to other sports-crazed cities because of its financial stability (e.g., Greg Bedard's Boston Sports Journal, The Athletic's former city verticals, etc.; Bucholtz, 2017; Finn, 2017). Substack subsequently brought niche content into the limelight due to its emphasis on replacing the murky parts of journalism (i.e., reliance on chain-of-ownership, clickbait, and the general advertising model) with individual monetization and lucid writing (Baker, 2020; Weiner, 2020).

Some media analysts consider Substack a "savior" (Shephard, 2021, para. 1) because it creates a culture of newsletter entrepreneurs who can target their audiences directly (Perlberg, 2020). The platform bills itself as an alternative to the corporate media route, emphasizing that an individual with an audience of, say, 1,000 subscribers each paying $5 per month can quickly turn writing into a full-time profession "without the hand-to-mouth hustle of freelancing" (Shephard, 2021, para. 1). Jobs in journalism may be dwindling, but Substack offers optimism, something that has only strengthened its appeal (Nover & Stenberg, 2021). Because of Substack, a furloughed media member, for instance, may no longer have to continue in the corporate media sector or potentially consider leaving the field altogether. Instead, the option to become one's boss and transition the social media following/reader base accumulated from the previous position is within reach, interviewees said—assuming the writer has a recognizable name.

For Craig Calcaterra, who writes about Major League Baseball via his newsletter, *Cup of Coffee*, the ability to sustain himself solely through Substack would not have been viable if he had not already cultivated a group of loyal readers (in the form of Twitter followers) during his tenure covering baseball at NBC Sports. A lawyer by trade who began blogging about baseball in 2007 for fun because he was "getting a little burnt out" by the law profession, Calcaterra's BlogSpot commentary quickly grew in popularity, and NBC Sports took note. After trying to replicate Mike Florio's blog-like Pro Football Talk website across its sports properties, NBC Sports executives contacted Calcaterra in the summer of 2009, asking if he would contribute written baseball content. The freelancing agreement went well, and by November of that year, Calcaterra was hired full-time to manage NBC Sports' former baseball website, Hardball Talk.

That position lasted until August 2020, when he was laid off in a move linked to COVID-19-related cost-saving measures. With the past 11 years spent in sports media, Calcaterra knew he did not want to return to the law sector. However, since outlets like The Athletic and ESPN also experienced COVID-19-related cutbacks, it was more logical, he said, to "take a stab of me going on my own." The issue was not what to do, but rather the most effective way to achieve the desired result of disseminating baseball writing to a curated audience in the most straightforward, most cost-effective manner. Calcaterra already had a personal WordPress website that he started when he first dove into blogging in the late-2000s. The process of taking an existing blog and monetizing it, though, seemed daunting, especially since he wanted to deviate from the advertising-exclusive model, which he said typically requires serious volume to be effective.

Mailchimp, an email marketing service, was an option. Still, there were aspects (e.g., implementing a paywall, content layout, etc.) associated with using the platform that Calcaterra did not want to handle. He said Patreon, which offers a subscription platform for content creators, needed more brand recognition. Calcaterra wanted a "turnkey solution," one that would allow him to quickly initiate the paywall model without the platform host taking too much of a revenue cut. Thus, Substack, which nets between 10 and 15 percent of total writer earnings (Barnett, 2021), met his need since it could deliver a newsletter that people could expect in their email inboxes on a set schedule, an aspect of publishing that he said enabled him to build a loyal reader base in his blogging days.

Back then, Calcaterra, who had toddlers at home and practiced law during the day, had to write first thing in the morning because it was his only free time. Whereas other baseball writers posted their content at night, filing a story immediately after a game's end, Calcaterra carved his niche by writing a news brief about the previous day's occurrences in baseball early in the morning. He said this provided a "one-stop shop" where readers could digest an overview of the sport in a few minutes while drinking their morning coffee. Even though he had drifted away from the condensed news brief format while employed by NBC Sports, it worked for his blogging routine and Calcaterra wanted to implement the strategy with Substack, giving subscribers everything they needed to know about the previous day in baseball, delivered by 7 a.m. Eastern each morning.

Calcaterra noted that his strategy, which has always been targeted at the busy M.L.B. fan, has allowed him to build a following of loyal readers at each stop of his writing career. Likewise, he admitted that his large Twitter following was a product of his tenure at NBC Sports and the profile that the sports media giant provided. Without accumulating this substantial social media following, an audience he could communicate the birth of his baseball-centric Substack to, Calcaterra said monetizing his newsletter would have been more difficult. The founders of Substack (Chris Best, McKenzie, and Jairaj Sethi), he said, realize that a content creator needs to have a recognizable name in media to make a living off newsletter subscriptions alone. However, as he put it, they "sort of want to play it down a bit" to sell their platform entirely as a "place where anyone can come in and be a member of the media."

As Calcaterra noted, Substack allows anyone to place their thoughts behind a paywall but promotes itself as a place where a blogger can funnel in enough subscription revenue to replace a salary in the corporate sector. Writers can be financially stable using Substack's subscription model. However, the guise that anyone can earn a steady living by putting out a bi-weekly newsletter leads to false assumptions being made about the profitability of Substack's individualized approach (Newitz, 2021). This lack of transparency regarding Substack's percentage cut from subscription revenue if a prominent writer takes an advance upfront (designated as a "Substack Pro"; McKenzie, 2021) has led to criticism from media pundits. The first occurred after it was reported that various writers (most notably former Vox writer Matthew Yglesias, who runs the *Slow Boring* perspectives newsletter) would have collected a higher income had they managed subscription revenue from the get-go and not negotiated complex deals (Ha, 2021; Knibbs, 2021; Smith, 2021).

The Substack model, in a way, is reminiscent of the notion of a business incubator—in which investors will provide accessible infrastructure, mentorship, and resources essential to a startup's growth with the hope that it blossoms into a financially viable platform so profits can be shared at a later date ("What is a business incubator," 2020). Because, as Doyle (2021) writes, Substack "makes choices as to who gets paid well and who doesn't" based on who receives "Pro" invitations (para. 10), the hope for a furloughed reporter of making a full-time living using the newsletter approach may sometimes seem like more of a pipedream than an achievable goal. Calcaterra banked on his following instead of taking an advance and said that his Substack has been a profitable business venture from the beginning, noting that his salary is higher now than it was while working for NBC Sports (full disclosure: he declined to state the range of this previous salary).

On the other hand, Justin Ferguson said he is happy to earn a living via Substack subscription rates and does not envision earning more than an average reporter's salary. Ferguson, The Athletic's former Auburn University football writer who was laid off in a June 2020 round of COVID-19-related cuts, said the editorial flexibility associated with being one's boss, coupled with the ability to "still pay my bills" working in media, made Substack a viable option. Unlike Calcaterra, who immediately conceived the idea for the *Cup of Coffee* newsletter on his own after being laid off, Ferguson was initially unsure of what to do when his position with The Athletic was terminated during what was supposed to be a standard weekly Zoom meeting during college football's off-season.

Like any modern sportswriter whose position gets axed, Ferguson took to Twitter to announce the news, writing that he was unsure what would come next but thanking his readers for "making what I've been able to do so far so much fun" (Ferguson, 2020). Shortly after that, his Twitter inbox flooded with direct messages from followers, most of whom informed Ferguson that they would pay to read his Auburn coverage at whichever media job he landed next. This reassuring feedback prompted Ferguson to explore the idea of independently branching out. However, he was not entirely sold on this entrepreneurial journalistic notion until speaking with early Substack adopter Matt Brown of the *Extra Points* newsletter, which is focused on the business of college athletics.

Realizing the apparent hole in the sports media landscape after The Athletic cut its Auburn coverage, Brown told his media peer to "jump on" the Substack approach because of his established audience. Although Ferguson's followers already knew his work from The Athletic, the pitch to drum up new subscriptions, he said, was to "treat the audience like people" by emphasizing reader expectations and wants rather than articles that solely move the click and pageview metric forward. Of note, The Athletic has not yet added another Auburn-specific beat writer to its staff as of 2024, with the only current consistent beat reporters being Ferguson and a handful of local Alabama-based media personnel (e.g., AL.com, *Montgomery Advertiser, Opelika-Auburn News*, etc.).

Though he labeled his short tenure with The Athletic as a "failed experience" because his position was ultimately cut, Ferguson was grateful for the experience because it gave him a "following of people that were willing to say, 'Hey, we'll throw a few bucks your way each month to keep reading your stuff.'" The true beauty of Substack, Ferguson said, lies in its ability to function as the "antithesis" of modern corporate media since the model is not rooted in exponential growth and profit margins. He pointed out that the *Auburn Observer* would not make him wealthy, but the income would be enough "to stay in my apartment and continue to live a pretty comfortable life here in Auburn." However, Ferguson is satisfied with his decision since "whatever [subscribers] invest in me, that's my salary."

This ability for writers to use their substantial social media following to garner subscription revenue for content hidden behind a paywall may be an appealing aspect of the Substack process for the former professional sportswriter. However, for those who have yet to work in mainstream media before launching a subscription newsletter, it can sometimes be difficult to entice the public to subscribe if they are unfamiliar with a sports reporter's work. That is why Jordan Sperber of *Hoop* Vision, a newsletter devoted to basketball analytics and film study, said he believes in the customer acquisition and conversion strategy of offering select content for free upfront—that way readers know what to expect before inputting their credit card information. Despite not possessing a traditional journalism background, Sperber noted that the key to financial stability on the Substack platform is turning the free, casual reader into a paid subscriber.

Substack may not have been Sperber's initial choice regarding a newsletter platform (he began delivering the subscriber emails using MailChimp). However, it was attractive because of the ability to start offering free content and switch to the paywall approach based on reader popularity. Unlike the other interviewees who operate a Substack based on subscriber revenue, Sperber is the only one whose audience acquisition strategy is rooted in the idea of freemium content. This plan, he said, enabled him to grow his reader base from one that was almost entirely college basketball coaches to an audience that is more of a "50/50" split, with the other half being general fans interested in learning more of the analytical approaches. Unlike in the past, when sports reporters were tasked with handling one function of a news organization's multifaceted approach (e.g., editorial, business, advertising, etc.), today's media entrepreneurs must be adept at not only producing written work but also navigating the intricacies of a sustainable business model. When a reporter can no longer rely on another person to determine how to turn a profit, he or she is forced to learn how much to charge for content, whether income will be supplemented by advertisers and/or marketing tactics to persuade the public to pay for the new product.

The thinking that a writer can be financially dependent on Substack sub-scription revenue by trusting that readers value a newsletter without getting to read its content needs to be revised, he said. Instead, the most effective formula equates to offering certain information for free and trusting that read-ers will convert to the paid format based on the overall quality of writing. Because of this, Sperber said he publishes a free newsletter each Friday, driven by a subscription conversion "hook" in the content that promotes a piece of news hidden behind the paywall. It is a "causal effect," one in which *Hoop Vision* typically receives a few new subscribers in the days after a free newslet-ter is disseminated and none during the Fridays when he forgets to publish. However, perhaps more critical than the freemium tactic, Sperber said, is the need to be upfront with readers about entrepreneurial sports journalism by "explaining how the business model works and educating our readership that you need to pay for this to maintain what we're doing here."

Whereas other sports Substack operators said that branching out on one's own enables quality journalism free from the clickbait constraints of the advertising model to flourish, Sperber quickly pushed back on this notion. As he put it, the more readers click on social media promotional posts for *Hoop Vision*, the more people become free subscribers—of which he con-verts "about one in every 10 free subscribers to paid subscribers." Although Calcaterra also offers select content for free as a way for potential subscribers to preview his work, he does not view his freemium writing as an extension of clickbait journalism. Sperber said this is naturally bred from the Substack model since it operates on the same incentives as clickbait, just on a slightly smaller scale (i.e., getting people to read the free posts and hopefully seeing enough value to warrant a subscription purchase). Of note, Ferguson does not offer freemium written content. Still, he does give non-subscribers access to a weekly Auburn football podcast with the incentive that this may incline a fan to consider becoming a paid subscriber. Regardless of one's take, the niche effectively allows a Substack writer to prioritize specialized content catering to only a handful of readers instead of a strategy targeting mass appeal.

Despite having what he deems to be an expensive subscription rate for a sports-focused Substack ($10 per month or $100 for a yearly rate) since finan-cial/business newsletters are typically the only ones successful at charging that rate, Sperber said, in 2021, that *Hoop Vision* was past its bottom goal of paying subscribers (of note, he declined to mention his newsletter's exact number of paying subscribers). Although he did not say his actual income figures, Sperber did note that Substack has a sports leaderboard sorted by annualized revenue, and the fact that *Hoop Vision* continually sits is continually near the top tells him that "there are not a lot of people on Substack writing about sports making a full-time living. I am, but there should be more people ahead of me." He said the ultimate goal is to grow *Hoop Vision* to a point where he does not rely solely on one business model (in this case, monthly subscription rates) for revenue generation. He said, "My next step is getting advertisers and diversifying a little bit if we can get it to a point going away from the subscriber model."

Sperber's above take, one centered on the eventual transition away from the subscriber-centric model and more toward one that brings advertising into the equation (presumably to either have *Hoop Vision* be more financially stable or to increase his overall profit margin), illustrates the difficulty that those who are established sports media brands can face when it comes to being a profitable entrepreneurial writer. Calcaterra, Ferguson, and Sperber had a niche audience before pivoting to Substack. Still, without their loyal reader base, each noted the struggle that would coincide with making Substack a full-time venture. This realization, coupled with Substack's lack of potential writer earning transparency, means that marketing itself as a platform where anyone can earn money through his or her writing may be more of a myth than a reality for those who lack large social media followings.

These viewpoints further negate how Substack promotes its image as an end-all, be-all to the corporate media grind when considering the focus of its initial 2017 welcome post. In this message, two of the company's three founders (Best and McKenzie) describe how legitimate journalism lost its "value—especially as measured in dollars" and explain how there has never been a better time to "bolster and project" the ideals that journalistic content should not be given away for free (Best & McKenzie, 2017, para. 2). Although Substack pushes this entrepreneurial narrative on the surface (even offering a profit calculator on its website that potential Substackers can use to estimate monthly earnings based on the projected number of subscribers and anticipated monthly subscription fee), the likely reality—one reflected by interviewees—is that career sustainability cannot be accomplished without already being a recognizable media personality in a specific reporting niche.

Testing the Waters: "If it doesn't turn into a full-time job, it can be a way to turn my writing into a little bit of side money"

As previously mentioned, the Internet effectively disrupted conventional pathways in journalism by giving anyone, regardless of professional training, a podium to present thoughts, analyses, and opinions to the public. Although there still are people who disseminate sports news as a hobby, there exists a growing faction of content creators whose goal is to parlay their blog-like writing into a livable income through either content monetization (Rizky & Pardamean, 2016) or full-time media employment. These individuals, Gil de Zuniga et al. (2011) write, perceive their blogging as an extension of traditional journalism.

The foundation behind the free information arm, thus, is one akin to the proverbial stepping stone present in any sector of business. If an individual can conjure brand recognition with a specialized audience based on his or her byline, sustaining oneself from a financial perspective may be simplified, even in today's uncertain media climate. Although there is generally a lack of mainstream print sportswriting jobs because of industry-wide layoffs and furloughs (Putterman, 2017; Strauss, 2020a), being able to construct an audience and promote sports content for free sheds light on the accessibility of self-publishing mediums, which Smith (2021) views as the "content-creation equivalent of Uber drivers" (para. 7). This type of dissemination may be perceived as an offshoot of blogging; however, when professional writing clips can be challenging to obtain, acting as a self-publisher can sometimes be a practical career kick-starter (Knox, 2021).

Perhaps nowhere is this notion of employing the do-it-yourself news strategy to get noticed more evident than with sports-centric Substack writers who use their free newsletters as a writing buffer until a more stable media opportunity arises. Though the following interviewees revealed that having a preestablished social media following is needed to earn a livable income as a one-man journalistic band, lost in the shuffle is how select Substackers perceive the platform's free subscriber function as an editorial training ground (either in the form of eventual paywall implementation or by serving as a corporate media audition for a stable position). It is not well documented how many writers parlayed their individual Substack presence into a full-time media position since most narratives focus on those who made the jump from corporate media to Substack (perhaps the most notable person to pivot to Substack has been former *New York Times* N.B.A. reporter Marc Stein; Casselberry, 2021). However, some sportswriters view Substack as a vehicle that can help get them noticed by larger news companies. One of the attractive features of Substack, therefore, is that it can gauge the feasibility of long-term journalism sustainability for the independent writer who needs both a substantial reader base and initial content monetization power.

For Matthew Kory, a former suburban Baltimore city planner who dove into online baseball writing simply because he needed an outlet while being a stay-at-home dad, Substack represented the perfect platform to test the potential paid sustainability of a Boston Red Sox newsletter. Like other interviewees, Kory possessed professional writing experience before his Substack's December 2020 launch. However, despite having a byline for significant organizations like Baseball Prospectus, Vice Sports, and The Athletic, Kory was only employed part-time as a journalist, branded as a contributing writer at each career stop. That is why the capability of Substack to function as a full-time writing position, assuming he or she has a large enough paid subscriber base, was appealing for someone who enjoyed the freedom of writing from home yet desired a livable yearly salary. The lifelong Red Sox fan did not want to jump into the paid model immediately, even though he garnered what he described as "mainstream credibility" while writing for the previously mentioned outlets. Instead, Kory found it problematic to ask Red Sox fans to pay a subscription fee for a newsletter that did not have an established reputation. Unlike Calcaterra, who turned on Substack's paywall during *Cup of Coffee's* initial launch, Kory wanted Red Sox readers to test the product for free—while giving himself at least one entire season to build a significant subscriber base—before hiding all content behind the paywall.

When he was a part-time contributing writer for large media conglomerates, Kory said the task of sitting down at his computer at night and spewing words onto a page seemed more like a chore than a relaxing activity since there were constraints regarding what he could write and the type of humor he could inject into his M.L.B. columns. Especially since these positions did not come with a full-time salary, Kory lost the enjoyment of writing about baseball for a corporate media organization. It was not until he researched Substack's ability to begin with the free model and eventually implement a paid version with the "money integration" feature, Kory said, that combining his two loves (Boston's baseball team and writing) made sense. Hence, in his initial welcome post, Kory billed *Sox Outsider* as a blog where fans can get Red Sox "analysis, opinion, whimsy" in one place (Kory, 2020, para. 1).

It is important to note that there is not much difference between the "paid" versus "money integration" model that Kory mentioned since a Substack user can toggle between the two. For example, writers using Substack as their primary mode of information dissemination can either launch the newsletter with the paywall in place from the onset (like Calcaterra, Ferguson, and Sperber) or can begin their publication using the free model and then switch to a paywall at a later date. According to an official post published on Substack's website, the company did not advise its newsletter users to follow the traditional approach of saving the "best work for their paying subscribers" ("Why free posts pay: Avoiding a tempting mistake," 2019, para. 2). Instead, Substack's leadership encouraged its publishers to make as much content freely available to any reader to allow as "many people as possible the chance to fall in love with your voice and worldview" ("Why free posts pay: Avoiding a tempting mistake," 2019, para. 4), with the rationale being that readers will be more open to paying for someone's work when they gain a sense of relationship with the publisher.

It is a direct approach, with the aim being that an audience needs to know what content offerings are available and experience it firsthand before they are likely to pay a monthly subscription fee. Substack's advice to newsletter entrepreneurs is akin to the former approach taken by the conglomerations of entertainment-based streaming media that typically allow free access to a library of Internet-based content before asking a consumer to pay a monthly or yearly subscription. For instance, when Netflix, Max, and Disney+ tried to grow an audience early in their platform's launch, all offered free trials that allowed users to try before you buy. Although Netflix and Disney+ no longer give free trials (most likely because the nameplates are associated with quality content worth the asking price), Substack openly advocated for more of an approach rooted in semi-free content, and readers are encouraged—but not required nor expected—to pay a subscription fee at the beginning.

This tactic, Substack maintained, helped market a newly established newsletter since it made content accessible to everyone and increased the likelihood of being shared online. This aligns with Kory's approach not to flip the paywall switch until he feels comfortable with *Sox Outsider*; that way, his reader base knows the specific type of content and slant to expect if they transition to a paying customer (of note, Kory still has not enabled a paywall as of May 2024). Botticello (2021), in his personal Substack titled *Blogging Guide*, stated that newsletter publishers who set up a paid publication are not forced to hide *all* content behind a paywall. Instead, the "monetization switch" gives the Substacker business flexibility since each time a post is published, he or she can decide "whether to make it free for everyone, or only for paying subscribers" (para. 8).

As a do-it-all writer responsible for creating and curating every newsletter, Kory admitted that it can sometimes be a challenge to tackle each piece of news on the Red Sox beat, the type of consistency that is often valuable when it comes to building a loyal reader base willing to pay a subscription fee. Being a husband and father who lives in the Pacific time zone means he sometimes cannot watch all 162 regular season Red Sox games and write an accompanying post for each. There are always story angles that he would like to explore or commentary that would be practical to write in regard to a player's performance. Still, he admits that it is not all doable as an entrepreneurial sportswriter.

Whereas other Red Sox-centric blogs and news outlets have multiple writers assigned to cover all aspects of the beat, Kory is a team of one and said the amount of information on *Sox Outsider* reflects this. He may have to watch highlights of certain games because he missed the live broadcast, but Kory mentioned that his voice, sense of humor, and love for baseball are conveyed in each newsletter that arrives in a fan's email inbox. Besides, he said it can be gratifying to wake up in the morning, after spending the previous night writing until 1 a.m., to comments from readers who enjoy his "for-now" free product.

Kory's decision not to charge a readership fee initially, yet eventually implement the practice after enough free subscribers sign up, leaves the door open for his Substack's future business moves. Right now, he may need to be more committed to providing readers with content regularly. However, he cannot make a full-time living with *Sox Outsider* until the paywall is initiated. His newsletter is a double-edged sword between the work-life balance of being a media entrepreneur and the financial benefits of a steady job. As a result, his Substack is what he makes of it, with the goal of eventually profiting from Red Sox writing seemingly within reach based on the success of other subscriber-only sports newsletter operators. As Kory said:

> When I started [*Sox Outsider*], I wanted to just get my name back out there and see how I would write about the team all the time. Everyone I talked to said I should start as a paid model, but I didn't feel like that would be fair to ask for people's money for something that didn't exist yet [. . .] As soon as you start asking people for money, there is the implication that you will provide something for that money, which is entirely fair. (M. Kory, personal communication, June 16, 2021)

Though not outwardly apparent at this point, it is plausible to believe that Kory's mindset of giving away content for free upfront before ultimately flipping the paywall switch may place *Sox Outsider* in a precarious position, one akin to the uphill battle currently facing the online product of legacy newspapers struggling to convince readers to pay for digital subscriptions (Adgate,

2021b; Owens, 2020). During the Internet's infancy, when news organizations were first constructing a web presence, a decision was made by a majority of gatekeepers to publish online articles for anyone to view, regardless of whether he or she purchased a print subscription (Spivak, 2011). Some media scholars and critics, like Chyi and Tenenboim (2019) and Shafer (2016), identify this as a critical error in the history of online news media because it inevitably placed the public under the perception that online newspaper content should be free. It is interesting, though, that the model of giving away free information has proved detrimental to various facets of journalism (sports media included) but has yet to yield as critical an effect on forms of entertainment-based media, specifically social media.

Despite rumors circulating over the previous decade that Facebook will eventually implement a subscription plan to use its social networking service, as advertising revenue on the platform is unstable and uncertain, it remains a free service, with the company even dedicating a page to its help section to this topic, writing "[...] we charge advertisers to show ads on the Facebook family of apps and technologies. This helps us make Facebook available to everyone without charging people for access to it" ("Does it cost money to use Facebook?" n.d., para. 1). Instead, Facebook—and other social media platforms—can sustain themselves financially by having users "pay with their data" (Horaczek, 2020, para. 11). Though this tactic of generating revenue through target marketing has proven successful for this type of media venture, in which the goal is to have as many active users as possible, news organizations whose bottom line revolves more around subscriptions than advertising are not afforded that type of luxury. In other words, the free model that has been successful for social media has had adverse effects on the news industry. It is plausible that the current climate of journalism, thus, is concerned more with dedicated audiences possessing disposable income to spend toward news consumption rather than accumulating sheer volume.

When news paywalls were first established, it was difficult to convince the masses that a product formerly available without a subscription was worthy of a production and distribution fee (Faulconbridge, 2019). Consequently, there persists the likelihood that some members of Kory's constructed audience of Red Sox readers—if or when the paywall is officially implemented in his newsletter—will not want to pay for something they were accustomed to receiving for free. If this occurred, it would most likely impact his financial bottom line and the revenue he can garner by pivoting *Sox Outsider* from a sportswriting hobby to a full-time, salaried media position.

Although lacrosse writer Kyle Devitte shared Kory's take that Substack can help media personalities affected by industry woes once again secure a livable wage writing about sport, his way of using the platform for career advancement differed from the typical narrative of current or eventual paywall implementation. When he officially launched his lacrosse-centric newsletter, branded *Lacrocity* (a combination of the first three letters of "lacrosse" with the word "atrocity"), the aim was to have an additional outlet where he could cover the game without traditional editorial constraints. However, because the former Division III lacrosse player and coach was able to accumulate more of a "quality audience" than just sheer volume of subscribers, the newsletter put his writing clips "in the shop window," displaying his tone and voice to media employers looking to fill a journalistic void. Roughly nine months after the first edition of *Lacrocity* hit email inboxes, Devitte secured an interview with the publisher of the *New England Lacrosse Journal* for a full-time job covering the sport on a regional level with a starting salary that was "more money than I have ever made in my life." Unlike the strategy implemented by Calcaterra, Ferguson, Sperber, and Kory—all of whom used Substack to write about a mainstream sport or team (e.g., Major League Baseball, Auburn University, basketball film breakdown, and the Boston Red Sox)—Devitte's approach differed since it focused on a sport that received little, if any, media attention from a vast majority of mainstream sports journalism (Sanchirico, 2009).

Whereas the Substack writers mentioned above were, in essence, competing with professionalized media for a share of the sports-consuming public, Devitte's take was not so much about the nuance of publicity and depth of coverage (i.e., finding unique angles on the same athletes/teams to differentiate newsletter coverage from mainstream sources) as it was to deliver pertinent news to the niche followers of lacrosse. This provided Devitte with audience segmentation since there is less competition with lacrosse media than there would be with a mainstream sport like professional baseball (as is the case with Calcaterra). Instead, the allure of Substack was its ability to capture the attention of a niche sports audience.

Blossoming a Substack newsletter into a sportswriting position at a print lacrosse magazine and online website may not have been Devitte's ultimate goal when he published the newsletter's first edition in July 2020. However, it was a way to add unfiltered clips to his portfolio in a creative manner that he was not permitted to explore in this then-position as gear and lifestyle editor for *Inside Lacrosse* magazine, one of the sport's premier publications. After being asked to take both a pay decrease and a diminished writing role by *Inside Lacrosse* after a series of cost-cutting measures by its parent company, American City Business Journals, Devitte wanted more to satisfy his hunger for lacrosse writing. He was happy to still have a job at the height of the COVID-19 pandemic but wanted to write the type of articles that pushed the needle forward regarding self-gratification. Therefore, through Brown and his *Extra Points* newsletter, Devitte found Substack to be a sanctuary where he could exercise complete control over the written word.

Knowing Brown from a mutual friend, Devitte sought advice about the potential sustainability of a lacrosse newsletter and decided to "go all in" on a paywall-free newsletter at a time when regular lacrosse content was virtually absent from Substack (of note, Brown has since migrated *Extra Points* from Substack to Ghost to Beehiiv, similar newsletter publishing platforms). This gap in terms of the lack of lacrosse-centric newsletters prompted McKenzie, Substack's co-founder, to send a "helpful email" to Devitte when *Lacrocity* was officially registered, conveying that a newsletter on this budding sport could "blow up" if he made it what he wanted (although there is no formulaic approach to gaining Substack subscribers if one does not possess a large social media following, it can be reasoned that finding a gap in coverage does help). So, Devitte took an unhampered approach to lacrosse writing, posting in-depth college season previews on each conference and evaluating player performance using a made-up statistic he dubbed the "Devitte matrix" (goals + assists – turnovers). Though it was an unconventional editorial plan, he admitted, the publisher of the *New England Lacrosse Journal* saw value in the approach, became a free subscriber to *Lacrocity*, and eventually hired him on the basis that he would transition his signature content to the new job.

Devitte maintained that building an audience of other lacrosse media members, coaches, and even Division I players and their parents via Substack helped secure his current position. Because the platform allowed him to see the names and email addresses of anyone who subscribed to email updates for free, Devitte built more of a "quality audience" than a quantity reader base. Even though *Lacrocity* served as the vehicle that transported Devitte to a full-time media position covering his favorite sport, he kept it active when switching professional affiliations. Devitte shifted the newsletter to focus more on professional and major college lacrosse since his current news organization only promotes youth, high school, and regional lacrosse. The content on his Substack may be readable entirely for free. Still, Devitte said he did receive a little financial kickback from his *Lacrocity* writing, mainly in the form of advertising and subscriber donation revenue (though, he noted, it is not enough to live off nor use to even "buy groceries"). Although he may not owe his entire career to Substack, Devitte said he is thankful for it since *Lacrocity* opened a "door that I didn't know was going to be opened."

Devitte, who used Substack to construct "an addition" to nearly a two-decade career, said writers without a professional media background could likely not earn a living solely using a paywalled newsletter. To him, this is a "unicorn dream," in which the expectation versus the reality is two completely different takes. Devitte said that a career as a professional sportswriter is built around "speed and efficiency." If an individual does not possess those two working characteristics, he or she will be unable to differentiate individual content from that of a sports blogger. In this regard, Devitte noted that Substack is the perfect platform for those looking to disseminate sports content for the pure enjoyment of writing and for professional journalists who want to expand their audience. He said it would be doubtful for a person without professional writing credentials to begin a subscription newsletter and stay relevant while turning a profit at the same time. The expectations of what someone wants to get out of Substack, thus, "need to be established, just like anything else in life, before you do it."

Content Catharsis: "It's nice to just kind of do something that is just for me"

In the current media landscape, filled with promoters, influencers, and web-cultivated personalities, the idea of an individual expressing himself or herself via mediated content without a monetary goal may seem outdated. Because of the paywall-driven corporate climate, in which most U.S. metropolitan newspapers limit what the public can read for free (Pattabhiramaiah et al. 2019), views toward the value of a news subscription have shifted, especially among the 18 to 39-year-old demographic. Kammer et al. (2015) posit that this age group's reluctance to pay for news, in any medium, can pose a future economic challenge for the journalism industry since its "future customers are opting out of not only the printed newspapers . . . but of fee-based news media altogether" (p. 117). Furthermore, Williams and Stroud (2021) maintain that the paywall incentivizes frugal news consumers to seek freely available information instead of purchasing a new subscription. This thinking that readers are likely to opt for free news instead of content with an associated cost coincides with visual artist Richard Serra's take on free forms of mass media. In the 1973 short film *Television Delivers People*, Serra states that those who receive free content are not consumers but the product itself (Oremus, 2018). Applying this concept to Substack means that readers of paywall-free newsletters (i.e., those who are not required to pay for the content itself) represent the product being pushed more than the consuming base because the niche, in this regard, carries more clout than sheer audience size.

However, this thought that legitimate journalism can only exist in a vacuum ultimately places those who write purely for the personal satisfaction of information dissemination at a disadvantage regarding reader appeal. Overall, trust in the mainstream gatekeeping process may have eroded; however, the hobbyist writers with no intention of implementing a paywall reinforce the value of placing personal gratification above profits. As the following interviewees noted, the ability to chase the cathartic release of writing, instead of profit, allows them to escape the daily grind of professionalized journalism. Writing for oneself aligns with the blogging boom of the Internet's infancy, when writers deviated from traditionalist media ideals to fulfill personal needs (Gill et al., 2009).

These interviewees said that Substack's most innovative feature is its ability to "make it what you want"—monetizing content or simply writing for fun. It is a passion project, initiated by the satisfaction of writing without having to "answer to paying subscribers." It may help that the following Substack writers all have full-time jobs outside their newsletters and, thus, possess the financial means required to write for a hobby. However, interviews with sports newsletter writers who do not currently have a paywall implemented reveal that Substack, from their perspective, is a superior alternative to the standard blog because of its functionality and ease of use. It is viewed as the perfect tool to freely disseminate hobbyist writing directly to the email inboxes of an invested niche audience.

One of the writers who used Substack for that purpose was Eric Nusbaum, co-operator of *Sports Stories*. While working as a sports editor at Vice, Nusbaum met illustrator Adam Villacin, noticed that the pair shared a common interest rooted at the intersection of sports and cultural history, and began bouncing ideas off one another regarding ways to publicize obscure sporting topics using both the written word and illustrated visual media. Before long, the idea of starting a newsletter as a creative outlet sprouted, with both opting not to place any commercial consideration on their work. Instead, the idea that guided the 2019 launch of *Sports Stories* was to create engaging content for fun and deliver it for free to a subscriber's email inbox.

Readers who appreciated the work could donate. Nusbaum and Villacin previously offered unique personalized postcards for those who contributed a specific dollar amount per year (of note, *Sports Stories* has yet to post a new entry since April 2022). However, all content hosted on *Sports Stories* was freely available. For he and Villacin, Substack represented something they did "for the love of it" and not because it had the potential to be a viable business model that could sustain a livable yearly income (only four interviewees, all of whom use a paywall, viewed Substack's financial model as being practical: Calcaterra, Ferguson, Sperber, and Jared Dubin, who is not directly quoted, but runs the N.B.A.-centric newsletter *Last Night, In Basketball*). This is because, as Nusbaum said, the work targeted such a niche audience that there needed to be more scale to pivot from a free to a paid-only model. He noted, though, that there was a "little money" from reader donations and that the giving was appreciated because it allowed him and Villacin to carve out the time needed to research, write, and design the content.

Whereas other content catharsis newsletter writers gravitated toward Substack because it represented a free, easy-to-use platform, Nusbaum said he did not "feel too strongly" about Substack. When he and Villacin searched for a newsletter platform, it seemed practical as a free option that could quickly be designed and initiated. Substack was also a more minor, lesser-known operation at the time, making it appealing. Nusbaum, however, admitted that he did not put a lot of consideration into the platform and instead gravitated toward it via word-of-mouth. The publication purpose, thus, was not rooted in the focus of the content nor the actual platform being used. Those were two thoughts Nusbaum—a self-employed journalist—said never crossed his mind. Instead, the underlying motive that drove *Sports Stories* was the appeal of collaborating with a personal friend who brought a different perspective. Nusbaum said Villacin enjoyed his writing style, and he appreciated his colleague's illustrations.

Whereas other Substack writers perceived the platform as bringing a revolutionary new idea to the media industry because it quickly allowed a user to send a curated newsletter to email inboxes, Nusbaum thought the tool was not that much different than the standard WordPress blog still used by select sports bloggers. He noted that Substack's concept (filling a niche void, constructing an audience, disseminating content, etc.) is simply an extension of blogging that is reimagined from an email-driven perspective since "you still have to build your audience, and you have to get email addresses and get them to sign up."

Substack's user-friendly interface, enabling anyone to disseminate his or her writing freely, can be equated to blogging 2.0 since it effectively does everything WordPress did for the blogging revolution of the early 2000s. However, the paywall function inevitably separates it from most standard blogs. That is not to say that a typical WordPress blog cannot have a paywall function added; however, doing so requires knowledge of web coding to allow the site to take payments. By signing up for a Substack account and beginning the newsletter creation process, anyone can either have their newsletter mimic a standard blog (with no paywall) or function as a more legitimized news source (with paywall activated). That is why, as interviewees elucidated, Substack represents more of a hybrid between a blog and a legitimate journalistic outlet because of its entrepreneurial approach.

What Nusbaum said Substack does differently from a business perspective, to segment itself from other do-it-yourself publication platforms, is its talent poaching strategy, similar to The Athletic during its initial growth spurt. Substack, in what Oremus (2021) calls the latest milestone in its "ascendance as a platform for high-profile journalism" (para. 2), used a round of venture capital funding (Kokalitcheva & Primack, 2021) to hire reporters, writers, and media commentators away from established outlets like *The New York Times*, Vox Media, and BuzzFeed. News coverage reveals that some writers defected to Substack because of the six-figure advances handed out to those with established followings (Ball, 2021). Others were lured by the guise of earning more than they did in traditional media (Monahan, 2020).

Smith (2021), in this manner, likens Substack's influence on the business of news in a post-COVID-19 world to a contradiction since its aim is to enable free-flowing journalism to flourish, yet at the expense of poaching talent under the belief that more money can be made in newsletter journalism. Substack, however, scaled back its "Pro" program in the summer of 2022 after co-founder Hamish McKenzie was quoted as saying, "We have to think ahead. We can't just bank on easy-to-get venture capital at good prices to be there, to be able to pass on to writers immediately" (Owens, 2022, para. 8). Regardless of an individual's motive for leaving mainstream media, Substack's former practice of buying the best talent raised questions about the identity it wanted to promote, whether as a newsletter hosting platform or as a new, multifaceted media production and distribution company. In this regard, being asked by the leaders of Substack to host a newsletter on the platform was seen as a status symbol, something that an established writer or journalist viewed as a personal benchmark.

Although he was not a Substack Pro poached by legacy media, Tim Haslam also viewed passion for the subject matter and positive feedback from readers as the driving force behind a successful free newsletter. Haslam, a father of four who publishes a regional newsletter on high school lacrosse in Utah (aptly named *Utah Lacrosse Report*), covers the intricacies of the sport, focusing on game recaps, top ten lists, and question-and-answer segments with players and coaches. Like Devitte, Haslam carved his territory in the regional lacrosse space, first writing about the sport for the University of Utah's student newspaper before parlaying that experience into a freelancing position for CollegeLax.us, a former news site centered on collegiate club lacrosse. Unlike Devitte, though, Haslam had a job outside of journalism and viewed his lacrosse writing as a hobby, something he did to stay close to a sport that he quit playing competitively after high school.

A web developer by trade, Haslam initially mimicked the *CollegeLax.us* formula to the high school level, constructing his website to cover all facets of a sport not officially sanctioned by the Utah High School Activities Association until 2017 (Donaldson, 2017). It was a passion project; however, Haslam and his four other reporters enjoyed the journalistic process, mainly since local media rarely covered boys' and girls' lacrosse during that time. After six years of essentially working what he described as "two jobs," Haslam felt burned out and jumped at an opportunity when a fellow lacrosse fan offered to purchase the brand domain from him.

His next foray into lacrosse media was working as a part-time sports information director and play-by-play announcer for the University of Utah's club program livestreams. However, that position was eventually transitioned to the athletic department when the school decided to elevate the team to N.C.A.A. Division I status in 2019 (of note, Haslam was hired by the University of Utah's N.C.A.A. Division I lacrosse team as director of operations in 2023). So, the following spring, Haslam hit a crossroads, wanting to write about lacrosse on a regional level—mainly since a void still existed in newspaper coverage of the newly sanctioned high school sport—but not wanting the type of commitment his previous news site required. Thus, The once-per-week email newsletter represented the perfect middle ground between staying connected with his writing hobby and not having it consume his free time.

With his background in web development, Haslam said that he could have quickly built another Utah lacrosse website from scratch if he wanted and run it using Mailchimp as the newsletter dissemination tool. However, what guided him to Substack was its straightforward approach (and the fact that it is free to use). Unlike Mailchimp, Substack does not charge a newsletter operator a fee each time his or her subscriber list grows, meaning that Haslam can send as many emails per day to as many subscribers on his list without having to pay a fee (Substack only charges newsletter users if a paywall is in place, in which case it takes 10 percent of total subscriber revenue; Ingram, 2021; Kafka, 2021).

Because lacrosse is a blossoming high school sport in Utah primarily played by athletes from a middle to upper-class background, he could profit if he asked readers to pay a nominal monthly fee. However, each time he thought of the benefits of charging readers to view the lacrosse news content that he produces as a hobby, Haslam was reminded of why he started the *Utah Lacrosse Report* Substack in the first place: for the flexibility that came with publishing only when he wanted to and not being bound to a forced schedule. Besides, he said, if the paywall were in place, he would need to please his paying subscriber base instead of himself, inevitably making it feel less like a diversion and "more like a job." The benefit of the hobby approach to Substack, he said, is the ability to post as often or as little as one desires. For Haslam, this means disseminating a weekly newsletter beginning in February, when the spring season commences, and ending his run after championship weekend in May (he takes a publishing hiatus during the other months).

In this sense, he saw his writing as a "switch that I can turn on and off," quickly toggling between periods of heavy content and the off-season, when virtually no high school lacrosse news occurs. Besides, if Haslam charged a monthly fee yet left the email inboxes of paying customers bare, he said he would feel guilty about this business practice. In other words, he does this purely for fun, feeling the greatest joy when someone he meets at a local high school lacrosse game recognizes him and his work with the newsletter. Haslam said it is not about the subscriber number; he finds joy in doing this because "I feel like it's making an impact."

For Michael Weinreb, a freelance journalist and nonfiction author who used the newsletter platform to write about the intersection of sport, culture, and history, Substack represented a "catch-22." From his perspective, the company's original aim was always to lift "up new voices" that had something to say yet needed a suitable platform for amplification. However, he noted Substack further contradicted the narrative that it helped establish within the writing community—that anyone could be an entrepreneurial journalist—by poaching writers with previously established followings. That is why Weinreb, the creator and curator of the *Throwbacks* newsletter, never wanted to monetize his Substack. It was never about doing it for profit, he said. Instead, the inherent idea was spurred by having an additional writing outlet where he could focus on "what's happening in the world through the lens of sports culture."

During the onset of the COVID-19 pandemic, Weinreb—whose work previously appeared in *The Atlantic*, The Athletic, and The Ringer—found it challenging to secure freelance writing work. Though he had professional journalistic clips and four nonfiction sports books attached to his byline, Weinreb was unsure what direction to take his career, whether continuing in journalism or pivoting full-time to screenwriting. He wanted to stay connected to the type of mainstream culture-based sportswriting that forged his professional identity if, for nothing else, as a cathartic writing release. Further, he desired to avoid the traditional reliance on audience cultivation via social media for blogs or other forms of web-based writing. Simply put, Weinreb wanted to move away from the "shallow" social media culture that was "deliberately devoid of depth" and viewed Substack as a way to write for himself—and no one else.

The approach, he said, came at the perfect time since he had grown tired of the freelance grind, in which each writing assignment was strategically taken for the paycheck. For the first time in a while, he could select the subjects he wanted to write about without regard for audience reaction, likelihood of clicks, or social media engagement. The simplicity of the paywall-free Substack model, Weinreb noted, aligned with the viewpoints of other interviewees, in which the environment was pressure-free since there was no demand for paying subscribers wanting a return on investment (although he did specify that some readers donate). Thus, by keeping each *Throwbacks* newsletter edition in front of the invisible paywall instead of locked behind it, Weinreb was not forced to put a quota on content output.

His Substack was purely motivated by personal gratification, writing about sports subjects that piqued his interest. It is not that the thought of "relentless promoting" to the point that *Throwbacks* could be a monetizable commodity never crossed his mind. Like Haslam and Nusbaum, he had at least considered flipping the paywall switch for profiting purposes. However, Weinreb thought the potential return on investment was only worth the time it would take to consistently research, write, and disseminate sports culture and history topics. This was because he did not like the primary tool—social media—needed to garner an audience large enough to provide a self-sustaining income (of note, he does have an X account but only posts sporadically). The underlying motive of Weinreb's Substack aligned more with his enjoyment of the process than audience attitudes after the fact.

All three interviewees' perspectives indicated Substack's perceived transformation by journalism outsiders from a writer-centric publishing entity to a full-fledged media arm aimed at competing with other comparable organizations. Because of its multi-pronged foray into actual media gatekeeping, Substack is no longer just a tool that one could use to project his or her thoughts to the masses. Instead, it is on the trajectory to become what it sought to combat in the first place: corporate media that values profits over individuality. Substack may have revolutionized the concept of self-sustaining sportswriting. However, creating a system in which only the most recognizable names make a profit places some at a disadvantage since it makes it seem as if the goal of achieving total time income is within reach of everyone.

This segmentation between actual earnings and profit perception is further exemplified when considering Substack's tactic as a publishing platform and editorial gatekeeper. With this approach, Substack divvied earnings to writers. It wanted to lure them away from other forms of mass media under the guise that their work would be more profitable as a newsletter brand instead of just a byline at a traditional journalistic outlet. However, doing this demonstrated that it actively chose which writers it wanted to promote on Substack. This, in turn, went against the principles of its editorial founding as a place where "anyone can make money on a newsletter" (Ha, 2021, para. 6). That is why Haslam, Nusbaum, and Weinreb may have the most practical viewpoint that Substack is best suited as a platform that promotes the cathartic release of hobbyist writing instead of one centered on content monetization linked to the one-man band approach to media.

The three collective themes that emerge from this chapter (Substack as an entrepreneurial form of journalism to make a living via implementation of the paywall, Substack as a stepping stone to full-time media employment, and Substack as a cathartic release hobby) provide added context to how sports journalism has evolved due to technology that may have rewritten the script on do-it-yourself information dissemination. Before Substack's official launch in 2017, sportswriters had few options for financially sustaining themselves. The path to becoming and maintaining full-time employment in journalism has long been rooted in the corporate media grind, in which an individual gains entry-level employment as a cub reporter before slowly climbing the hierarchical ladder of a mainstream newsroom.

As previously mentioned, there were journalists before 2017 who took an entrepreneurial approach to journalism using the online sports news subscription model developed before, yet popularized by, The Athletic (e.g., Dejan Kovacevic's D.K. Pittsburgh Sports, Greg Bedard's Boston Sports Journal, etc.). However, before Substack, the one-man sports journalism band concept was only feasible for those with the capital needed to fund the development of an independent sports news website. What Substack perfected, consequently, was the ease of use and accessibility for anyone who wanted to write about a niche topic and charge a subscription fee in the process. This drastic alteration to the sports media landscape, one that effectively gave anyone the ability to become a paid information disseminator by charging any monthly/yearly fee (assuming there was enough of a loyal audience willing to pay), further closed the gap between the corporate media sector and the niche entrepreneurial sportswriter.

Furthermore, Substack not only has the potential to create a new breed of paid sportswriters via its subscription method but also can help sportswriters gain mainstream employment by acting as somewhat of a writing portfolio to showcase work. Whether an individual uses the free, subscription-less version of Substack to determine if he or she can construct enough of a readership to warrant paywall implementation (as is the case with Kory and his *Sox Outsider* newsletter) or perceives the newsletter as a stepping stone to potential corporate media employment (similar to Devitte's take), the platform's versatility to function in whatever manner a writer deems fit may be its most positive effect.

Its most noticeable downfall, though, is that the likelihood of an unknown reporter with no prior media experience jumping on the Substack bandwagon and earning a living wage is virtually nonexistent, as revealed by most interviewees. Substack, on its website, brands itself as the platform where you can "start your Substack at breakfast; start bringing in revenue by lunchtime" ("The home for great investing and business writers," n.d., para. 14). However, interviewees noted this was only possible if a writer carried a substantial social media following from a legacy media position. The rationale is that to garner enough readers who would be willing to pay a nominal monthly subscription fee, a sportswriter would need to be already established in his or her career and have a sizable audience vested in the work since only a fraction of social media followers would likely pay for content.

Therefore, the Substack paywall is positioned to cater to journalists who lost their jobs in mainstream media yet still want to write about sports for a living and those who do not wish to use Substack as a profit-making tool. The group it is not as friendly to are the unestablished and unproven sportswriters who either envision turning on the paywall from the very beginning or those who want to use Substack as a vehicle to get their bylines to the masses in hopes of garnering a legitimate job in media as a result of the newsletter function.

Despite this perceived flaw to the do-it-yourself paid publishing genre that Substack ushered in, its most noticeable contribution to sports journalism may be its ability for sportswriters to remain in the field after a layoff or buyout instead of being forced to take a position in an unrelated communication sector. At a time when print sportswriting positions are more difficult to obtain because of various financial setbacks (effects from the COVID-19 pandemic being one of them), Substack represents a beacon of light in an otherwise bleak sports media landscape.

References

Adgate, B. (2021b, August 20). Newspapers have been struggling and then came the pandemic. *Forbes*. https://www.forbes.com/sites/bradadgate/2021/08/20/newspapers-have-been-struggling-and-then-came-the-pandemic/?sh=71d5442212e6

Allyn, B. (2020, December 2). *Tired of the social media rat race, journalists move to writing Substack newsletters*. NPR. http://www.npr.org/2020/12/02/941020719/tired-of-the-social-media-rat-race-journalists-move-to-writing-substack-newslett

Baker, K. (2020, November 13). *Niche sports reporting finds a home*. Axios. https://www.axios.com/independent-sports-journalism-newsletters-791eb509-a391-4c94-b88e-87cad52b9a63.html

Ball, K. (2021, May 2). *Substack: How the game-changer turned poacher*. The Guardian. https://www.theguardian.com/media/2021/may/02/substack-how-the-game-changer-turned-poacher

Barnett, D. (2021, September 3). *Why authors are turning down lucrative deals in favour of Substack*. The Guardian. http://www.theguardian.com/books/2021/sep/03/authors-lucrative-deals-substack-salman-rushdie-dc-marvel

Best, C., & McKenzie, H. (2017, July 17). *A better future for news*. Substack. https://on.substack.com/p/a-better-future-for-news

Botticello, C. (2021, July 7). *Substack F.A.Q s and tips*. Blogging Guide. https://bloggingguide.substack.com/p/substack-faqs-and-tips

Bucholtz, A. (2017, July 26). *Dejan Kovacevic talks about D.K. Pittsburgh Sports' third anniversary and their differences from other local plays*. Awful Announcing . https://awfulannouncing.com/online-outlets/dejan-kovacevic-talks-dk-pittsburgh-sports-third-anniversary-and-their-differences-from-other-local-plays.html

Casselberry, I. (2021, June 25). *N.B.A. reporter Marc Stein leaving New York Times to produce Substack newsletter.* Awful Announcing. https://awfulannouncing.com/nba/nba-reporter-marc-stein-leaving-new-york-times-produce-substack-newsletter.html

Chyi, H. I., & Tenenboim, O. (2019). From analog dollars to digital dimes: A look into the performance of U.S. newspapers. *Journalism Practice, 13*(8), 798–819.

Davis, P. (2017, March 15). 7 surprising facts about the history of email marketing. *Tower data.* http://www.towerdata.com/blog/history-of-email-marketing.

"Does it cost money to use Facebook?" (n.d.). *Facebook.* https://www.facebook.com/help/1865 56401394793.

Donaldson, A. (2017, May 4). *It's official: Lacrosse is the 11th sport sanctioned by U.H.S.A.A. for both boys and girls.* Deseret News. http://www.deseret.com/2017/5/4/20611657/it-s-official-lacrosse-is-the-11th-sport-sanctioned-by-uhsaa-for-both-boys-and-girls#0

Doyle, J. E. S. (2021, March 12). *In Queers we trust. All others pay cash.* Doyles. https://doyles.substack.com/p/in-queers-we-trust-all-others-pay

Drezner, D. W. (2021, February 17). *Everything old is new again in the mainstream media.* The Washington Post. http://www.washingtonpost.com/outlook/2021/02/17/everything-old-is-new-again-mainstream-media/

Ekdale, B., Tully, M., Harmsen, S., & Singer, J. B. (2015). Network within a culture of job insecurity. *Journalism Practice, 9*(3), 383–398.

Faulconbridge, G. (2019, June 11). *The media has a big problem, Reuters Institute says: Who will pay for news?* Reuters. http://www.reuters.com/article/us-global-media/the-media-has-a-big-problem-reuters-institute-says-who-will-pay-for-the-news-idUSKCN1TC2WV

Ferguson, J. [@JFergusonAU]. (2020, June 5). *The Athletic laid off 46 people today. I was one of them* [Tweet]. Twitter. https://twitter.com/jfergusonau/status/1268951246926479 362?lang=en

Finn, C. (2017, July 18). *Greg Bedard launching Boston Sports Journal website.* Boston.com. https://www.boston.com/sports/media/2017/07/18/greg-bedard-launching-boston-sports-journal-website/

Fischer, S. (2024, February 22). *Substack says it now has more than 3 million paid subscriptions.* Axios. https://www.axios.com/2024/02/22/substack-3-million-paid-subscriptions

Gil de Zuniga, H., Lewis, S. C., Willard, A., Valenzuela, S., Lee, J. K., & Baresch, B. (2011). Blogging as a journalistic practice: A model linking perception, motivation, and behavior. *Journalism, 12*(5), 586–606.

Gill, A., Nowson, S., & Oberlander, J. (2009). What are they blogging about? Personality, topic, and motivation in blogs. *Proceedings of the International AAAI Conference on Web and Social Media, 3*(1), 18–25.

Glickhouse, R. (2020). *Journalists get left behind in the industry's decline.* NiemanLab Predictions for Journalism 2020. http://www.niemanlab.org/2020/01/journalists-get-left-behind-in-the-industrys-decline/

Ha, A. (2021, March 18). *Substack faces backlash over the writers it supports with big advances.* Tech Crunch. https://techcrunch.com/2021/03/18/substack-backlash/

"The home for great investing and business writers." (n.d.). *Substack.* https://substack.com/investing-and-business

Horaczek, S. (2020, July 1). *Don't expect to pay for Facebook any time soon.* Popular Science. https://www.popsci.com/story/technology/pay-for-facebook/

Ingram, M. (2021, April 1). Substack raises more money, but is that a good thing? *Columbia Journalism Review.* http://www.cjr.org/the_media_today/substack-raises-more-money-but-is-that-a-good-thing.php

Kafka, P. (2021, March 19). *Substack writers are mad at Substack. The problem is money and who's making it.* Vox. http://www.vox.com/recode/22338802/substack-pro-newsletter-controve rsy-jude-doyle

Kalaf, S. (2018, January 25). *Pittsburgh's cutting-edge sports site is a meat grinder of a workplace.* Deadspin. http://www.deadspin.com/pittsburghs-cutting-edge-sports-site-is-a-meat-grin der-1821797940

Kammer, A., Boeck, M., Hansen, J. V., & Hauschildt, L. J. H. (2015). The free-to-fee transition: Audiences' attitudes toward paying for online news. *Journal of Media Business Studies, 12*(2), 107–120.

Knibbs, K., (2021, June 7). Why are writers fleeing Substack for Ghost? *Wired* . https://www. wired.com/story/ghost-substack-platforms-publishers/.

Knox, S. (2021, January 29). *How to kick-start your freelancing career during the pandemic.* Journalism.co.uk. http://www.journalism.co.uk/news/how-to-kick-start-your-freelancing-career-during-the-pandemic/s2/a791558/

Kokalitcheva, K., & Primack, D. (2021, March 30). *Scoop: Substack is raising $65 million amid newsletter boom.* Axios. https://www.axios.com/substack-andreessen-horowitz-newsletter-36cb98ea-a7b3-43b1-883a-fa45586eaad4.html

Kory, M. (2020, December 8). *Red Sox analysis, opinion, whimsy.* Sox Outsider. https://soxoutsi der.substack.com/

Lareau, L. (2010). The impact of digital technology on media workers: Life has completely changed. *Ephemera: Theory and Politics in Organization, 10*(3–4), 522–525.

Lee, S. K., Lindsey, N. J., & Kim, K. S. (2017). The effects of news consumption via social media and news information overload on perceptions of journalistic norms and practices. *Computers in Human Behavior, 75*(1), 254–263.

McKenzie, H. (2020, May 18). *What's next for journalists?* Substack. https://on.substack.com/p/ whats-next-for-journalists

McKenzie, H. (2021, March 12). *Why we pay writers.* Substack. https://on.substack.com/p/why-we-pay-writers

Monahan, S. (2020, November 17). *Why are public thinker flocking to Substack?* The Guardian. https://www.theguardian.com/commentisfree/2020/nov/17/substack-media-platform-pub lishing

Moore, G. A. (1999). *Crossing the chasm: Marketing and selling high-tech products to the mainstream customer.* HarperCollins.

Newitz, A. (2021, March 17). *Here's why Substack's scam worked so well.* The Hypothesis. https:// thehypothesis.substack.com/p/heres-why-substacks-scam-worked-so

Newman, N. (2023, June 14). *Overview and key findings of the 2023 Digital News Report.* Reuters Institute Digital News Report. https://reutersinstitute.politics.ox.ac.uk/digital-news-rep ort/2023/dnr-executive-summary

Nover, S., & Stenberg, M. (2021, April 15). *Newsletter platform Substack goes local.* AdWeek. http://www.adweek.com/media/newsletter-platform-substack-goes-local/

Oelrichs, I. (2023). Adoption of innovations in digital sports journalism: The use of Twitter by German sports journalists. *Communication & Sport, 11*(2), 288–312.

Oremus, W. (2018, April 27). Are you really the product? *Slate.* https://slate.com/technology/2018/04/are-you-really-facebooks-product-the-history-of-a-dangerous-idea.html

Oremus, W. (2021, April 23). What Substack is doing to the media. *Slate.* http://www.slate.com/business/2021/04/substack-media-new-york-times-subscriptions-poaching.html

Owens, S. (2020, February 28). *Why local news outlets struggle with digital subscriptions.* What's New in Publishing. https://whatsnewinpublishing.com/why-local-news-outlets-struggle-with-digital-subscriptions/

Owens, S. (2022, October 5). *Substack found its unfair advantage.* Simon Owens's Media Newsletter. https://simonowens.substack.com/p/substack-found-its-unfair-advantage

Pattabhiramaiah, A., Sriram, S., & Manchanda, P. (2019). Paywalls: Monetizing online content. *Journal of Marketing, 83*(2), 19–36.

Perlberg, S. (2020, July 1). *How Substack has spawned a new class of newsletter entrepreneurs.* D.I.G.I.D.A.Y. http://www.digiday.com/media/how-substack-has-spawned-a-new-class-of-newsletter-entrepreneurs/

Putterman, A. (2017, August 24). *Saying bye to sportswriting: Amid industry chaos, ex-reporters explain why they're leaving the profession.* Awful Announcing. https://awfulannouncing.com/online-outlets/saying-good-bye-sportswriting-industry-chaos-reporters-leaving.html

Rizky, A., & Pardamean, B. (2016). Critical success factor in monetizing blog. *Telkomnika, 14*(2), 757–761.

Rogers, E. M. (1962). *Diffusion of innovations.* Free Press.

Sanchirico, D. (2009, May 27). *A manifest destiny: Lacrosse's success rides on non-traditional areas.* Bleacher Report. https://bleacherreport.com/articles/185894-a-manifest-destiny-lacrosse-success-rides-on-non-traditional-areas

Schrager, Al. (2020, September 28). The Substack superstar system. *City Journal.* http://www.city-journal.org/unbundling-trend-in-media-and-economy

Shafer, J. (2016, October 17). What if the newspaper industry made a colossal mistake?" *POLITICO Magazine.* https://www.politico.com/magazine/story/2016/10/newspapers-digital-first-214363/

Shephard, A. (2021, March 19). *What is Substack?* The New Republic. https://newrepublic.com/article/161764/substack.

Smith, B. (2021, April 11). Why we're freaking out about Substack. *The New York Times.* http://www.nytimes.com/2021/04/11/business/media/substack-newsletter-competition.html

Spivak, C. (2011). Pay to play. *American Journalism Review, 33*(1), 34–39.

Stober, R. (2004). What media evolution is: A theoretical approach to the history of new media. *European Journal of Communication, 19*(4), 483–505.

Strauss, B. (2020a, May 14). *Amid layoffs and furloughs, sportswriters wonder what will be left of a storied profession.* The Washington Post. http://www.washingtonpost.com/sports/2020/05/14/amid-layoffs-furloughs-sportswriters-wonder-what-will-be-left-once-storied-profession/

Strauss, B. (2020b, June 1). *Out-of-work sportswriters are turning to newsletters, hoping the economics can work*. The Washington Post. https://www.washingtonpost.com/sports/2020/06/01/out-of-work-sportswriters-are-turning-newsletters-hoping-economics-can-work/

Weiner, N. (2020, February 4). *The girl in the huddle*. S.B. Nation. https://www.sbnation.com/2020/2/4/21119144/elinor-kaine-penna-giants-jets-sportswriter

"What is a business incubator." (2020, May 22). *Draper University*. https://www.draperuniversity.com/blog/what-is-a-business-incubator

"Why free posts pay: Avoiding a tempting mistake." (2019, April 30). *Substack*. https://on.substack.com/p/why-free-posts-pay-avoiding-a-tempting

Williams, K., & Stroud, S. R. (2021, February 15). *The ethics of news paywalls: Should we pay for news in our digital democracy?* The University of Texas at Austin Center for Media Engagement. http://www.mediaengagement.org/research/the-ethics-of-news-paywalls/

THE VIRTUAL SPORTS BAR: S.B. NATION COMMUNITIES AS SPORTS MEDIA'S CORPORATE BLOGOSPHERE

The concept of an ardent sports fan having an open forum platform to discuss, debate, and speculate real-world topics centered on a specific professional or major collegiate sports team may seem like a revolutionary idea only made possible by the Internet. Besides, to an extent, the Internet allows those with a shared identity, yet not living in the same geographic area, to connect in a virtual, communal-like setting (Kirmayer et al., 2013). However, the basis behind what is now known as the networked sports blogging community—whether existing on a specific website or social media platform—can most likely be traced to the type of dialogue standard at the stereotypical hometown sports pub in the pre-Internet age. During this time, the local sports-centric bar/restaurant represented one of the only places, besides attending an actual game in person, where sports fans could congregate to gauge perspective on a team's upcoming schedule, roster moves, and/or discuss the game at hand. Being surrounded by like-minded individuals meant that sports fans had a physical, interpersonal space where community and belonging could be continually reproduced through social connection (Allison, 2021).

That is not to say, though, that the idea of in-person communal sports discussion disappeared whenever fans first figured out the intricacies of early online message board forums (of note, the COVID-19 pandemic did further illustrate the value of transitioning team sports talk further into the online and social media sphere; Pollack & Peck, n.d.; Wakefield, 2020). However, the beauty of the Internet as a communicating tool is that it allows the joy— and sometimes frustration—of being a fan to be magnified on a much larger scale through interpersonal interaction (Mastromartino et al., 2020; Romero-Jara et al., 2023). Further, those who utilize the web to facilitate fan discussion tend to have increased social capital from association with the in-group than those whose sports conversation is limited to a face-to-face setting (Mathwick et al., 2008).

One specific social-based platform that sports fans use to drive the sporting conversation forward is team-specific Twitter, a general term used to encompass the X presence of a particular sports organization's leading voices (e.g., a team's athletes, its hometown beat writers/television commentators, fervent fans with social influence, etc.). This type of organic sport-centric X (formerly known as Twitter) community is what Maese (2018) describes as "a sports bar that doesn't close, a barbershop with unlimited seating" (para. 4). There are no barriers to entry for one to become engaged with team Twitter; rather, the only requirement, Maese (2018) writes, is for fans to follow social media closely and not be afraid to "jump in a conversation that moves quickly and has no boundaries" (para. 8).

The collection of a team's most vocal social media voices provides a forum where fan dialogue can be conveyed in a pseudo-social setting (Williams et al., 2014). However, because of the vastness of X, in which a fan would plausibly stumble upon thousands of mentions from many accounts by searching hashtags of a mainstream professional sports team, it may not be the ideal online home base for fans. Instead, as this final interview-based chapter illustrates, those affiliated with S.B. Nation communities believe their websites uniquely position themselves as a modern mecca of sports conversation in a way no other content distribution organization or platform can match.

S.B. Nation Domination: The impact of Vox Media's blogosphere on fan-centric sports content

There may be a handful of fan community websites, blogs, and/or forums that all cater to the fan-first mentality (see Minute Media's *FanSided*, *Sports Illustrated*'s FanNation site, the Locked on Sports podcast network, etc.);

however, perhaps nothing compares to the stronghold that Vox Media subsidiary S.B. Nation—and its fan-centric websites (Strauss, 2020)—has on both the written word and multimedia segment of the fan community. Whereas the aforementioned sports community platforms generally implement the same type of editorial direction and style as S.B. Nation (most notably insight, analysis, and lighthearted takes tailored to the sports geek; Mullin, 2017b), interviewees noted that they pale in comparison. Instead, the individual S.B. Nation editors and managers interviewed said the copycat fan communities housed within a larger corporate structure lack a true sense of togetherness in the comment section, recognizable brand name, and editorial flexibility—the central tenets S.B. Nation brought to the sports journalism forefront nearly two decades ago (Lichterman, 2016).

S.B. Nation never intended to kick-start the networked fan community movement; the original sports blog that eventually led to the creation of Vox Media was meant to serve as an online home for the Oakland Athletics, an utterly biased news source where "passionate and obsessive" A's fans could consume content about the team "24/7/365" (Sutton, 2015, para. 12). However, the vision of giving fans a voice—one that countered routines of traditional media by effectively making sports journalism a two-way communication street—was welcomed by all parties involved (Bleszinski, 2011; Mullin, 2017a). This formulaic approach, which is similar to partisan political media, took advantage of what Plambeck (2010) describes as a group of "unapologetically biased sports sites" functioning as a "digital water cooler for the like-minded" (Plambeck, 2010, para. 2). It struck when the sports sections of daily newspapers were shrinking, using the fan-first selling point to challenge the status quo of the traditional sports media model by filling the content generation void left by downgraded legacy media sports departments. Additionally, S.B. Nation took an unorthodox stance on the conventional journalistic norm of impartiality, something its reader base preferred.

Whereas most sportswriters working for mainstream newspapers must adhere to the ethical guidelines set forth by the Associated Press Sports Editors (A.P.S.E.), a national association that "strives to improve professional standards for sports departments of professional news organizations" ("About us," n.d.), S.B. Nation writers are not necessarily bound to these traditional journalistic ideals. This is because they are classified as bloggers and not as legitimate reporters by the teams they cover. It is important to note that some S.B. Nation personnel are given media credentials to cover home games while others are not (Gold-Smith, 2014). The lack of firsthand interviews, however, allows an S.B. Nation blog to cover its team (whether overly optimistic or hypercritical) without the same fear of access repercussions that mainstream sportswriters face.

Further, while other conglomerate sports media properties (e.g., Gannett newspapers, The Athletic, ESPN Insider, etc.) have recently implemented (or have always had) some paywall structure prohibiting who can view what content, S.B. Nation remains a free media entity reliant exclusively on advertising—and not subscription revenue (a tactic offset by the Vox Media model, in which most site personnel only receive a small stipend for their work and not a full-time yearly income; Bucholtz, 2017; Wagner, 2018). Simply put, the corporately managed fan community is different from the conventions of modern sports media, something Vox Media CEO Jim Bankoff told *The Washington Post* is predicated on "being by, of and for the fan" since writers "embrace bias and check objectivity at the door" (Overly, 2010, para. 4).

The reader and writer appeal to individualized S.B. Nation sports communities, thus, more closely aligns with the motives guiding select Substack newsletter operators mentioned in the previous chapter. Like the Substack writers guided by writing satisfaction and not a paycheck (e.g., Eric Nusbaum, Tim Haslam, and Michael Weinreb), most associated with S.B. Nation blogs are involved because of the fulfillment associated with being a thought leader for a specified sports community. Of note, some former S.B. Nation corporately employed writers have transitioned to more mainstream forms of sports media—most notably The Athletic's San Francisco Giants reporter Grant Brisbee, who founded the *McCovey Chronicles* site, and Charlotte Wilder, a former S.B. Nation and *Sports Illustrated* staffer now with FOX Sports.

As is the main focus of this chapter, how the sports-centric communities of S.B. Nation navigate their place within the already crowded online marketplace sheds light on sports media's overall transition toward fulfilling the niche. The community-driven approach of the S.B. Nation network, as a whole, embodies an altered form of online news engagement that runs parallel to the content/audience standards of most other mainstream sports media organizations. Instead of focusing on a bold strategy aimed at steering readers away from the page of the local sports newspaper section (i.e., The Athletic) or one centered on cutting out the media middleman (e.g., team-run information dissemination), interviewees revealed that the overall goal of S.B. Nation is to supplement what a fan consumes from legacy and online-only sports news sites—rather than trying to be a one-stop shop in terms of team-specific news. Further, since the site editors/managers quoted generally agree that targeting a niche subset of the fanbase enables coexistence, it can be construed that S.B. Nation has uniquely positioned itself as *the* central communal-centric blogging platform in the sports media sector.

This chapter's theoretical basis is grounded in the updated uses and gratifications work of Sundar and Limperos (2013), which formulates a new approach to studying media usage motives. Applying this concept (U&G 2.0), which modernized the seminal uses and gratifications work of Katz et al. (1973), to the study of emergent sports media technologies demonstrates how sports fans have transitioned from a culture of passive media consumers (i.e., no direct role in the content consumed) to that of an active Internet user, in which those consuming the content may also play a part in its creation (Hubbard, 2010; Kemp, 2019). Instead of simply consuming sports news related to an individual's favorite team and delivered via the standard print newspaper, today's fans can play an active role in the dissemination process (Kroon & Eriksson, 2019). S.B. Nation's unique approach to user-generated content in the sports blogging sphere facilitates this ease of use, enabling anyone to post in the fan forum and, potentially, work their way up to a stipend-paid writing and/or editorial role.

Uses and gratifications 2.0, furthermore, connects to the main ideas conveyed in this chapter since what one gets out of a media interaction is often influenced by the use of emerging technologies as a sense of gratification. Simply put, the type of interactive media that the Internet affords has transitioned how motive-driven consumption habits are assessed. Now, the gratification is almost instantaneously. Since different people can use the same medium in various ways (e.g., one as a passive user, the other taking a more active approach), the focus is "not only how users can interact with the interface, but also how they can contribute and construct content by using that interface" (Sundar & Limperos, 2013, p. 511). Regarding S.B. Nation, browsing a specific sports team's comment thread or online newsfeed can be construed as a passive approach, more akin to non-interactive traditional sports media. However, once someone assumes the role of a content creator, whether in the fan posts section or as a paid or unpaid contributor, his or her gratification is more apparent, especially since the fan perspective helps to shape so much of the editorial direction of the blogs under the S.B. Nation umbrella.

From Niche Baseball Blog to Networked Publishing Platform: S.B. Nation's Ascent to Sports Media Power Player

It may have a humble origin, one that demonstrates the ability of a sports media startup to blossom under the direction of budding entrepreneurs. However, S.B. Nation's ascent from a niche blog focused on a single A.L West team to a network of interconnected fan communities was methodical, taking advantage of sports fans' desire for communal connection during a time when a majority were shifting their information consumption habits from the physical to the virtual. The former startup's story began in 2003 when Tyler Bleszinski, an ex-*Orange County Register* sportswriter and lifelong Oakland Athletics fan (Yu, 2013), perceived bias against his favorite team—one that often led Northern California mainstream sports media to blatantly ignore the A's in favor of the crosstown rival San Francisco Giants (Deckard, 2015). The local legacy press, furthermore, would stop covering baseball at the end of October; yet, Bleszinski yearned for year-round discussion on his team, and he knew other devout fans likely wanted it as well.

So, the groundwork for this fan-centric vision, which would spur a future conglomerate of networked sports blogs and the entire Vox Media brand, was laid in November 2003 when Bleszinski's brainchild, *Athletics Nation*, went live. At the time, it was a standalone entity, a blog that shared the same passion for the hometown perspective as ardent Oakland Athletics supporters. Expansion may not have been on Bleszinski's agenda. However, when he received encouragement and a little financial support from friend and political blogger Markos Moulitsas, founder of the left-leaning *Daily Kos* blog, the goal seemed within reach (Terdiman, 2005).

First, S.B. Nation's strategy focused on baseball, bringing other independent M.L.B. bloggers at the time—like Chicago Cubs fan Al Yellon, who was interviewed for this research—into the mix. Yellon, a former television news director in the Chicagoland area with an affinity for the city's Northside M.L.B. team, began a personal blog in 2003 simply because "some of my friends were doing it." Soon, his page grew to be "about 95 percent about the Cubs"— partly because of the franchise's deep postseason run that year, which ended in the National League Championship Series. Armed with the desire for expansion, Moulitsas—whom Yellon described as a "Big Cubs fan"—asked him and his blog to join the network as one of the "original six" S.B. Nation fan sites (of note); Yellon said the original blogs, in addition to *Athletics Nation* and his

Bleed Cubbie Blue site, were *McCovey Chronicles* (San Francisco Giants), *Reds Reporter* (Cincinnati Reds), *Lookout Landing* (Seattle Mariners), and *D Rays Bay* (Tampa Bay Devil Rays).

After forming fan communities for all 32 M.L.B. teams, Bleszinski and Moulitsas expanded into the territory of other sports and sports leagues—both by creating new blogs and also bringing existing team-centric bloggers under the Sports Blog Nation (as it was called at the time) umbrella. One of those fans tasked with beginning a community from scratch was Christopher Gates, a lifelong Minnesota Vikings supporter from North Dakota who noticed the team was missing from S.B. Nation's original coverage repertoire. His S.B. Nation indoctrination may not be a "romantic story," Gates admitted. Still, it illustrates how streamlined the network was during its infancy when there were "10 or 12 other N.F.L. sites that S.B. Nation had put together." Gates said he initially discovered S.B. Nation in 2006, when he stumbled across the Chicago Bears blog, *Windy City Gridiron*, and grew impressed with the fan-first product after "poking around" on the member sites that existed in its first two years. Noticing, however, that S.B. Nation did not have a Vikings blog, Gates sent Bleszinski, the founder and lead man in charge, a cold email to gauge potential interest in a new addition. Bleszinski was naturally interested in blanketing the professional sporting landscape with S.B. Nation communities. After exchanging a few writing samples to show potential fit, Gates was brought on board.

However, if Bleszinski represents the brains behind the operation's humble beginnings and subsequent editorial expansion, Jim Bankoff was the financial brawn because he enabled S.B. Nation to become what, at the time, was described as the "largest, fastest growing network of fan-centric online sports communities" (Dubois, 2010, para. 1). Bankoff, the former AOL executive who helped launch some of its most notable entities (e.g., MapQuest, Moviefone, and TMZ; Heath, 2014), moved from Vox Media advisor to CEO in late 2008 (Kramer, 2010). During this time, he ushered in a new business era of networked sports blogging by structuring "equity swaps for each of the S.B. Nation sites in which the company acquires all the content, URLs and related assets, and the bloggers then share the ad revenue" ("Former AOL exec raises funding for sports blogs network," 2008, para. 3). Bankoff had a keen business sense, transforming what he saw as "more of a good idea than it was a business" under Bleszinski's leadership into an investor-led media conglomerate (Dubois, 2010, para. 6). The acquisition of capital funding led then-S.B. Nation president Bleszinksi to write, in a 2008 *Athletics Nation* post, that this "is just going to enable us to do a lot of things like further iterate on our magnificent technology [. . .] If it weren't for the success and passion of A's fans, Sports Blog Nation would have never gotten to this point" (Dubois, 2010, para. 2).

In his first year, Bankoff changed the then-perceived advertising narrative of blogs, which allowed S.B. Nation to grow its revenue base and, more importantly, secured venture capital funding by "raising money for the bloggers and techies who would help boost the content and make S.B. Nation fun" (Heath, 2014, para. 27). Using his AOL network, Bankoff brought investor Andrew Braccia—affiliated with Silicon Valley venture capital firm Accel Partners—into the fold, leading to a $4 million investment. Next came two more fundraising rounds in the subsequent two years, allowing S.B. Nation to amass close to "23.5 million [dollars] in backing from Accel Partners, Khosla Ventures, and Comcast Interactive Capital" (Carr, 2011, para. 19). From there, the Vox Media brand expanded, venturing outside the sports realm in 2011 by launching six other culture and lifestyle websites.

Vox Media—which continued to acquire media properties well after its rounds of highly successful venture capital funding over a decade ago—remained in what Bankoff told *Vanity Fair* at the end of 2020, a "really strong position" (Pompeo, 2020, para. 2). This allowed Vox to purchase lifestyle website conglomerate Group Nine Media in December 2021 in a deal *The New York Times* wrote may be influenced by how "digital media companies have been looking for ways to pay back investors and compete with Google and Facebook, which dominate online advertising" (Robertson, 2021, para. 9). Like other media companies, however, Vox was not immune to the typical industry woes that plagued some other similarly-oriented outlets, like downsizing, slashed advertising budgets, layoffs, etc. (a problem only magnified by the COVID-19 pandemic).

When Bankoff's tenure began, S.B. Nation had 150 individual blogs (Ratner, 2008); two years later, that number grew to 275 total, including 20 region-specific sports communities (Dubois, 2010). Presently, S.B. Nation's niche fan sites include one for each N.F.L. and M.L.B. team, as well as select Power-Five college athletic programs and specialty blogs dedicated to niche sporting interests (i.e., DraftKings Network, which centers on gambling, Cageside Seats, dedicated to pro wrestling and M.M.A. coverage, etc.). Although S.B. Nation, before a January 2023 round of cuts by parent company Vox Media, had a team blog for each N.B.A. and N.H.L. team, there are currently only fan communities for 21 of the 30 total N.B.A. teams and seven of the 32 entire N.H.L. teams (Cash, 2023; Wagner, 2023).

During this 2023 round of cuts, Vox laid off seven percent of its staff in revenue, editorial, operations, and core services (Robertson, 2023). The layoffs affected those who worked for the S.B. Nation flagship site (as full-time employees) and independent contractors writing and editing content on most M.L.S., N.B.A., and N.H.L. fan communities, as well as most S.B. Nation-sponsored podcasts (Wagner, 2023). It is important to note that most team blogs that were cut continue to operate independently (operating under the same site name) despite not receiving funding from S.B. Nation. One such site is Japers' Rink, a Washington Capitals fan community affected by Vox's 2023 cuts. In one of the last posts published to the site while it was still affiliated with S.B. Nation, the editorial team wrote that it had no plans to "shutter" altogether. Instead, the priority remained to "provide coverage of the team and sport we love, and continuing to maintain the great community we have built here over the years" ("A message from your Japers' Rink team," 2023).

Where Everybody Knows Your (Screen) Name: "You kind of get to know people even though you never actually meet them in person"

When Bleszinski first launched *Athletics Nation* nearly two decades ago, the idea to form a website catered to the fan perspective of one specific team may not have seemed that revolutionary—mainly because sport-specific websites had existed since the mid-1990s (of note, the term blog did not regularly appear in the Internet lexicon until the beginning of the twenty-first century; Safire, 2002). Although it is not known, specifically, which fan-founded/managed sports website began the trend of sportswriting that counters the ideal of impartiality, Hoag (2010) maintains that two former independent hockey sites (InTheCrease.com, circa 1996, and San Jose Sharks blog *Sharkspage*, circa 1998) are evidence that the web had been used to give fans an alternative home to read sports news.

However, what *Athletics Nation* did bring to the sports media forefront was the idea that fans wanted to consume biased team opinions from other likeminded individuals—and not information filtered by mainstream media gatekeepers. Thus, Bleszinski envisioned his site operating more like an online forum than a full-fledged news organization because of the ability for any fan to comment and/or publish his or her writing on the message board. In an introductory post announcing the formation of *Athletics Nation*, Bleszinski equated his communal sports dialogue to an online sports bar, believing that it would function as a "place where everyone knows your name and where the swivel chair at your computer becomes a bar stool upon which we will pontificate and ruminate together" (Bleszinski, 2004, para. 1).

Additionally, he noted that the intention of his site, which was to fill the news hole left by Northern California mainstream sports press, was not to compete with legacy media by focusing on legitimate journalism but rather to provide biased takes on the Athletics. Bleszinski further elaborated on this in the same post welcoming readers to the website, writing, "I am only capable of viewing the world as an A's follower. I consider myself a fan-columnist, in that order. That is what this blog is, and that's what you'll receive here in AN" (Bleszinski, 2004, para. 1).

Although over 20 years have passed since Bleszinski created the fan-driven blog that led to this eventual national network, John Butchko said the communal aspect of sports fandom that S.B. Nation was founded upon is as strong as ever. Butchko, the site manager for S.B. Nation's *Gang Green Nation*, a New York Jets community, viewed his platform as a virtual *Cheers* for Jets fans. The 1980s NBC sitcom, whose "where everybody knows your name" tagline has become infused in the pop culture lexicon of classic television, centers on patrons at a Boston bar who meet to "drink, relax, and socialize" (Gibson, 2021, para. 7). Similar to the friendly, neighborhood pub atmosphere that the fictional *Cheers* evoked, Butchko noted that his site feels more like a group of regulars who informally know each other than unrecognizable commenters on a website. *Gang Green Nation*, he said, is the common thread that unites a diverse group of people who otherwise would not have the opportunity to interact in a friendly, virtual manner. It may not have the verbal, in-person dialogue present in all 275 episodes of *Cheers*, but Butchko maintained the sports pub-like exchanges of *Gang Green Nation*, where everyone knows each other's (screen)name, is not far behind.

Like most physical sports bars, Butchko said the site has its own set of inside jokes, witty comments about the Jets' on-field misfortunes that are increasingly easy to make about a team that last qualified for the N.F.L. playoffs in 2010. Additionally, as with any regular meeting place, if someone went on a temporary hiatus without conveying information related to his or her planned leave of absence, others became worried; for instance, Butchko said it is common to see a post asking, "Has anybody heard from Broadway Jose?" or "Whatever happened to JB45?" It is this sense of a tight-knit fan community, one that other sports media properties have tried to emulate yet not succeeded on the same magnitude, that Butchko said is the most marketable strength of his Vox Media subsidiary.

The comment section of *Gang Green Nation* (and other S.B. Nation fan communities like it, for that matter) permeates a heightened sense of social identity among its members. What readers comment on a post following a Jets' win, or more frequently a loss, is an extension of themselves, Butchko maintained, since Jets fandom is often formed during childhood and strengthened in adulthood. Consequently, the site is viewed as a place where one's affinity toward the New York Jets can be reproduced via online engagement.

Similar to the discussion in the chapter focused on The Athletic, in which interviewees noted that the paywall-drive sports site is meant to serve the displaced sports fan, S.B. Nation also serves that niche because not every New York Jets fan lives within the team's geographic radius of New York City, Northern New Jersey, and/or parts of Connecticut. The ability for both local and displaced Jets fans to assemble in a virtual space further illustrates the importance of sports media as a socializing agent that bridges the gap between the casual observer and the diehard supporter.

When describing the sense of communal camaraderie that the fan community fosters, Butchko cited Vox Media's 2020 decision to revamp the layout and feel of each blog's comment section and how *Gang Green Nation* used it as a rallying cry not to let fan engagement slip. In short, while other S.B. Nation communities—Butchko said—lost some degree of comment participation because of reader disdain toward altering conventionality, *Gang Green Nation* advocated for its group of loyal followers to stick together because of the strong community they built. Instead of simply lamenting over corporate frustration and coming to terms with the notion that some fans would take their Jets fandom to another online home, Butchko conveyed a sense of transparency to his readers, reiterating that corporate changes do not define the blog's track record of quality fan engagement. The steady readership despite this overall S.B. Nation hiccup, he said, is a testament to the type of community that Butchko has built during his tenure as team brand manager, one that reflects how his readers value him and how he appreciates what each member brings to the site.

Above all else, though, the thing that he viewed as separating each S.B. Nation fan site from the work produced by the stereotypical hometown newspaper beat writer is the "institutional knowledge" that only comes with being a fan of one specific team. In essence, Butchko sees the "pro-quality, fan perspective" slogan that S.B. Nation trademarked early in its existence as still holding true. He said this is because fans do not always want to read balanced coverage from someone with no rooting interest in their team's success:

> The guy who is doing this for a paycheck, who rooted for your rival as a kid and is now the beat writer, they're doing it for a job. When I write something, you know that I care. You know that I'm feeling the same things that you are after a big win or a significant loss. And I think there's a connection you build with your reader base that isn't there with somebody who does it in more of a professional sense. (J. Butchko, personal communication, January 11, 2022)

From Riley Feldmann's perspective, the community does not necessarily have to replicate the standard *Cheers*-like mentality, where the commenters are familiar with one another. Instead, the desired sense of community can still be maintained if an S.B. Nation reader base is composed of a less homogeneous group of fans in terms of their level of affiliation. For a team like the Milwaukee Bucks, the focal point of the *Brew Hoop* blog (of which Feldmann is one of the editors), the type of fan reading the content is only sometimes one who grew up following the team. Instead, because the Bucks feature superstar Giannis Antetokounmpo, coupled with the fact that the team won an N.B.A. championship in 2021, Feldmann noted that the site attracts a diverse range of readers. This wide net of Bucks fans gravitating toward *Brew Hoop* may also be attributed to the N.B.A.'s younger and generally more impressionable fanbase (one more likely to be active on Internet platforms; Thompson, 2014).

The name recognition of Antetokounmpo, nicknamed the "Greek Freak" because of his nationality and atypical height/skillset, means that *Brew Hoop* functions as a community of fans interested in the superstar mixed with those whom he classified as the "thinking man's Bucks fan" (i.e., the analytically minded supporter of the team). This, in turn, means the formula for creating engagement on a level akin to a virtual sports bar is twofold. For one, it equates to focusing on content mapping season-long trends—what he branded as the site's "bread and butter." Secondly, editorial efforts must be centered on the team's and its players' day-to-day happenings. This type of information drums up discussion in the comment threads between even the most casual of Antetokounmpo and/or Bucks fans.

The key to a thriving sports fan community, Feldmann said, is giving readers the specific nuggets of news that can ultimately be used as discussion forum points since the "community thrives best when people in the comments, the readers, they're engaged with each other." Whereas the diehard Bucks fan may be vested in season trends and more statistical-based information, those who only visit *Brew Hoop* for the Antetokounmpo connection, for example, may be less accustomed to following N.B.A. basketball, mainly if they are overseas. Therefore, the challenge to maintaining and strengthening community for a team with diehard and bandwagon fans is catering to both perspectives tastefully. For example, the *Brew Hoop* writing staff generally wants to throw the critical statistics at the casual fan since it is information they will need in the broader sense. However, at the same time, it is vital to let these individuals know that the existing dialogue in the comments section is less severe of a conversation. Feldmann noted, "We want to help bring [the casual fans] in and continue to build them up so they can make their analysis based on the information presented and add to the conversation that way."

Like Butchko, Feldmann realizes the community draw of the S.B. Nation network equates to the platform's user-friendly commenting system, which he argued has not been as easily mimicked by other copycat fan blogs. Having the ability for fans to engage in discussion on a fan community that has existed since October 2007 comes with a mark of prestige, one perceived to be the lifeblood that differentiates *Brew Hoop* from virtually every other Milwaukee Bucks blogging competitor. Feldmann said the other fan-centric online-only sports outlets that focus on Bucks coverage (e.g., *Cream City Central* and Substack's *GSPN* newsletter, written by four former members of FanSided's Bucks site) tend to migrate the conversation to the Twittersphere instead of keeping it directly on each respective website.

This concept of a "thought leader" purposely transitioning two-way sports engagement (i.e., direct conversation between the reader and gatekeeper) to X can lead to lessened host-participant conversation since navigating a thread occurring in the mediated online sphere of microblogging can often be challenging. In other words, the comment section is more intimate on the S.B. Nation network because each site's reputation, Feldmann said, has led to a community of its own:

> [*Brew Hoop*] has been around so long. People have been there for over a decade at this point. I've known these people since I started commenting there; at least I know their usernames. I think that's the big differentiator. We've just been around long enough. We have a well-established community where everybody gets along and knows each other. (R. Feldmann, personal communication, November 17, 2021)

Feldmann's take represents the prestige that most S.B. Nation editors/ site managers perceive their site to hold over other similarly structured fan blogs, communities (most notably those connected to FanSided), or social media accounts that cover the same team. Whereas a new fan entity aimed at driving traffic away from the more established virtual home for a select fanbase is likely to enter the conversation, the shared belief is that it is not a threat to the sustainability of individual S.B. Nation websites because it is not connected to a long-standing corporate establishment that has been caving its niche in the fan sector since the early-2000s. Butchko and Feldmann view community as essential to the fan-driven sites they help lead. However, as revealed, the community's strength is predicated on its ability to keep fans wanting to revisit the virtual gathering place regularly. Therefore, the history and distinction of each S.B. Nation fan site (most of which have been around for over a decade-plus) are the foundation for getting users to return each time. Like the typical hometown sports bar, whose business would falter if its regular customer base fled to the newer watering hole across the street, long-time readers and commenters serve as the livelihood of S.B. Nation's team-centric blogs. This, in turn, makes it apparent why the brand's selling point is so often rooted in its sense of community.

That is different from saying that the comments section of S.B. Nation, an aspect of the news product that interviewees noted is unique to its model, is not sometimes rife with noise or distractions akin to virtually every other online comments section. Although it can be a primary draw, with interviewees mentioning how there are specific individuals whose contributions to the comments section are the main reason why others visit the site, divisiveness can be present. As *Acme Packing Company* (Green Bay Packers) editor Evan Western said, monitoring the comments of branded "bad actors" is a challenge of the job. Like any physical or virtual community, disagreements are bound to occur; yet how *Acme Packing Company* asks for reader feedback regarding how to monitor the comments section ultimately enables the communal feel to persist, despite potential trolling. Western's approach to commenting forum monitoring is twofold, with it being tied to S.B. Nation's network guidelines for general moderation while also being unique to his site and the overall Packers fanbase. As he put it, "There's a handful of specific words or derogatory terms toward specific rival teams, for example, that we've said, point blank, aren't acceptable. So any time one of those pops up, that gets automatically removed, and the person gets a warning."

Corporate Recognizes Corporate: "We're all about creating better, more interested, more engaged fans"

From its modest beginning as a lone, one-man blog that transformed into a full-fledged media conglomerate, S.B. Nation has experienced two vastly different perspectives in sports media. Unlike most legacy news organizations, which have always been corporately run in a management style that can best be categorized as a top-down approach, S.B. Nation has traditionally promoted individuality among its member blogs (Bena, 2012; Ellis, 2012). Despite its position within the information marketplace, site managers and editors still possess total autonomy without S.B. Nation's corporate oversight instructing what can or cannot be written. At the same time, though, they said the benefits of being attached to the S.B. Nation brand (e.g., connection to a national network, ability to collaborate with other team sites for content distribution, having a credible byline, etc.) are present if needed.

In a way, the success of attracting top-level fans to lead the direction of S.B. Nation's team-centric sites may equate to the notion of individuality infused with corporate brand power. It may be cliché to say that S.B. Nation's approach brings in the *best of both worlds*—being hands-off with the day-to-day operation yet giving blogs a nameplate that yields a sense of credibility. However, what one gets out of working with an S.B. Nation blog is a byproduct of what he or she feeds into the fan-driven machine and the motives looking to be gained. Interviewees said this individualistic philosophy of providing a solid brand name while giving its properties editorial and structural leeway is a win-win, a professional tactic that some noted would have pushed them elsewhere if S.B. Nation implemented a more controlling form of oversight.

One of the site managers who said S.B. Nation's "side hustle" mentality kept him in his editorial role was Joe Mullinax, former site manager of the Memphis Grizzlies blog *Grizzly Bear Blues*. Like most of his S.B. Nation counterparts, Mullinax developed a rooting interest in his then-local team while living in the Greater Memphis area. He joined as a staff writer before being promoted to site manager two years later. However, unlike other interviewees, he continued to run the editorial side after moving away from his team's primary geographic region (of note, Mullinax was the only interviewee who managed his staff from a fully remote position). This is because Mullinax, whose day job is a social studies teacher/head high school football coach, enjoyed the degree of freedom that S.B. Nation afforded since it was a passion project and not his "literal job." Instead, he gravitated toward S.B. Nation simply because it did not conjure the same stressors associated with sports media editorial management in a full-time role (of note, since moving on from *Grizzly Bear Blues*, Mullinax became a co-host for the *Locked on Grizzlies* podcast).

Rather than being forced to focus on web traffic metrics (e.g., article clicks, bounce rate, etc.) traditionally associated with the business of journalism, Mullinax said he did not have to worry about these in his stipend-paid position. This is because there were no incentives for hitting a specific benchmark regarding page views or increasing social media following. Thus, his mindset was to provide the best possible news-consuming experience for the type of Grizzlies fan seeking alternative story angles that differ from what *The Commercial Appeal* and *The Daily Memphian*—the city's two mainstream press outlets—regularly published. The hobbyist outlook, in turn, shifted the standard media management emphasis away from budgeting, expense reports, and everything else that would fall within the job description of a professional sports editor and, instead, placed priority on "making good content." From Mullinax's perspective, being a fan who did this solely for passion—and not for the accompanying small monthly stipend—was a philosophy without consequence.

This flexibility allowed him to experiment with content angle, focus, and delivery more than a conventional legacy media sports editor ever could. If S.B. Nation corporate ever deemed his approach as not correctly serving the fan-first mentality, he could have gotten fired from his post. However, if that had happened, he would still have had a steady income and health benefits via his primary job in public education. This type of alternative thinking championed by S.B. Nation that went against previously held notions of sports journalism is what Mullinax credited as the network's most apparent benefit. Whereas most other arms of sports media have found ways to offset costs by charging for content, S.B. Nation remains a free entity, something Mullinax attributed to its relative popularity among readers.

The other editor-first element that made S.B. Nation successful, he said, was its "hodgepodge" of fans with different sporting interests and backgrounds using their free time to publish fan-first content. Some writers, Mullinax said, perceived S.B. Nation to be their career jump starter in journalism, beginning as a contributor before leaping to a paid position (either with one of S.B. Nation's networked sites or another comparable sports media entity) when the byline gets recognizable enough. Others had a sports media presence because of the passion it provoked. As Mullinax put it, S.B. Nation was "able to mix and match and merge all those different philosophies on what this is supposed to be," providing a platform and the possibility of small financial benefits in a way that "offers enough to keep you holding on, but at the same time it's just enough for people like me that I don't feel like I'm wasting my time doing it."

Whereas Mullinax valued the hobbyist flexibility of the network, R.J. Ochoa of *Blogging the Boys* saw S.B. Nation's attachment to a corporate structure as one of its chief advantages over other sports blogging entities since it led to his salaried position. Ochoa, the manager and editor-in-chief for the Dallas Cowboys blog, may have an S.B. Nation origin story similar to other editorial personnel in terms of first discovering his favorite team's community and later becoming a loyal reader. However, unlike his counterparts, the South Texas native did not travel the typical path to a managerial role (i.e., beginning as a contributor during the site's infancy before slowly climbing the editorial ladder after the departure of those in a more leadership position).

Ochoa—a lifelong Cowboys fan—first met *Blogging the Boys* founder David Halprin at training camp as a high school student in 2007, two years after the site's creation, and had an opportunity to begin writing at that time. Since *Blogging the Boys* was a newly added member of the S.B. Nation sports network, the hesitation was natural, mainly because he did not want to "burn" his shot by "being awful." A few years later, after working at a regional Cowboys brick-and-mortar team store, Ochoa decided to go the blog route to gain practical experience. In his words, this opportunity allowed him to be a "yes man" by volunteering to write five articles per week and co-hosting the website's podcast—roles that allowed the former Texas A&M University engineering student to increase his position as an authoritative voice within Cowboys social media.

From there, he transitioned to local broadcast sports media in 2016 as a part-timer with a San Antonio sports talk radio show after winning the station's "Rock the Mic" competition. He began to expand his growing list of contacts within the Cowboys organization since his then-employer was one of the team's official media partners. Eventually, Ochoa felt he had established himself enough within the Cowboys' media circle to finally write for *Blogging the Boys*. So, in 2017, he reached out to Halprin via the business card acquired at training camp 10 years prior and got "brought on staff as a contributor at first," tasked with handling the blog's Facebook streams before being hired full-time when a position opened the following year. As Ochoa put it, his current role as a full-time S.B. Nation employee is to oversee all aspects of the blog—from written, podcast, and YouTube channel content to its social media presence—in a way that he likened to "serving as the face of the *Blogging the Boys* name and overall brand."

Although his ascent from passionate Cowboys fan to salaried site manager may not represent the standard path taken by a majority of the other interviewees, it does illustrate the benefit of S.B. Nation having a corporately subsidized model, one that gives it the funding to transition select site managers running highly trafficked blogs from stipend to salaried employees. Indeed, one cannot deny that a visible divide does exist between those whose S.B. Nation existence is limited to a hobbyist approach and the lucky few who have transitioned this passion into full-time employment with Vox Media (this tactic of paying a majority of its side job writers and editors unfair compensation for hours incurred will be critically examined later in this chapter). However, Ochoa's interview sheds light on the notion that S.B. Nation's duality to make it what you want—content production, pay, or both—is one of its chief attractions.

For Andrew Mearns of *Pinstripe Alley*, the ability to receive a small monthly stipend for writing about his favorite baseball team at night, while working for The Brookings Institute during the day, makes S.B. Nation such a unique player in the sports media sphere. Although the concept of a writer juggling multiple projects at once is not new in the legacy media sphere, especially since journalists have become accustomed to taking on added responsibilities because of newsroom layoffs and furloughs, it can sometimes be an adjustment for those lacking a traditional media background. However, Mearns said it is easy to find time to manage S.B. Nation's New York Yankees blog, despite having a separate career outside writing in the public policy research sector, because of the enjoyment that it produces.

The need for his staff to "buy in" to the process comes down to mutual understanding that each person who writes for *Pinstripe Alley* has priorities (i.e., a family, a career, etc.) outside S.B. Nation. If Mearns, who has been associated with the site since his senior year of college in 2012, has something "pop up" at work unexpectedly—meaning he is unable to post content promptly—those below him via *Pinstripe Alley's* chain of command are understanding since this is something he does for fun. At the same time, though, he said that his day job is aware of his hobbyist role, making it a two-way street of mutual understanding that allows him to effectively balance both without being forced to abandon the baseball writing because of time constraints.

In a way, S.B. Nation's ability to make blog management a part-time position that individuals flock to because of the opportunity to receive minor financial compensation for writing about their favorite sports team is a system rooted in trust. For one, members of the fan community trust that those in charge will cater content to fit their perspective best. Moreover, Vox Media likely trusts that each site editor will post a regular stream of content during that sport's season to feed fan appetites. These individuals, in turn, put their faith in S.B. Nation to have a forum to promote the fan agenda in a flexible way that works with their schedules. This cycle of confidence, therefore, gives Mearns the ability to reach Yankees fans in any way he sees fit without being bound to a generic templated approach to site content.

Aside from the job flexibility that his role as managing editor provides, Mearns further explained that an additional benefit of having *Pinstripe Alley* connected to the S.B. Nation brand is that it makes cross-site collaboration with others in a similar position possible. Because it can sometimes be challenging to plan for a consistent stream of content for a baseball fan community, having access to a network of 29 other M.L.B. site managers via a Slack group chat eases this process. If, for instance, the Yankees have an upcoming three-game series against a divisional opponent, Mearns noted how he can team up with his counterpart at that site for an interview-based preview article, similar to how newspaper sports sections will sometimes write "know your enemy" articles.

This kind of agreement, he suggested, is in the same vein of a quid pro quo deal, with the implication that if he interviews an editor who blogs about a team the Yankees are slated to play, he will eventually return the favor at a later date. The mutualism between specific baseball site editors for content collaboration can be broadened to exemplify the corporate fan blogging model as a whole. S.B. Nation, for instance, provides each of its sites with credibility and name recognition in a way that helps elevate its properties in the search engine rankings because of the institutional backing (of note, *Pinstripe Alley* is typically on the first page of results that Google yields whenever someone searches "New York Yankees news"). Each site staffer, in turn, produces the amount of sports content needed to keep audiences interested in the shortened news cycle era of modern media, although often not at a fairly compensated rate for the time invested (this will be further explored in the following section).

The overarching benefit for most, including Mullinax, Ochoa, and Mearns, is that S.B. Nation provides a sports media platform for those lacking the skills and education needed to be a mainstream legacy media sportswriter. However, for someone like Sean Corp, who was previously a newspaper reporter, S.B.

Nation provides both the nameplate and editorial freedom to write about a team in ways that newspaper beat writers could not replicate—either because of a lack of time, editor approval, and/or knowledge of fan culture and wants. Corp, who spent five years working as a newspaper reporter and editor for daily newspapers in Northwest Ohio and Michigan, said he could target the niche, analytically-driven Detroit Pistons fan in his role as editor for S.B. Nation's *Detroit Bad Boys* (aptly named after the team's edgy, on-court personality throughout the 1980s). This is because his readers "appreciative of the top-level form of analysis" that is not offered by the newspaper beat writers covering the team.

When Corp began his tenure with *Detroit Bad Boys*, first as a writer in 2012 before making the jump to site manager six years later, he said there was more of a divide between the type of coverage that Pistons fans desired and the content being disseminated by *The Detroit Free-Press* and the *Detroit News*, the city's two daily newspapers. Where the concept of sports blogging was most effective in its earliest incarnations, Corp noted, was being aware of the need to differentiate its work from the mainstream by providing a level of detail and analysis that dove "into these super nerdy, arcane topics that nobody else was going to make time for, the type of material that would resonate with certain fans." However, because more specialized facets of online-only sports media have recently implemented this approach (Corp mentioned The Athletic and ESPN as being two of the most notable outlets to bring this type of sportswriting into more of a mainstream light), sports blogs have been forced to evolve into more of a multimedia hub.

To do this, the current University of Michigan content strategist has forayed the site into the realm of basketball film breakdown and play analysis by recruiting an ex-Division I player to talk about the game via written and video content in a way that few newspaper beat writers would ever have the time, resources, or knowledge to accomplish. Now, Corp has Bryce Simon—a former American University forward who was searching for a creative outlet to talk about the game after his playing days were over—produce short online highlight videos from each Pistons game, complete with voiceover narration, that dissects important plays in layman's terms in an article series entitled "Film don't lie." As he saw it, Simon became "an integral part of this community because he's providing that passion and high level of analysis that fans respond to."

Corp admitted that the most read piece of content on the *Detroit Bad Boys* site on any given day is usually the standard game recap, chiefly because the general Pistons fan gravitates toward the basic information of who won, who lost, and who played well (from his perspective, this is why newspapers have been adamant of sticking to this classic, yet effective, editorial formula). However, his intent as a stipend-paid site manager is to grow the Pistons fan base any way he deems fit, noting the most effective way to do this is by playing into S.B. Nation's flexible strategy of putting complete editorial control into the hands of those at the individual level. Simply put, Corp wants to turn each *Detroit Bad Boys* visitor into a repeat reader and believes that the best way to accomplish this is by focusing on the type of content that fans "can appreciate and they're not going to get from anywhere else" (like the "Film don't lie" breakdown). Of note, a majority of other S.B. Nation communities have not borrowed this idea, opting instead to stick with the standard game preview-recap approach in a manner that further illustrates the individuality that S.B. Nation allows each fan site to operate under.

It is fair to brand Corp's site as a blog, primarily since it is housed under a company whose initial name was Sports Blog Nation. Like a handful of other interviewees, though, he dislikes being branded as a blogger since the line differentiating perceived legitimate and non-legitimate writing is blurred in the modern sports media ecosystem. While *Detroit Bad Boys*, along with most other S.B. Nation fan communities, may not receive full-time media credentials Corp said he approaches writing for his site the same way he would if he were covering the Pistons for a more mainstream outlet, like Detroit's local newspapers, since the same basic journalistic principles (e.g., telling a complete story, standing behind your analysis, conveying accurate information, etc.) apply, no matter the medium.

S.B. Nation's Smokescreen: "If you're not able to be exploited long enough to hope that it turns around, then it really can't work for you there"

As referenced above, the model of networked sports blogging managed at the individual level, yet structured within the corporate domain, is generally seen as a positive complement to the otherwise legacy feel of sports media's more traditional forms of gatekeeping. For one, S.B. Nation fan sites are better equipped to meet the news-consuming needs of a particular fanbase, interviewees said, since they possess the institutional knowledge, wit, and overall perspective needed to promote the fan agenda. Additionally, it was revealed that being connected to the S.B. Nation brand name invokes recognition and credibility in the eyes of the sports-consuming public in a way that independent or standalone hobbyist sports sites cannot match. However, interviewees acknowledged that among the benefits that one can be entitled to if one writes for an S.B. Nation blog is the flexibility to register for and/or manage a fan community for a small stipend in one's spare time.

Despite the relatively small paycheck, the notion that a sports fan can translate a passion for a favorite team into a paid endeavor is appealing since S.B. Nation could be used to monetize fandom. Most interviewees saw value in the S.B. Nation approach, realizing that they were not going to become wealthy through their role as a fan community manager or even earn enough to make it a full-time venture (Ochoa, of *Blogging the Boys*, aside), yet appreciating the platform that it provided since it gave a somewhat authoritative voice in their favorite team's media ecosystem. It was summed up as a give-and-take relationship, with site managers and editors expressing that their respective positions require a bit of compromise—personally, professionally, or both—to effectively balance the time commitment of working a full-time career while being an independent blogging contractor.

Not all interviewees agreed that S.B. Nation's primary approach of relying on stipend-paid labor for content generation in exchange for a byline was beneficial. Matthew Miranda said the S.B. Nation nameplate does provide an advantage for those looking to foray blog writing into a potential full-time media position in the sense that "corporate recognizes corporate," meaning it can be easier to transition from one mainstream sports outlet to another if someone already has that legitimized byline. However, for the amount of work required to effectively manage one of S.B. Nation's blogging properties as a side job, this type of position can sometimes be a lose-lose situation, one in which a site staffer must choose loyalty to either having a healthy work-life balance or investing the effort needed to grow the fan community itself. It was rare, Miranda suggested, to have both priorities met because of the network's inherent quota system. S.B. Nation, he noted, represents a smoke screen that blinds new writers from its actual danger, attracting them under the guise of being able to legitimize a byline through association, yet paying this labor very little.

To illustrate this, Miranda—formerly one of two mid-level editors for S.B. Nation's New York Knicks site *Posting, and Toasting*—recalled the unusual predicament that arose after the N.B.A. officially ceased league operations on

March 12, 2020, at the onset of the COVID-19 pandemic. During this initial sports stoppage, Miranda said he "took a break" from writing and editing for the *Posting and Toasting* site since his S.B. Nation agreement only stipulated that he was required to produce content while the Knicks were actively playing. Around this time, Miranda said he got "double pneumonia" and, for the sake of his health, took a hiatus from writing. Not realizing that he violated his contract for not blogging about the Knicks during the standard timeframe of an N.B.A. season (even though the team's schedule was paused from March to July 2020), Miranda noted how "that was the only time in eight years that I had heard from anyone personally at S.B. Nation about anything."

The communication came via an email from a higher-up, informing him that if he did not increase his publication rate, his monthly editorial pay would be decreased. Ultimately, this prompted Miranda, who now writes for another Knicks blog, *The Strickland*, to send a follow-up, pointing out that his contract specifies that he is not bound to write if the Knicks are not playing, which they were not at that time because of the N.B.A.'s league-wide shut down.

It is "that kind of thing," Miranda noted, that demonstrates how S.B. Nation corporate management can sometimes be out-of-touch with the well-being of its contracted writers and editors, most of whom, he said, are not given a substantial paycheck for the number of hours incurred in this side job. He added that it is a case of needing to understand the situation's realities. Whereas the lower levels of management are often more involved with what transpires among their staff (similar to how Mearns discussed that he and his writers understand that S.B. Nation writing is merely a passion project and, thus, should be treated as one), Miranda suggested that S.B. Nation's hierarchical pyramid is what ultimately detracts from its basis as a strong sports blogging entity for the typical fan's editorial involvement. The idea of using S.B. Nation as exposure, he said, is "horseshit" since the writer's exploitation (in a manner that is a step above free labor) often does not outweigh the negative consequences of doing the work.

That is why, despite his continued affiliation with S.B. Nation after this incident, Miranda sees the future of sports blogging shifting toward worker-owned and worker-managed sports websites that can counter S.B. Nation's stronghold on the market. One of these sites that he mentioned was *The Strickland*, an independent Knicks Patreon site with the tagline "new site designed for Knicks fans, minus any Vapid Media overlords" that Miranda and other ex-*Posting and Toasting* writers founded in August 2020 after they grew "dissatisfied with some of the realities working for S.B. Nation." Although those affiliated with *Posting and Toasting* did have what Miranda branded as "free rein" to run their site in any way deemed fit (similar to the sentiment expressed by every other interviewee), he called it "exacerbating circumstances" that led to this group of writers leaving S.B. Nation.

Not being bound to a corporate umbrella means that Miranda and *The Strickland* are more committed to focusing on the type of news not widely covered by other Knicks outlets. Above all else, though, being a writer-owned entity means *The Strickland* can give a greater sense of editorial feedback during the process, something that Miranda noted did not always occur at *Posting and Toasting* because S.B. Nation's lack of editors often meant that no one was available to edit his work before they got posted.

Miranda further went on to explain that one of the main reasons why *The Strickland* came into existence was because of growing "disgust" over the fact that S.B. Nation classified its writers as freelancers instead of actual employees (this stripped entitled benefits and pay increases from those who worked more than freelance hours). In early 2020, California enacted a law requiring any media network with non-employees who wrote more than 35 articles per year to be classified as staffers entitled to benefits (Levy & Sherman, 2019). S.B. Nation's subsequent response to this was to cut the stipend-paid writers of its N.B.A. team sites in California. The move on S.B. Nation's part, Miranda said, was to downsize and start over with people who were willing to do the same type of work for less money:

> You can be paid in exposure. But the reality is that, if you're not able to be exploited long enough to hope that it turns around, then it really can't work for you there [. . .] Everyone benefits from more voices and more access to voices in sports media. And one way you could democratize voices in sports media would be not to have this exploitative model that only allows people who are willing to get screwed over to have any chance of advancing. (M. Miranda, personal communication, December 2, 2021)

Although he did not delve into the specifics regarding his monthly financial earnings through S.B. Nation, Miranda noted that he made "much less than minimum wage per hour." However, Mullinax, formerly of *Grizzly Bear Blues*, did specify the pay structure of S.B. Nation. He mentioned that his blog received a budget ($1,200 per month) to divide among its staff. After paying each of his three associate editors, and ten paid writers underneath them, Mullinax said his monthly take home was $620. Thus, he pushed against the notion that very few people could live off the side job income that S.B. Nation pays—unless a site editor takes the entirety of the $1,200 monthly budget for him or herself without paying the staff (of note, Mullinax did say that blogs covering larger market teams typically receive a slightly larger budget, but not by much).

This issue of S.B. Nation writer exploitation and lack of pay was first made apparent by Deadspin writer Laura Wagner in a 2017 exposé that anonymously interviewed former site editors to dissect how the corporation treated the media conglomerate's content creators and editorial staff. In this article, it was revealed that the work of individual S.B. Nation site managers "adds up to a demanding job—or, in some cases, close to a full-time one—but site managers are independent contractors who are paid a monthly stipend that varies widely" (Wagner, 2017, para. 6). Although these individuals are not classified as professional media members, the alleged issue was that they were expected "to meet such professional expectations as keeping the site updated and covering news as it happens, no matter when that is" (Wagner, 2017, para. 5). Additionally, since those who worked for S.B. Nation at the time often clocked long hours and received "only token sums for work against which Vox sells ads," it was surmised that this type of employee-business approach "could, according to labor lawyers, conflict with labor laws" (Wagner, 2017, para. 3). Subsequently, former and then-current members of the S.B. Nation part-time editorial staff filed a class-action lawsuit shortly after the publication of Wagner's piece to recoup owed wages that they were supposedly entitled to since it was ultimately deemed that Vox Media's "compensation methods violated federal and state employment law" (Perez, 2020, para. 2).

Nearly three years after its filing, the lawsuit was settled in August 2020, paying a $4 million settlement to the 450 individual blog employees (though, after the ruling, these individuals were left with $2.5 million to split since $1.5 million went to covering legal fees; Hayes, 2020; Wagner, 2020). According to Front Office Sports, site managers were given a payout between $5,000 to $7,500. At the same time, contributors were expected to receive anywhere in the range of $2,100 to $2,500, with total individual payout value ultimately being impacted by the number of hours worked and where one lived (those in California and New Jersey received a higher cut because of more apparent alleged violations of individual state labor law; Perez, 2020). Despite the lawsuit's ruling, S.B. Nation—in a statement—wrote that "there was no admission of liability" and that it "weighed the costs of continued litigation and made a business decision that this settlement amount was reasonable and would enable the company to put these cases behind it and move on" (Kelly, 2020, para. 6).

The criticism of S.B. Nation's stipend model and the lawsuit that it created was echoed by Mark Brown, editor of the Baltimore Orioles fan site *Camden Chat*. During his interview, the S.B. Nation veteran cited the lawsuit as signaling a positive for how the company treats its contracted workers. Brown, who was not part of the lawsuit yet admittingly wished he was, noted how it signaled a step in the right direction for S.B. Nation since it began increasing monthly stipends in a "go-figure" manner. Despite this criticism toward Vox Media's business culture, he said the increased pay that each site manager now receives demonstrates that S.B. Nation has "gotten a little bit more serious as there's been more money and more expectations."

This internal struggle that S.B. Nation site managers and editors face, one at a crossroads between actively catering content to a sports team's fan base and not wanting to be exploited for unfair employment practices, can be a caveat for future user-generated content. For one, the corporate-centric philosophy of a network of sports blogging communities like S.B. Nation tends to benefit the fans the most because it functions as a legitimate sports news organization. On the other hand, though, lost in the shuffle is almost always the position of those who serve as the writing and editorial staff. When the mentality for each S.B. Nation fan community is to crank out as much content as possible to remain competitive in an industry like sports media, the content producers are the ones who get overlooked in favor of click rates, page views, and other web metrics.

The flaws in the S.B. Nation system, thus, are even more reason—Miranda said—for sports media to go back to the individualized, worker-cooperative blogging routines of the Internet's infancy. He maintained that the viability of the sports fan community may lie in the abandonment of corporate affiliation, despite the perceived name recognition that it affords, and more toward a pivot back to the basics (i.e., the independent sports news site in which those who own it are also the content producers). In a way, it aligns with the philosophy set in motion by Bleszinski with the original incarnation of *Athletics Nation*: to give fans a way to stay engaged with others who shared the same bond with their favorite team in an unfiltered manner. Although S.B. Nation has continually evolved throughout its existence, Miranda is confident that getting back to the root of the "by fans, for fans" mentality is the next move for fan communities.

References

"About us." (n.d.). *Associated Press Sports Editors*. https://www.apsportseditors.com/history/

Allison, R. (2021). Becoming fans: Socialization and motivations of fans of the England and U.S. women's national football teams. *Sociology of Sport Journal, 39*(3), 287–297.

Bena, J. (2012, September 7). *A sneak peek at the future of MHR—and SB Nation.* Mile High Report.   https://www.milehighreport.com/2012/9/7/3299338/SBNation-United-Mile-High-Report

Bleszinski, T. (2004). *Athletics Nation manifesto.* Athletics Nation. http://web.archive.org/web/20040612045644/http://www.athleticsnation.com/about.html

Bleszinski, T. (2011). *Happy 8th birthday AN and SB Nation!* Athletics Nation. https://www.athleticsnation.com/2011/11/6/2541778/happy-8th-birthday-an-and-sb-nation

Bucholtz, A. (2017, August 14). *SB Nation contracts, site managers go against execs' assertion all contributors are paid.* Awful Announcing. https://awfulannouncing.com/online-outlets/sb-nation-contracts-managers-go-against-execs-assertion-all-contributors-are-paid.html

Carr, D. (2011, April 3). No longer shackled by AOL. *The New York Times.* https://www.nytimes.com/2011/04/04/business/media/04carr.html

Cash, M. (2023, March 30). *After Vox Media cuts created "huge crisis" at SB Nation, a new alliance is now further consolidating women's pro sports coverage.* Business Insider. https://www.insider.com/womens-sports-media-partnership-next-ice-garden-sparked-by-crisis-2023-3

Deckard, D. (2015, February 2). *An interview with SB Nation's Tyler Bleszinski.* Blazer's Edge. https://www.blazersedge.com/2015/2/2/7968917/an-interview-with-sbnations-tyler-bleszinski

Dubois, L. (2010, August 20). *The evolution of Sports Blog Nation.* Inc. https://www.inc.com/news/articles/2010/08/interview-with-jim-bankoff-ceo-of-sbnation.html

Ellis, J. (2012, September 25). *Building a better sports bar: SB Nation redesigns its blog network.* NiemanLab.   http://www.niemanlab.org/2012/09/building-a-better-sports-bar-sb-nation-redesigns-its-blog-network/

"Former AOL exec raises funding for sports blogs network." (2008, October 29). *TechCrunch.* https://techcrunch.com/2008/10/29/former-aol-exec-raises-funding-for-sports-blogs-network/

Gibson, D. (2021, August 12). *Showbiz CheatSheet.* https://www.cheatsheet.com/entertainment/is-the-bar-cheers-real.html/

Gold-Smith, J. (2014, October 28). *Blazer's Edge rejects second-tier media credentials from Trail Blazers.* Awful Announcing. https://awfulannouncing.com/2014/blazers-edge-rejects-second-tier-media-credential-trail-blazers.html

Hayes, P. (2020, August 18). *SB Nation bloggers, Vox Media seek approval of $4 million deal.* Bloomberg Law. https://news.bloomberglaw.com/daily-labor-report/sb-nation-bloggers-vox-media-seek-approval-of-4-million-deal

Heath, T. (2014, December 7). *Vox Media's Bankoff tries to keep creativity alive as investments roll in.* The Washington Post. https://www.washingtonpost.com/business/economy/as-investments-roll-in-vox-medias-bankoff-tries-to-keep-creativity-alive/2014/12/06/14e34fba-7a66-11e4-b821-503cc7efed9e_story.html

Hoag, D. (2010, June 21). *What is the oldest sports blog? It sure isn't SportsbyBrooks*. On the Forecheck. https://www.ontheforecheck.com/what-is-the-oldest-sports-blog-it/

Hubbard, S. (2010). *Exploring the virtual communities of college football fans: The uses and gratifications of online message boards* [Unpublished master's thesis]. https://mospace.umsystem.edu/xmlui/bitstream/handle/10355/44835/research.pdf?sequence=1&isAllowed=y

Katz, E., Blumler, J. G., & Gurevitch, M. (1973). Uses and gratifications research. *Public Opinion Quarterly, 37*(4), 509–523.

Kelly, K. J. (2020, August 19). *Vox Media agrees to $4M settlement with SB Nation writers*. New York Post. https://nypost.com/2020/08/19/vox-media-agrees-to-4m-settlement-with-sb-nation-writers/

Kemp, N. (2019). *The end of the passive fan: Sports marketing's social shift*. US Campaign. https://www.campaignlive.com/article/end-passive-fan-sports-marketings-social-shift/1523542

Kirmayer, L. J., Raikhel, E., & Rahimi, S. (2013). Cultures of the Internet: Identity, community and mental health. *Transcultural Psychiatry, 50*(2), 165–191.

Kramer, S. D. (2010, November 8). *SB Nation ups its funding to nearly $24 million with new round*. GIGAOM. https://gigaom.com/2010/11/08/419-sbnation-ups-its-funding-to-nearly-24-million-with-new-round/

Kroon, A., & Eriksson, G. (2019). The impact of the digital transformation on sports journalism talk online. *Journalism Practice, 13*(7), 834–852.

Levy, A., & Sherman, A. (2019, December 16). *Vox Media to cut hundreds of freelance jobs ahead of changes in California gig economy laws*. CNBC. https://www.cnbc.com/2019/12/16/vox-media-to-cut-hundreds-of-freelance-jobs-ahead-of-californias-ab5.html

Lichterman, J. (2016, January 6). *Built on passion: How Vox Media grew from its roots as an Oakland A's blog into one of the Internet's biggest publishers*. NiemanLab. https://www.niemanlab.org/2016/01/built-on-passion-how-vox-media-grew-from-its-roots-as-an-oakland-as-blog-into-one-of-the-internets-biggest-publishers/

Maese, R. (2018, May 31). *NBA Twitter, a sports bar that doesn't close where the stars pull up a seat next to you*. The Washington Post. https://www.washingtonpost.com/news/sports/wp/2018/05/31/nba-twitter-a-sports-bar-that-doesnt-close-where-the-stars-pull-up-a-seat-next-to-you/

Mastromartino, B., Ross, W. J., Wear, H., & Naraine, M. L. (2020). Thinking outside the "box": A discussion of sports fans, teams, and the environment in the context of COVID-19. *Sport in Society, 23*(11), 1707–1723.

Mathwick, C., Wiertz, C., & De Ruyter, K. (2008). Social capital production in virtual P3 community. *Journal of Consumer Research, 34*(6), 832–849.

"A message from your Japers' Rink team." (2023, January 20). *Japers' Rink*. https://www.japersrink.com/a-message-from-your-japers-rink-team-01-20-2023/

Mullin, B. (2017a, March 3). *SB Nation names first editor in chief in push for growth*. Poynter. https://www.poynter.org/business-work/2017/sb-nation-names-first-editor-in-chief-in-push-for-growth/

Mullin, B. (2017b, May 1). *With its redesigned website, SB Nation wants fans to geek out with them*. Poynter. https://www.poynter.org/tech-tools/2017/with-its-redesigned-website-sb-nation-wants-fans-to-geek-out-with-them/

Overly, S. (2010, December 20). *SB Nation's sports blogger collective sees bias as a plus.* The Washington Post. https://www.washingtonpost.com/wp-dyn/content/article/2010/12/17/AR2010121706202.html

Perez, A. J. (2020, August 18). *Vox Media agrees to $4 million settlement with SB Nation workers.* Front Office Sports. https://frontofficesports.com/vox-media-agrees-to-4-million-settlement-with-sb-nation-workers/

Plambeck, J. (2010, June 6). *Sports-centric web sites expand, and bias is welcome.* The New York Times. https://www.nytimes.com/2010/06/07/business/media/07fans.html

Pollack, H., & Peck, D. (n.d.). *Meet the new sports fans in the Twitter stands.* Twitter Marketing. https://marketing.twitter.com/en/insights/twitter-sports-community-research-2020

Pompeo, J. (2020, December 11). *Forget Buzzfeed and the Times, Vox Media chief Jim Bankoff wants to follow in Disney's footsteps.* Vanity Fair. https://www.vanityfair.com/news/2020/12/vox-media-chief-wants-to-follow-in-disneys-footsteps

Ratner, A. (2008, March 30). *True devotion: Blogging about the Orioles.* The Baltimore Sun. https://www.baltimoresun.com/news/bs-xpm-2008-03-30-0803300060-story.html

Robertson, K. (2021, December 13). *Vox Media and Group Nine, digital media giants, have agreed to merge.* The New York Times. https://www.nytimes.com/2021/12/13/business/media/vox-media-groupnine.html

Robertson, K. (2023, January 20). *Vox Media to cut 7 percent of workers.* The New York Times. https://www.nytimes.com/2023/01/20/business/media/vox-media-layoffs.html

Romero-Jara, E., Solanellas, F., Muñoz, J., & López-Carril, C. (2023). Connecting with fans in the digital age: An exploratory and comparative analysis of social media management in top football clubs. *Humanities and Social Sciences Communications.* https://doi.org/10.1057/s41599-023-02357-8

Safire, W. (2002, July 28). *The way we live now: 7-28-02: On language; blog.* The New York Times. https://www.nytimes.com/2002/07/28/magazine/the-way-we-live-now-7-28-02-on-language-blog.html

Strauss, B. (2020, April 17). *SB Nation faces murky future after Vox Media furloughs national writers for three months.* The Washington Post. https://www.washingtonpost.com/sports/2020/04/17/sb-nation-faces-murky-future-after-vox-media-furloughs-national-writers-three-months/

Sundar, S. S., & Limperos, A. M. (2013). Uses and grats 2.0: New gratifications for new media. *Journal of Broadcasting & Electronic Media, 57*(4), 504–525.

Sutton, K. (2015, December 14). *Tyler Bleszinski, co-founder of SB Nation, to leave Vox Media.* POLITICO. https://www.politico.com/media/story/2015/12/tyler-bleszinski-co-founder-of-sb-nation-to-leave-vox-media-004319/

Terdiman, D. (2005, April 18). *A blog for baseball fans builds a league of sites.* The New York Times. https://www.nytimes.com/2005/04/18/technology/a-blog-for-baseball-fans-builds-a-league-of-sites.html

Thompson, D. (2014, February 10). *Which sports have the whitest/richest/oldest fans?* The Atlantic. https://www.theatlantic.com/business/archive/2014/02/which-sports-have-the-whitest-richest-oldest-fans/283626/

Wagner, L. (2017, August 14). *How SB Nation profits off an army of exploited workers.* Deadspin. https://deadspin.com/how-sb-nation-profits-off-an-army-of-exploited-workers-1797653841

Wagner, L. (2018, July 31). *SB Nation is paying workers as little as $3 per blog post.* Deadspin. https://deadspin.com/sb-nation-is-paying-workers-as-little-as-3-per-blog-po-1827998745

Wagner, L. (2020, August 18). *Vox Media agrees to settle worker-exploitation lawsuits for millions.* Vice. https://www.vice.com/en/article/v7gjmb/vox-media-agrees-to-settle-worker-exploitation-lawuits-for-millions

Wagner, L. (2023, January 20). *Vox Media layoffs wipe out most SB Nation hockey, MLS sites.* Defector. https://defector.com/vox-media-layoffs-wipe-out-most-sb-nation-hockey-mls-sites

Wakefield, K. (2020 April 1). Evidence from the Internet: How the pandemic sparks sports fans on Twitter. *Forbes.* https://www.forbes.com/sites/kirkwakefield/2020/04/01/evidence-from-the-internet-how-the-pandemic-sparks-sports-fans-on-twitter/?sh=2c0c8afa43f5

Williams, J., Chinn, S. J., & Suleiman, J. (2014). The value of Twitter for sports fans. *Journal of Direct, Data and Digital Marketing Practice, 16*(1), 36–50.

Yu, R. (2013, October 19). *Vox Media grows with focus on video.* USA Today. https://www.baltimoresun.com/news/bs-xpm-2008-03-30-0803300060-story.html

· 5 ·

REIMAGINING THE FUTURE OF DIGITAL SPORTS JOURNALISM

This research shows that catering to the niche can allow for coexistence in digital sports journalism. This aligns with the findings of Kleineberg and Boguñá (2015), who write that the "competition-colonization trade-off"—in which each platform competes for different peer groups (para. 4)—can be essential to maintaining a sense of stability. Interviews with 100 sports reporters inform these findings, focusing on the coexistence of varying sports news platforms and sports journalism's future market stability. Although each interviewee had different perspectives, the insight gained provides a snapshot of the field's issues and opportunities.

This book first examined how digital sports journalists position themselves within media competition, using gatekeeping, niche gratification theory, diffusion of innovations, and journalistic boundary work as the guiding theoretical concepts. However, because each group of interviewees brought different viewpoints to light, this research evolved from a book focused on outlet competition to one that examines how the niche can lead to editorial coexistence among modern sports journalistic outlets. The five themes uncovered through the qualitative interview process (detailed below) illustrate commonality among sportswriters from team-run media, The Athletic, Substack, and S.B. Nation. Despite Dimmick et al. (2000) writing that two media with a high degree of niche overlap (assuming one is superior to the other in terms of the fulfillment of certain gratification) will compete until the superior one replaces the other, interviewees suggested otherwise. Rather, despite the existence of a degree of niche overlap between the editorial approaches of Substack newsletters and S.B. Nation blogs, it was revealed that sportswriters generally believe coexistence is possible via the niche.

Generally, most sportswriters want to avoid seeing outlets squashing their competitors. Instead, as Buzzelli et al. (2020) note, a healthy sports journalism ecosystem is often favored because it means more job opportunity (i.e., an *everyone is in this together* mindset). Interviewee Jenny Vrentas of *The New York Times* echoed this sentiment when discussing how those in sports journalism—because of layoffs and furloughs—want to see other outlets survive. Competition, Vrentas said, is still a variable at play because of the inherent idea that a reporter wants to provide the reader "with something they can't get anywhere else" and be the first to have a scoop. However, because she has been around organizations that have laid off talented journalists (most notably, she survived a round of cuts while writing for *Sports Illustrated*), Vrentas said sportswriters should support other outlets because there generally are not enough reporters to cover all of the essential sports topics and news stories that arise. She said, "I don't know how you could care about sports journalism and want other outlets to fail. I want all outlets to succeed and more good jobs so people can have careers in this business."

Marketplace Coexistence via the N.G.T. Lens

Media generally operate under the assumption that they must actively compete with those in the same coverage realm "to collect the highest number of followers" (Quattrociocchi et al., 2014, para. 7). This is because more significant audience cultivation can often lead to a more attractive news product for advertising; in turn, this equates to more revenue being directed back to the news organization (Elejalde et al., 2019; Radcliffe & Wallace, 2021). According to a Pew Research Center report, digital advertising, in 2022, encompassed nearly 75 percent of all advertising revenue in news—compared to just 64 percent in 2020 ("Digital news fact sheet," 2023). It is apparent, therefore, why journalistic competition among similarly structured organizations would be a pertinent topic for journalists (and those who study journalism) since marketplace saturation means there are additional forms of consumption that reader attention could, in theory, be devoted toward (Choi & Yang, 2021).

However, interviewees noted that they rarely perceive direct media competition (two or more outlets targeting the same audience and/or advertisers; Levin, 1954). Despite the thinking that journalistic outlets covering the same sports beat would be highly competitive since they "operate within the same or different industries in local markets" (Dimmick, 2006, p. 346), more than 10 interviewees said direct competition is not as outward. One of the main reasons for this is the shared view that emphasis on niche sports content has led to a state of coexistence. This is because most organizations now cater to a more focused sports viewpoint instead of adhering to the "one-size-fits-all approach to sports journalism," which no longer exists since fans now use multiple forms of media for specific purposes ("How digital media has changed sports journalism," 2021, para. 18). Online news, in this regard, can breed specialization since consumption habits illustrate that mediated sports content can capture both mass and niche audiences ("The power play: How sport captivates mass and niche audiences alike," 2023).

Anderson (2004), in a *Wired* magazine article dubbed "The long tail," sees this as the updated economic model created by the Internet since access to niche titles created a shift from "hit-driven culture" to one centered on the "misses" (para. 5–6). He argues that the power of unlimited selection reveals what consumers value. The more alternative content one discovers, the more it becomes apparent that mainstream tastes in media offerings are the byproduct of mass marketing tactics. Physical media existed in a world of scarcity, with media gatekeepers being forced to select what perspectives to push since not everything could remain relevant. Online distribution, however, ushered in an era of abundance that caters to virtually every taste. This, Anderson (2004) writes, constitutes the "long tail" (p. 27) of modern media, a concept maintaining that as long as the content is accessible online, it will be consumed—even if the audience for said content is only one person.

Applying the long tail principle to sports journalism helps illustrate the rise of niche sports content (e.g., blogs, newsletters, etc.) as a direct alternative to mainstream sports media. This is because a market with a variation of product offerings, Brynjolfsson et al. (2006) write, allows consumers to "cultivate deeper tastes for these niche products" (p. 69). Therefore, even if a sports news outlet has a small audience, it will likely still cultivate a dedicated reader base since the niche permits tailored content in a general climate that is more inviting for sportswriters. This overall theme, additionally, aligns with both Dimmick (2003) and Gaskins and Jerit (2012), who noted that a key to survival in an overcrowded digital marketplace is to serve a specialized segment (i.e., the niche) of media consumers whose coverage tastes are primarily ignored by other outlets.

Most interviewees said their individualized editorial strategies effectively secure readership because of content differentiation, in which everyone tries to write about *their* team differently. Although a professional sports team likely has multiple external sportswriters assigned to the beat at any given time, meaning competition can be plentiful, the niche enables each reporter to locate an editorial hole and write for a dedicated targeted audience of sports consumers, which Carmody (2011) notes mainly consists of men. If, for instance, one specific sports news site takes a more analytical approach, another of comparable structure, delivery, and/or lean will slightly adjust its editorial strategy so the overlap is less pronounced. The saying, "There's room at the table for everyone," may be cliché. However, fulfilling the niche makes this possible since varying forms of sports journalism can peacefully coexist without fighting for survival. That table, however, turned out to be larger than imagined because the Internet demonstrates that sports fans' thirst for content is a constant churn.

Regarding newspapers, carving a coverage niche is sometimes tricky, Lori Riley admitted, because of the constrained resources associated with current newspaper journalism. Riley, a high school sportswriter with the *Hartford Courant* since 1988, said she wishes her newspaper could have more flexibility regarding the type of sports coverage (high school athletics) that does not receive much media attention. Riley noted that the tactic of just printing submitted box scores of select high school games—instead of having more depth to the coverage—is a byproduct of a small sports staff (of note, she said she is one of three sportswriters for The *Courant*, Connecticut's largest daily newspaper, which had a 2022 print circulation of less than 34,000; Storace, 2022). Because the main emphasis is getting the newspaper out each morning, the sports staff typically does not have time to "reinvent things or think of new ideas" since "everybody's running around like a chicken with their head cut off." Therefore, although Riley said a more innovative editorial approach could benefit her newspaper, the lack of time (and sports reporters) means that niche-focused coverage is not always possible.

It was also revealed that editorial overlap sometimes exists between team-run media and The Athletic. However, interviewees said their main content offerings differ in length and depth, illustrating that both serve a specific niche and/or type of fan. Those who manage a Substack newsletter, conceivably the most niche sports media platform represented, also viewed their writing specialization as a factor that makes coexistence possible. For Matthew Kory, carving a niche of humoristic writing via *Sox Outsider* allowed him to build what he called a loyal reader base of Boston Red Sox fans. Tim Haslam of *Utah Lacrosse Report* felt the same since few other news outlets covered a niche high school sport in a state not traditionally viewed as a lacrosse hotbed. He said having a small (but dedicated) audience of people who want Utah high school lacrosse news, which they cannot get from local newspapers, makes it possible for his newsletter to remain relevant.

Justin Ferguson of *Auburn Observer*, a Substack dedicated to the university's football and men's basketball team, faced a similar situation when deciding how to forge his niche on an already crowded beat. Unlike Red Sox analysis from a witty perspective or coverage of high school lacrosse in Utah, there is plenty of competition on the Auburn beat. Ferguson, however, noticed that few provided analyses and podcasts. This void prompted the editorial basis for his paywalled Substack, which he said can maintain strong readership because it covers the beat slightly differently than comparable outlets (of note, Ferguson had over 3,000 total subscribers in 2024, according to data on his Substack page). Therefore, the niche nature of modern sports journalism means the competitive stance of the past is no longer as universal since interviewees revealed that space exists for various sports outlets—as long as each frames its writing slightly differently. Niche gratification theory, in this regard, does not just explain media outlet survival; instead, it can also be applied to the coexistence of sportswriting from a niche perspective. This coexistence between old and new forms of sports journalism, McCollough (2018) writes, can be uncomfortable at times, though.

It is also conceivable to believe that coexistence via the niche is possible because of the distinct boundaries that each outlet has to continually negotiate in terms of establishing professional identity. As previously mentioned, Gieryn's (1983, 1999) concept of boundary work rationalizes how specific groups occupying the same space compete by creating boundaries that specify who does (and does not) belong in a work-related group. From a more narrowed lens, Gieryn (1983) maintains that three types of boundary work exist:

- Expansion (a group claiming a new task).
- Expulsion (said group refusing entry to the perceived out-group).
- Protection of autonomy (safeguarding the boundary against those who seek to redefine it).

Because most interviewees said they did not perceive other sports journalism as direct competition because each generally had a different editorial approach, predefined boundaries that established hierarchical trends were less prevalent. Applying the work of Gieryn (1983) to sports journalism coexistence can mean that the most apparent boundary is expansion since each tries to claim an editorial and audience area, yet in a manner that permits the proverbial seat at the table to remain open. More specifically, the changing boundaries of sports journalism can be linked to the overall question of "What is sports journalism?" since digital media has bred other avenues of consumption. As Rojas-Torrijos and Nölleke (2023) note, the "superiority of established media is increasingly being challenged by competitors from the field's periphery" (p. 853). With that, the lack of a formal professionalized barrier means non-trained writers can become disseminator of sports news. In turn, this opens the door for more niche perspectives to exist online.

It is important to note that boundary work is wider than the individual and routine levels. Instead, boundaries also encompass organizations and their inherent structures since an individual moving from one area of sportswriting to another must navigate the specific objectives and metrics valued in each sphere. From an organizational level, gatekeeping and boundary work are factors based on what each organization values and how that influences professional identity. For example, in-house reporters who were originally newspaper sportswriters before working for a sports team typically have to navigate the boundary of how they perceive themselves, their work, and the role of their employer from a journalistic standpoint (Mirer, 2019). Interviewees (John Oehser, Jacksonville Jaguars; Darren Urban, Arizona Cardinals; and Jim Wyatt, Tennessee Titans) said their role aligns with journalism because the job is still predicated on the basics that all current journalists possess (i.e., accuracy/integrity, writing/proofreading, multimedia skills, ability to work under pressure, etc.; Wenger & Owens, 2013). Although some in external media may disagree that in-house reporters are journalists, Mirer (2023) notes that "independent reporters are arguably less likely to disparage [those who write for a team's website] as it becomes a more acceptable option" for employment in sports journalism (p. 451).

The same can be said for sportswriters who transitioned from corporate to entrepreneurial sports media via Substack. These interviewees, too, had to negotiate their values when making the switch. As a former writer in corporate sports journalism, Craig Calcaterra (of the *Cup of Coffee* M.L.B. newsletter) had to think about his objectives when transitioning from NBC Sports to Substack. This is because NBC Sports valued page views and article clicks, whereas Calcaterra built his Substack on subscription conversions from free-mium content and his established social media following. For Calcaterra and Ferguson, of the Auburn Observer, the gatekeeping process switched from a hierarchical structure specifying the organization's direction to the content creator having autonomy. Professional identities, like boundaries, constantly evolve. Because of this, Perreault and Bell (2022) note that journalists should familiarize themselves with outlet and audience trends to grapple "with a ten-sion between tradition and turbulence of change" (p. 409).

The Niche Negates a Sense of Perceived Direct Competition

Monitoring a news organization's editorial output to "outmaneuver specific competitors" (Lowrey & Woo, 2010, p. 44) may be a competitive advantage. Interviewees, however, clarified that the niche negates a sense of perceived direct competition. As previously mentioned, modern sports fans benefit the most from a saturated sports journalism marketplace because they can access as much content as desired (e.g., blog posts, daily coverage, video breakdowns, etc.) from any perspective. This makes it apparent that fans "are no longer pleased with a single source of information" (Galily, 2018, p. 3). According to Deloitte's 2023 "Sports fan insights" survey, sports fans under 40 are just as engaged in mediated content as those over 40. However, the content con-sumed by Gen Z and Millennial fans is more likely from social media (e.g., game highlights, interview videos, and athlete posts; Ryan, 2023). These altered media consumption habits make coexistence possible.

This approach is evident in brick-and-mortar stores, with businesses like The Home Depot and Whole Foods specializing in a specific product segment that generally cannot be found elsewhere (Arnold, 2018; Schroeder, 2021). There are businesses like Wal-Mart, Target, and even Amazon where consum-ers can likely find everything in a one-stop shop. Just because a big-box store can carry thousands of products catering to all needs, however, does not neces-sarily mean that specialized retailers perceive direct competition with general retailers. This concept can be applied to sports media since most interviewees said there is little perceived direct competition (and subsequent content mon-itoring) among the more specialized forms of sports news (i.e., The Athletic, Substack, S.B. Nation). Conversely, those working for newspapers—which may represent the *one-stop-shop* of journalism—viewed digital outlets like in-house reporters and The Athletic as more of the opposition than Substack or S.B. Nation (of note, neither in-house writers nor interviewees from The Athletic perceived newspapers as competition). Newspaper sportswriters and editors were more likely to perceive digital media as a competitor, to some degree, than the other sports journalism platforms examined. This is likely because competition has traditionally been a critical element of objective journalism in the twentieth century, with traditional news organizations competing for story scoops and subscription and advertising revenue (Graves & Konieczna, 2015). Further, because local newspapers have seen their staff shrink (partly due to layoffs, budget cuts, and talent poaching) at an accelerated rate (Bauder, 2023), it makes sense why there would be most robust views toward competition in this capacity.

This is because the standard editorial approach of newspaper journalism—incremental coverage to stay informed on a team's day-to-day happenings—has some overlap with in-house media, despite English (2022) writing that the latter tends to be "more promotional, positive and substantially less critical" (p. 866). Perhaps one reason why newspaper and in-house coverage is similar is because many ex-print sportswriters shifted to internal media, meaning they were trained in the traditional editorial routines of newspaper journalism. Whereas most newspapers typically have some form of news paywall that limits who can view content without purchasing a subscription, team-run media is not bound to the traditional constraints. This is because sports organizations operate under a different business model, typically rooted more in sales, stakeholder investments, and television broadcasting rights than pure advertising revenue (Mathewson, 2019; Pittz et al., 2021).

These interviewees said they do not view themselves as competing against print journalists since they still know people on that side; they noted it is more of a friendly relationship than an adversarial one. Additionally, in-house reporters have an inherent advantage when building relationships with sources (but not necessarily in terms of increased access) since they interact with players and coaches more frequently. That, coupled with the thinking that being on the inside represents a more stable sportswriting position than those in newspaper journalism, may lead to less of a view on direct competition. Although O'Boyle and Gallagher (2023) state that some newspaper sportswriters have a negative view of colleagues who transition from external to internal media because of the perception that they may have "forgotten their roots as journalists," most acknowledge that the move is often motivated by a desire for more excellent career stability (O'Boyle & Gallagher, 2023, p. 673).

What was made evident by team-employed journalists, though, was that competition with other beat writers was less direct since internal media have more leeway in finding newer storytelling methods. Instead of focusing on the editorial strategy of game preview, recap, and analysis, some in-house reporters (e.g., John Boyle of the Seattle Seahawks and Matthew Tabeek, formerly of the Atlanta Falcons) viewed their role as an extension of the marketing department. This is because internal reporters can use content on a team's official website to increase brand impressions, awareness, and overall engagement.

It is also important to note that the perception of competition for newspapers was not solely limited to editorial routines. Instead, interviewees said competition persisted in the form of staff retention because of digital media's poaching from legacy news. Although the most notable form of talent competition was previously the team itself, a shift occurred when The Athletic began to lure journalists away from local newspapers under the guise of greater writing flexibility and increased salary in 2016 (Buzzelli et al., 2022). All newspaper sports editor interviewees said they lost at least one sportswriter, if not multiple, to The Athletic during their tenure (as mentioned in the introduction, Bud Geracie of the *Bay Area News Group* lost four of his top beat writers to The Athletic whenever it entered the Northern California media market).

The reason those writing for The Athletic, Substack, or S.B. Nation did not view sports journalism as hypercompetitive is most likely because each caters to such a specialized segment of the sports-consuming public. Interviewees from The Athletic said that focusing more on contextual reporting than daily coverage makes their work stand out since only a few outlets take this approach. Also, they generally perceived themselves as being in a class of their own regarding freedom, flexibility, and content produced. Sports-centric Substack newsletter writers, likewise, mentioned that their editorial lean is so narrow that no one else approaches sportswriting similarly. Although S.B. Nation is not the only sports blogging community platform on the web (the tone, voice, and structure of individual FanSided blogs are very comparable), site managers/editors said brand credibility and a long-standing, loyal following means the same readers keep coming back.

S.B. Nation's niche is the fan community since it has famously touted the "for fans, by fans" tagline (Plambeck, 2010). Additionally, not having a paywall places more emphasis on the professional identity of its staff since it must also cast a wide net about the target audience. Navigation of The Athletic's niche (in-depth and feature-style coverage) is also partly influenced by its business model rooted in subscriptions since it knows that its audience will pay. When The Athletic launched, it changed the traditional business and editorial structure of sports media (Ferrucci, 2022); yet looking at it through the lens of journalistic boundary work can mean that the niche content being produced and the organization's overall primary revenue generation structure are more closely aligned than previously thought.

Technology Breeds Newer Opportunity in a Somewhat Financially Unstable Industry

Before the Internet, a sportswriter could rise through the ranks of professional sports journalism through the industry standards of obtaining a journalism degree, gaining entry-level employment, or climbing the hierarchical sports beat ladder (Hardin et al., 2009). During this time, there were only three types of media—print, radio, and broadcast—meaning that employment was sometimes challenging since positions were limited. The Internet, however, offered more opportunities for those wanting to develop a career in sports journalism (Boyle, 2017; Butler et al., 2013). An up-and-coming sportswriter can still go the traditional route if he or she wants to work for legacy or more professionalized forms of online-only sports media (i.e., team-run, The Athletic, ESPN, etc.). However, those are not the only options for breaking into this field since Substack, S.B. Nation, and other sports blogging platforms represent an alternative to mainstream sports journalism (McCarthy, 2014).

S.B. Nation, for instance, offers those with limited professional experience the ability to turn a sports blogging habit into a stipend-paid side job (as previously mentioned, the pay is not substantial, though; Strauss, 2020c). Substack, similarly, makes it possible for someone with a recognizable media brand or byline to monetize his or her sportswriting in newsletter form, signifying a trend for some laid-off sportswriters (Briggs, 2023; Strauss, 2020d). Both approaches are different than the standard do-it-yourself sports blogging era of the early 2000s since it has become easier for a writer to profit, even if it is a small monthly amount. As referenced in Chapter Three, Substack allows anyone with a specific interest to create an email newsletter that can support a paywall function, thus allowing the manager to earn potential revenue (Tracy, 2020). Substack's co-founder, Hamish McKenzie, notes that the platform accommodates writing talent not "well supported by the dominant media structure" (McKenzie, 2021, para. 7) because it adds increased job opportunities in a field that has suffered from financial setbacks exacerbated by the COVID-19 pandemic. Similarly, the corporate blogosphere of S.B. Nation allows fans to write fan posts as a media audition before slowly working toward a stipend-paid position (Kuehn & Corrigan, 2013). This enables those with a specific sports team interest to earn money (albeit insignificant) via a side job that functions through the hobbyist lens.

However, despite the increased editorial opportunities that new media entrants like Substack and S.B. Nation offer, personal financial stability in sports journalism has suffered because full-time positions are less readily available. The Arena Group, which owns *Sports Illustrated*, laid off nearly 40 editorial staffers when it purchased the magazine in October 2019 from publishing conglomerate Meredith (Strauss, 2020b). In February 2023, *Sports Illustrated* then laid off 17 employees (including editors) and was alleged (in November of that year) to have published product reviews under fake bylines accompanied by artificial intelligence-generated writer headshots in a report by Futurism (Harrison, 2023; Kludt, 2023). Another round of mass layoffs occurred in January 2024, with The Arena Group cutting "a majority of its workforce in what many see as the end of the publication" (Kraft, 2024, para. 4).

ESPN announced layoffs in November 2020 that cut positions for 300 total employees of the self-branded "worldwide leader in sports" (approximately six percent of its entire staff) because of both cord-cutting and COVID-19-related financial setbacks (Draper, 2020). It then laid off 20 additional sportscasters in a July 2023 cost-saving measure (Tapp, 2023). Even N.F.L. Media cut 132 positions in 2021 after it inked deals of "$1 billion with Amazon, $2.1 billion with CBS, $2.7 billion with ESPN, $2.2 billion with FOX, and $2 billion with NBC" in March of that year (Traina, 2021, para. 6).

Job opportunities exist in mainstream sports journalism. However, as illustrated above, job security in an ever-evolving landscape is not guaranteed—even when working for a notable or prestigious sports news outlet (Curtis, 2023; Robertson & Koblin, 2023). Substack, for instance, sells itself as an easy way for "writers to break away" despite a "fast-growing collection of competitors" existing (Hsu, 2022, para. 35). What is not as quickly transparent, though, is that the pay is often insufficient for one to sustain himself or herself without an added source of income. For instance, interviewees who had the Substack paywall in place made it clear that their ability to earn a livable income on the platform would not be possible if they did not already have an established reader base. This is because only a fraction of a loyal audience sees value in paying a nominal monthly fee for content (of note, approximately 5–10 percent of free Substack subscribers convert to paying subscribers; "A guide to paid subscriptions," n.d.).

S.B. Nation interviewees also clarified that sportswriting opportunities and financial stability are entirely different since the former is readily available and the latter is only available to a select few. This lack of economic opportunity manifests itself in writers and site managers being expected to constantly hit a content quota yet earning very little from their work. This is further evident by Vox Media's settling of a $4 million class-action lawsuit filed by 450 writers and site managers who claimed they were not fairly compensated for their work (Kelly, 2020). A few interviewees (notably Matthew Miranda, formerly of the New York Knicks blog *Posting and Toasting*) noted that S.B. Nation's corporate mentality emphasizes profit margins over writer well-being.

The opportunity bred by digital sports journalism represents a double-edged sword since it can benefit those looking for a platform yet also creates the false illusion that stable financial positions are readily available. From the perspective of more mainstream forms of sportswriting, the opportunity and economic prospects are more closely correlated. Therefore, the most stable position in digital sports journalism, Mirer (2019) writes, lies in team-run media. Of note, interviewees were not asked questions about their annual earnings, meaning there is no way to substantiate which path in written sports journalism is genuinely the most lucrative financially. A few S.B. Nation site managers did disclose this information without being prompted; however, the pay was only stipend form (according to a 2017 report by *Deadspin*, the last time data on this was made public, the typical S.B. Nation site manager received $600 per month, which also doubled as a budget to pay contributors; Wagner, 2017).

Further, the perception of a boundary in sports journalism is more dynamic since individuals can now supplement their name, work, and image on various platforms. A national example of this is Ken Rosenthal, the longtime Major League Baseball personality who writes a column for The Athletic while also working as a field reporter for M.L.B. on FOX (Futterman, 2023). Rosenthal, in this regard, effectively navigates his identity as both a broadcast and print journalist simultaneously. On a more local level of this cross-boundary navigation is Bob Sturm, The Athletic's former Dallas Cowboys writer, who was laid off in June 2023 in a shift that cut four percent of its newsroom (Perez, 2023). When The Athletic employed him, Sturm also worked as a radio personality in the Dallas-Fort Worth Metroplex—meaning he had two separate roles in sports journalism. Though a different type of media, the two often overlap in coverage, meaning Sturm had fluidity via this boundary since he could supplement his sportswriting earnings.

Concerning boundary navigation among hobbyist sportswriters, those who write a sports-centric Substack newsletter or manage an S.B. Nation fan community had mixed feelings regarding their professional identity. Although S.B. Nation brands itself as a fan blogging platform, there was disagreement regarding whether editorial staff considered themselves bloggers, journalists, or blogger-journalist hybrid. Whereas some S.B. Nation interviewees said their work aligns with the concept of sports blogging because the content is more observational than reporting-based, others wanted to distance themselves from the commonly held "blog" stereotype because the word can sometimes conjure a negative connotation. This is because blogging has typically been associated with spreading rumors and other unverified information (Hansell, 2008). Some S.B. Nation interviewees, therefore, said that labeling their fan community as a blog can detract from its built-up public credibility in sports journalism. However, as McEnnis (2015) illustrates, live bloggers retain a sense of core journalistic value by perceiving their professional identity as "community builders and mediators of discussion" (McEnnis, 2015, p. 967).

It is important to note that those who manage Substack newsletters were less interested in how their professional identity was categorized. The terms "writer" and "reporter" were both generally accepted by Substack interviewees, with only Kyle Devitte of the *Lacrocity* professional lacrosse newsletter having a label preference. Devitte said he does not view himself as a reporter—only a writer—since he is not breaking news or conducting interviews for his newsletter. All other Substack interviewees, however, considered themselves both writers and reporters. This may be because most Substack interviewees previously held paying positions within mainstream sports journalism (the only two who did not were Jordan Sperber of *Hoop Vision* and Tim Haslam of *Utah Lacrosse Report*). Even though these interviewees did not have source access, like Devitte suggested, having that former professional mindset may guide one's perception of him or herself within a new sports media platform.

This notion of a former professional sportswriter maintaining that mindset aligns with the take of team-employed reporters who were former print newspaper sportswriters. Having switched from legacy to new media, these individuals still perceive themselves as legitimate journalists, even though they can no longer report on controversial or breaking news (Mirer, 2022).

Despite not being tethered to the team's public relations department nor being branded as a PR staffer, the in-house reporters who are ex-print sportswriters still saw themselves as journalists (even though the definition of sports journalism is fluid; Perreault & Nölleke, 2022).

Market Adaptation Is Ongoing

At a surface level, the common saying, "complacency breeds contempt," may not seem like it has practical value in sports journalism since news outlets have been forced to adapt to Internet dissemination. In a way, this refutes their ability to even be complacent in the first place. However, if the current uphill battle of subscriber acquisition and retention has demonstrated anything, it is that news outlets unwilling to wither the storm of innovation are often left behind in the wake of disruption (Oelrichs, 2023; Rojas-Torrijos & Nölleke, 2023). Just because the niche enables coexistence does not mean outlets should become complacent under the assumption that they will survive simply by covering a team in a way that no one else does. Instead, as Pantic (2022) writes, news organizations should focus efforts on producing original content that fulfills a niche function. This is because it can be "among the main drivers of reader engagement, subscriptions, and donations to websites" (Christensen et al., 2001, p. 1736). Instead, interviewees reasoned that long-term stability is predicated on a willingness to stay ahead of, and not behind, the curve. Call it experimentation, origination, or adaptation. Whatever the case, interviewees said preparedness for change is an essential principle of modern sports journalism.

This mentality of trying to get ahead of the curve aligns with N.H.L. hall-of-famer Wayne Gretzky's famous quote: "Skate to where the puck is going, not where it's been" (Christensen et al., 2001). The goal in any industry is to be an innovator who can both recognize—and capitalize on—the next trend (Noice, 2015). This thinking, however, can sometimes spur mass migration, with smaller industry players chasing after their larger counterparts when the latter makes a move viewed as ground-breaking. When this occurs, most smaller outlets may not gravitate to where the puck will ultimately skirt. Instead, they will likely try to pick up clues from the more established sports journalism conglomerates and follow in their footsteps.

Sturm, The Athletic's Dallas Cowboys analytics writer laid off in 2023, said his former employer was one of the leading drivers of adaptation. For one, Sturm said that sports journalism as a whole, because of The Athletic's innovative approach, has been forced to improve reporting standards and pay higher salaries to retain editorial employees. This, in turn, made readers expect higher-quality reporting from all outlets. The phrase, "rising tides raise all boats," may seem overused. Still, this perspective fits modern sports journalism since journalistic innovators sometimes need to set the pace for everyone else (Strauss, 2020a). The Athletic's most significant impact on the market, though, has been reminding the sports-consuming public that quality reporting costs money and, thus, is worthy of a subscription. Sturm's take that his employer has normalized the sports journalism paywall is a bit ironic given that it was made one year before *The New York Times'* January 2022 acquisition of The Athletic.

However, innovation to keep pace with changing consumer demand is broader than newspaper sports departments and The Athletic. Part of market adaptation is knowing one's intended audience, and those in team-run media also mentioned that they have altered their reporting strategy to appeal to younger fans. Miami Heat manager of basketball content Couper Moorhead said his adaptation strategy is to have more of a personal social media presence to build community with the team's followers through relationship establishment. This shows the audience "there's a person behind what's going on" so they can better relate. In journalism, innovation is more than just being stuck in the repetitive cycle of daily news production. Instead, innovation can mark a news outlet's competitive advantage (Baregheh et al., 2009), which means that media must continually develop approaches to disruptive industry changes (see *The New York Times'* internal newsroom memo on innovation).

Sports Journalism's Future is Cemented, yet Precarious

Sports journalism will likely always exist in some form. However, the unknown is where sports journalism is headed and what the role of the sportswriter will be—mainly because of the impact of artificial intelligence. Although all interviewees were asked what the future of sports journalism holds, each response is speculative since no one knows the exact direction. The one commonality was that sportswriting will always exist because of fans' desire to stay informed. More specifically, newspaper interviewees speculated about the type of access teams will grant external journalists in the future. In journalism, relationship building is essential to telling impactful stories, and newspaper sportswriters are fearful that diminished locker room and interview access in the future will lead to a lesser product. Randy Miller, NJ.com's New York Yankees beat writer, said it is not far-fetched that U.S. sports media will eventually move toward a post-access approach to media relations, in which source access in an open locker room setting will be limited. If this is the case, he reasoned, legitimate journalists will not have as much of an edge over sports bloggers since access is the fundamental thing that helps to differ their coverage.

The uncertainty of sports media's future regarding interview access is a sentiment not just limited to those in newspaper sports journalism. For example, Tennessee Titans.com senior writer Jim Wyatt said he could also see a public relations department restrict future access to in-house reporters. From the journalistic perspective, it is no secret that sportswriters value a free-rein mentality regarding postgame locker room access (Glier, 2022; Han, 2022). He said players and coaches have gotten acclimated to not having media constantly present after a game because of the increased levels of privacy they are now afforded, though.

For a veteran sportswriter like Geoff Hobson, who spent nearly ten years covering the Cincinnati Bengals for local newspapers before writing for the team's official website, the question is not whether sports media will exist in the future (because of the public's insatiable desire for sports information, Hobson is confident that the overarching umbrella of sports media will always live). Instead, he said the three fundamental questions are:

(1) Will the public desire more video content in the future?
(2) Will sportswriters place more emphasis on social media?
(3) Will the written word be all but extinct in favor of multidimensional modes of storytelling?

Perhaps one reasonable take on Hobson's questions lies in Moritz's (2022) view of sports gambling's impact on journalism. Since the language of sports journalism "has always been deeply influenced by gambling" (para. 20), Moritz sees newsrooms devoting more resources toward pregame reports and roster news than feature reporting and human-interest-type journalism. This is because the mainstreaming of sports gambling after *Murphy v. N.C.A.A.* (the landmark 2018 Supreme Court case that paved the way for legalization) brought increased attention to sports information deemed valuable to betmaking (Diamond, 2023; Morais, 2023). In a way, if the future of sports journalism shifts to more of a basis of insider information (akin to what Adam Schefter and Adrian Wojnarowski deliver to social media followers), it can lead to a fundamental change that significantly impacts public perception of sportswriting. The audience ultimately determines the value of mediated sports content; if readers desire a shift in coverage routines toward information that helps with betting, then media may adhere to this ideal since it can mean more eyeballs on the content (Moritz, 2022; Rodriguez & Salao, 2022).

Although the lines between hard news and sports coverage have become somewhat blurred since the definition of what constitutes legitimate journalism has expanded, both types of reporting have similar overlap. From a theoretical standpoint, Shoemaker and Reese (1996) maintain that sports and news coverage are the same because the gatekeeping process of reporting (one that decides which news will be available for public consumption) does not shift based on attention. However, as evidenced by niche gratification and boundary work, the reporting approach is more interchangeable than previously thought. Although the journalistic requirement of publicizing newsworthy topics (based on impact, proximity, relevance, or timeliness) remains the same, the job routine is inherently different based on the nature of sourcing and reporting (i.e., the beat system). That is not to say that the beat system in the more traditionalist view of news is ineffective; however, maintaining source access in sports journalism is more critical than in other subsets of reporting, despite these relationships sometimes being tense (Mirer, 2023).

Another uncertainty regarding the future of sports journalism is whether more will be done to close the gender gap. Sports journalism remains a predominantly male field, which can impact the coverage women's sports receive in the typical news cycle. Despite small growth in the past few years, women still face barriers to entry. Lapchick's (2021b) Associated Press Sports Editors (A.P.S.E.) study on hiring diversity among member newsrooms did note a slight increase in sports journalistic roles, with women holding 36.3 percent of all positions. However, the sports media field still received a failing grade on its diversity hiring report card because a quarter of all female sports editors worked for ESPN, meaning that diversity was not as widespread among legacy news organizations (Lapchick, 2021b).

Chicago Sun-Times sportswriter Annie Costabile raised an interesting point regarding the lack of gendered representation in mainstream sports journalism. Costabile said that before college, she did not realize opportunity existed for women in sportswriting since there were few female sports to idolize growing up in the Chicago suburbs in the 1990s (aside from Melissa Isaacson, whom she said is a "legend in her own right"). Costabile, who covers the Chicago Sky (W.N.B.A.) and Red Stars (N.W.S.L.), was able to look at female sportscasters during this time and say, "I could do that" because of representation in terms of women working in broadcast news. Despite not being told that female sportswriters did exist, Costabile "just had it in my mind that sportswriting was a man's game. That's just this idea I had in my head—even in college." This thought, she noted, still sometimes persists when she is in certain situations with few other female reporters and is something that she has "actively gotten rid of."

This lack of mainstream representation sometimes dissuades women from entering sports journalism, which aligns with the other potential deterrents brought to light by Whiteside and Hardin (2013), who found that some of the barriers women face are either sexism and/or nontraditional hours that can take away from one's ability to raise a family. For ESPN producer Megan Flood, the atypical work schedule can answer the common question, "Why don't we see more female SportsCenter producers?" The standard hours (in this case, the "rigid" 5 a.m. to 2 p.m. shift) make it "a little harder to find female representation" among producers and production assistants for ESPN's live studio shows because the schedule is often not conducive to raising a family.

Industry Implications

This book uncovered five overlapping themes among various subsets of written sports journalism. For instance, it was revealed that interviewees did not perceive themselves as being in direct competition with other sportswriters covering the same beats. This was, interviewees said, because writing about a team in a slightly different manner than other outlets (thus targeting the niche) enables coexistence since the Internet exists to serve all types of sports fans and interests (Mahan & McDaniel, 2006). Although a few interviewees (most notably newspaper journalism veterans) did perceive direct competition with digital media for a localized sports audience, most saw their work catering to a different type of sports information niche. Substack and S.B. Nation interviewees viewed their work not as competition, but as a supplementary component to mainstream outlets.

Similarly, another finding was that interviewees rarely monitor the content of other outlets covering the same beats. The niche, they said, allows content offerings to be so distinct that there is no need to survey the editorial approach of others occupying the same space. Additionally, it was revealed that the ability for an entrepreneurial sportswriter to monetize his or her writing (no matter how small the revenue may be) has somewhat shifted the conventional power of the balance of sports journalism. A paid sportswriter, by definition, is no longer someone who must follow the typical career trajectory of working one's way up the corporate ladder. Instead, as evident by Substack and S.B. Nation, it is easier to generate income from sportswriting—assuming he or she has a significant following—based on these platforms (Strauss, 2020d).

It is a move that goes against the old guard's media view of what constitutes a gatekeeper since those who lack formalized training no longer have a barrier to entry into sports journalism. That is not to say that full-time sportswriters no longer influence sports conversations. However, the ability of alternative sports journalism approaches to net a market share (no matter how small, as illustrated by the long tail concept) demonstrates how the industry may slowly be moving toward content specialization instead of generalized coverage. There may be room at the table for sports media outlets that produce a slightly different form of content; nonetheless, carving a niche does not permit a sportswriter to disregard innovation by believing that he or she will always have an audience.

References

Anderson, C. (2004, October 1). The long tail. *Wired*. https://www.wired.com/2004/10/tail/

Arnold, K. (2018, January 22). *Retailers find niche success for brick-and-mortar shops as online sales grow*. The Orlando Sentinel. https://www.orlandosentinel.com/business/os-cfb-retail-brick-mortar-niche-20180122-story.html

Baregheh, A. Rowley, J., & Sambrook, S. (2009). Towards a multidisciplinary definition of innovation. *Management Decision, 47*(8), 1323–1339.

Bauder, D. (2023, November 16). *Decline in local news outlets is accelerating despite efforts to help*. Associated Press. https://apnews.com/article/local-newspapers-closing-jobs-3ad83659a6ee070ae3f39144dd840c1b

Boyle, R. (2017). Sports journalism: Changing journalism practice and digital media. *Digital Journalism, 5*(1), 493–495.

Briggs, J. (2023, July 21). *Sportswriter Bob Kravitz blasts The Athletic in a new newsletter*. AXIOS Indianapolis. https://www.axios.com/local/indianapolis/2023/07/21/sportswriter-bob-kravitz-the-athletic

Brynjolfsson, E., Hu, Y., & Smith, M. D. (2006). From niches to riches: The anatomy of the long tail. *Sloan Management Review, 47*(4), 67–71.

Butler, B., Zimmerman, M. H., & Hutton, S. (2013). Turning the page with newspapers: Influence of the Internet on sports coverage. In P. M. Pedersen (Eds.) *Routledge handbook of sport communication*. Routledge.

Buzzelli, N. R., Gentile, P. Billings, A. C., & Sadri, S. R. (2020). Poaching the news producers: The Athletic's effect on sports in hometown newspapers. *Journalism Studies, 21*(11), 1514–1530.

Buzzelli, N. R., Gentile, P., Sadri, S. R., & Billings, A. C. (2022). "Cutting editors faster than were cutting reporters": Influences of The Athletic on sports journalism quality and standards. *Communication & Sport, 10*(3), 417–437.

Carmody, T. (2011, May 23). *Both the short and long of it: How sportswriting is taking over the web through innovation and adaption.* NiemanLab. https://www.niemanlab.org/2011/05/both-the-short-and-long-of-it-how-sportswriting-is-taking-over-the-web-through-innovation-and-adaptation/

Choi, J. P., & Yang, S. (2021). Investigative journalism and media capture in the digital age. *Information Economics and Policy, 57.* https://doi.org/10.1016/j.infoecopol.2021.100942

Christensen, C., Raynor, M. E., & Verlinden, M. (2001). Skate to where the money will be. *Harvard Business Review.* https://hbr.org/2001/11/skate-to-where-the-money-will-be.

Curtis, C. (2023, July 31). *A list of the names and shows reportedly affected by ESPN layoffs.* For the Win. https://ftw.usatoday.com/lists/espn-layoffs-shows-names-2023

Diamond, J. (2023, September 20). Journalists have inside information. Gamblers may be trying to get it. *The Wall Street Journal.* https://www.wsj.com/sports/journalists-inside-information-gambling-4e560bc6

"Digital news fact sheet." (2023, November 10). *Pew Research Center.* https://www.pewresearch.org/journalism/fact-sheet/digital-news/

Dimmick, J. (2003). *Media competition and coexistence: The theory of the niche.* Lawrence Erlbaum.

Dimmick, J. (2006). Media competition and levels of analysis. In A. B. Albarran, S. M. Chan-Olmsted, & M. O. Wirth (Eds.), *Handbook of media management and economics.* Lawrence Erlbaum Associates.

Dimmick, J. W., Kline, S., & Stafford, L. (2000). The gratification niches of personal email and the telephone: Competition, displacement, and complementarity. *Communication Research, 27*(1), 227–248.

Draper, K. (2020, November 5). *ESPN to lay off 300 employees.* The New York Times. https://www.nytimes.com/2020/11/05/sports/espn-layoffs.html

Elejalde, E., Ferres, L., & Schifanella, R. (2019). Understanding news outlets' audience-targeting patterns. *EPJ Data Science, 8*(16), 1–20.

English, P. (2022). Sports newsrooms versus in-house media: Cheerleading and critical reporting in news and match coverage. *Communication & Sport, 10*(5), 854–871.

Ferrucci, P. (2022). Covering sports when there's no sports: COVID, market orientation, paywall, and the *Athletic. Newspaper Research Journal, 43*(4), 389–406.

Futterman, D. (2023, June 13). *Ken Rosenthal built a career on bowties and credibility.* Barrett Sports Media. https://barrettsportsmedia.com/2023/06/13/ken-rosenthal-bowties-and-credibility/

Galily, Y. (2018). Artificial intelligence and sports journalism: Is it a sweeping change? *Technology in Society, 54*(1–2), 1–5.

Gaskins, B., & Jerit, J. (2012). Internet news: Is it a replacement for traditional media outlets? *The International Journal of Press Politics, 17*(2), 190–213.

Gieryn, T. F. (1983). Boundary work and the demarcation of science from non-science: Strains and interests in professional ideologies of scientists. *American Sociological Review*, 48(1), 781–795.

Gieryn, T. F. (1999). *Cultural boundaries of science*. University of Chicago Press.

Glier, R. (2022, July 21). *Passing gas, building bridges: Why sports journalism is stronger and better with locker room access*. Global Sport Matters. https://globalsportmatters.com/culture/2022/07/21/why-sports-journalism-stronger-better-locker-room-access/

Graves, L., & Konieczna, M. (2015). Sharing the news: Journalistic collaboration as field repair. *International Journal of Communication*, 9(1), 1966–1984.

"A guide to paid subscriptions." (n.d.). *Substack*. https://substack.com/going-paid-guide

Hardin, M., Zhong, B., & Whiteside, E. (2009). Sports coverage: "Toy department" or public service journalism? The relationship between reporters' ethics and attitudes towards the profession. *International Journal of Sports Communication*, 2(1), 319–339.

Harrison, M. (2023, November 27). *Sports Illustrated published articles by fake, AI-generated writers*. Futurism. https://futurism.com/sports-illustrated-ai-generated-writers

Han, N. (2022, June 15). *As pandemic continues, locker room access a concern*. Sports Journalism Institute. https://www.sportsjournalisminstitute.org/latest-news/a-return-to-locker-room-access-is-slow-to-return-as-the-pandemic-continues

Hansell, S. (2008, March 16). *What I've learned as a blogger for The New York Times*. The New York Times. https://archive.nytimes.com/bits.blogs.nytimes.com/2008/03/16/what-ive-learned-as-a-blogger-for-the-new-york-times/

"How digital media has changed sports journalism." (2021, March 16). *St. Bonaventure University Online*. https://online.sbu.edu/news/sports-journalism

Hsu, T. (2022, April 14). *Substack's growth spurt brings growing pains*. The New York Times. https://www.nytimes.com/2022/04/13/business/media/substack-growth-newsletters.html

Kelly, K. J. (2020, August 19). *Vox Media agrees to $4M settlement with SB Nation writers*. New York Post. https://nypost.com/2020/08/19/vox-media-agrees-to-4m-settlement-with-sb-nation-writers/

Kleineberg, K., & Boguñá, M. (2015). Digital ecology: Coexistence and domination among interacting networks. *Scientific Reports*. https://www.nature.com/articles/srep10268

Kludt, T. (2023, December 20). *"The worst that it's ever been": Inside Sports Illustrated's winter of discontent*. Vanity Fair. https://www.vanityfair.com/news/sports-illustrated-future

Kraft, N. (2024, January 21). Mass layoff appears to be the end of Sports Illustrated. Forbes. https://www.forbes.com/sites/nicolekraft/2024/01/21/mass-layoff-appears-to-be-the-end-of-sports-illustrated/?sh=378c719f75e5

Kuehn, K., & Corrigan, T. (2013). Hope labor: The role of employment prospects in online social production. *The Political Economy of Communication*, 1(1), 9–25.

Lapchick, R. (2021b). *The 2021 Associated Press Sports Editors racial and gender report card*. Tides: The Institute for Diversity and Ethics in Sport. https://43530132-36e9-4f52-811a-182c7a91933b.filesusr.com/ugd/8af738_b1530694d56142cc8a684649497f4746.pdf

Levin, H. J. (1954). Competition among mass media and the public interest. *The Public Opinion Quarterly*, 18(1), 62–79.

Lowrey, W., & Woo, C. W. (2010). The news organization in uncertain times: Business or institution? *Journalism & Mass Communication Quarterly, 87*(1), 41–61.

Mahan, J. E., & McDaniel, S. R. (2006). The new online arena: Sport, marketing, and media convergence in cyberspace. In A. A. Raney & J. Bryant (Eds.) *Handbook of sports and media* (pp. 443–469). Taylor & Francis.

Mathewson, T. J. (2019, March 7). *TV is the biggest driver in global sport league revenue.* Global Sport Matters. https://globalsportmatters.com/business/2019/03/07/tv-is-biggest-driver-in-global-sport-league-revenue/

McCarthy, B. (2014). A sports journalism of their own: An investigation into the motivations, behaviors, and media attitudes of fan sports bloggers. *Communication & Sport, 2*(1), 65–79.

McCollough, J. B. (2018, October 9). *Sports journalists battle for relevancy.* NiemanReports. https://niemanreports.org/articles/sports-journalists-battle-for-relevancy/.

McEnnis, S. (2015). Following the action: How live bloggers are reimagining the professional ideology of sports journalism. *Journalism Practice, 10*(8), 967–982.

McKenzie, H. (2021, May 13). *Growing the pie for writers.* Substack. https://on.substack.com/p/growing-the-pie-for-writers?utm_source=url

Mirer, M. (2019). Playing the right way: In-house sports reporters and media ethics as boundary work. *Journal of Media Ethics, 34*(2), 73–86.

Mirer, M. (2022). Just how they drew it up: How in-house reporters fit themselves into the sports media system. *Communication & Sport, 10*(3), 438–455.

Mirer, M. (2023). "The media answer": How athletes conceptualize their relationship to the press in the Players' Tribune. *Communication & Sport.* https://doi.org/10.1177/2167479523 1217169

Morais, B. (2023, August 18). ESPN's big gamble. *Columbia Journalism Review.* https://www.cjr.org/the_media_today/espn_penn_sports_betting.php

Moritz, B. (2022, January 11). *What happens to sports media when everyone is a gambler?* Global Sport Matters. https://globalsportmatters.com/business/2022/01/11/what-happens-sports-media-sports-betting/

Noice, M. (2015, November 24). *5 ways to spot and capitalize on trends.* Entrepreneur. https://www.entrepreneur.com/growing-a-business/5-ways-to-spot-and-capitalize-on-trends/253101

O'Boyle, N., & Gallagher, A. (2023). Sports organizations and their defensive mediatization strategies: The sports journalist's perspective. *Journalism and Media, 4*(1), 665–678.

Oelrichs, I. (2023). Adoption of innovations in digital sports journalism: The use of Twitter by German sports journalists. *Communication & Sport, 11*(2), 288–312.

Pantic, M. (2022). Local media in a digital market: Establishing niche and promoting original reporting to ensure sustainability. *Journalism Practice, 16*(8), 1736–1752.

Perez, A. J. (2023, June 12). *The Athletic lays off 20 journalists in reorganization.* Front Office Sports. https://frontofficesports.com/the-athletic-lays-off-20-journalists-in-reorganization/

Perreault, G., & Bell, T. R. (2022). Towards a "digital" sports journalism: Field theory, changing boundaries and evolving technologies. *Communication & Sport, 10*(3), 398–416.

Perreault, G., & Nölleke, D. (2022). What is sports journalism? How COVID-19 accelerated a redefining of U.S. sports reporting. *Journalism Studies, 23*(14), 1860–1879.

Pittz, T., Bendickson, J. S., Cowden, B. J., & Davis, P. E. (2021). Sport business models: A stakeholder optimization approach. *Journal of Small Business and Enterprise Development*, 28(1), 134–147.

Plambeck, J. (2010, June 6). *Sports-centric web sites expand, and bias is welcome*. The New York Times. https://www.nytimes.com/2010/06/07/business/media/07fans.html

"The power play: How sport captivates mass and niche audiences alike." (2023, May 25). *PRWeek*. https://www.prweek.com/article/1823971/power-play-sport-captivates-mass-niche-audiences-alike

Quattrociocchi, W., Caldarelli, G., & Scala, A. (2014). Opinion dynamics on interacting networks: Media competition and social influence. *Scientific Reports*. https://www.ncbi.nlm.nih.gov/pmc/articles/PMC4033925/

Radcliffe, D., & Wallace, R. (2021, October 7). *Life at local newspapers in a turbulent era: Findings from a survey of more than 300 newsroom employees in the United States*. Tow Center for Digital Journalism. https://www.cjr.org/tow_center_reports/life-at-local-newspapers-in-a-turbulent-era-findings-from-a-survey-of-more-than-300-newsroom-employees-in-the-united-states.php

Robertson, K., & Koblin, J. (2023, July 10). *The New York Times to disband its sports department*. The New York Times. https://www.nytimes.com/2023/07/10/business/media/the-new-york-times-sports-department.html

Rodriguez, A., & Salao, C. (2022, December 26). *How sports betting is changing the media industry*. Business Insider. https://www.businessinsider.com/how-us-sports-betting-is-changing-media-companies-partnerships-ma-2021-12

Rojas-Torrijos, J. L., & Nölleke, D. (2023). Rethinking sports journalism. *Journalism & Media*, 4(3), 853–860. https://doi.org/10.1177/21674795231217169

Ryan, T. J. (2023, July 6). *EXEC: Deloitte study finds sports fandom getting more immersive*. SGB Media. https://sgbonline.com/exec-deloitte-study-find-sports-fandom-getting-more-immersive/

Schroeder, B. (2021, December 29). As a startup or small business, don't sell to everyone—Do what Whole Foods, Gatorade and Volcom did. *Forbes*. https://www.forbes.com/sites/bernhardschroeder/2021/12/29/as-a-startup-or-small-business-dont-sell-to-everyone--do-what-whole-foods-gatorade-and-volcom-did/?sh=deff15c34dba

Shoemaker, P. J., & Reese, S. D. (1996). *Mediating the message: Theories of influences on mass media content*. Longman.

Storace, B. (2022, May 23). Amid news industry struggles, CT's media landscape faces significant changes. *Hartford Business Journal*. https://www.hartfordbusiness.com/article/amid-news-industry-struggles-cts-media-landscape-faces-significant-changes

Strauss, B. (2020a, March 4). *Sportswriting's future may depend on the Athletic, which is either reassuring or terrifying*. The Washington Post. http://www.washingtonpost.com/sports/2020/03/03/the-athletic-sports-media-future/

Strauss, B. (2020b, March 30). *Sports Illustrated endures another round of layoffs, this time prompted by the coronavirus*. The Washington Post. https://www.washingtonpost.com/sports/2020/03/30/sports-illustrated-endures-another-round-layoffs-this-time-prompted-by-coronavirus/

Strauss, B. (2020c, April 17). *SB Nation faces murky future after Vox Media furloughs national writers for three months*. The Washington Post. https://www.washingtonpost.com/sports/2020/04/17/sb-nation-faces-murky-future-after-vox-media-furloughs-national-writers-three-months/

Strauss, B. (2020d, June 1). *Out-of-work sportswriters are turning to newsletters, hoping the economics can work*. The Washington Post. https://www.washingtonpost.com/sports/2020/06/01/out-of-work-sportswriters-are-turning-newsletters-hoping-economics-can-work/

Tapp, T. (2023, July 31). *ESPN layoffs: Here's updated the list of on-air talent who were let go*. Deadline. https://deadline.com/2023/07/espn-layoffs-list-talent-fired-1235428485/

Tracy, M. (2020, September 23). *Journalists are leaving the noisy Internet for your email inbox*. The New York Times. https://www.nytimes.com/2020/09/23/business/media/substack-newsletters-journalists.html

Traina, J. (2021, July 15). NFL inks massive TV deals, promptly undergoes round of layoffs: Traina thoughts. *Sports Illustrated*. https://www.si.com/extra-mustard/2021/07/15/nfl-media-undergoes-massive-layoffs

Wagner, L. (2017, August 14). *How SB Nation profits off an army of exploited workers*. Deadspin. https://deadspin.com/how-sb-nation-profits-off-an-army-of-exploited-workers-1797653841

Wenger, D., & Owens, L. C. (2013). An examination of job skills required by top U.S. broadcast news companies and potential impact on journalism curricula. *Electronic News, 7*(1), 22–35.

Whiteside, E., & Hardin, M. (2013). The glass ceiling and beyond. Tracing the explanations for women's lack of power in sports journalism. In P. M. Pedersen's (Ed.) *Routledge handbook of sport communication*. Routledge.

APPENDIX A

LIST OF INTERVIEWEES

Note: Each interviewee's job title/news outlet affiliation at the time of the interview is listed.

Name, job title, and news outlet affiliation of newspaper interviewees

Name	Job title	News outlet
Joe Baird**	Sports editor	*Salt Lake Tribune*
Paul Barrett	Sports editor	*Seattle Times*
Bill Bilinski**	Sports editor	*South Bend Tribune* (IN)
Chris Carr	Sports editor	*Star Tribune* (Minneapolis, MN)
Annie Costabile	Beat reporter (Chicago Sky/ Red Stars)	*Chicago Sun-Times*
Bud Geracie	Executive sports editor	*Bay Area News Group*
Ryan Gorcey*	Sports editor	*San Francisco Examiner*
Bill Hartlep	Sports editor	*Tribune-Review* (Greensburg, PA)

Name	Job title	News outlet
Jason Hoffman	Senior sports editor	*Cincinnati Enquirer*
Tom Housenick	Senior sports reporter	*The Morning Call* (Allentown, PA)
Amie Just	Sports columnist	*Lincoln Journal Star* (NE)
Ainslie Lee	Beat reporter (Auburn)	*AL.com*
Kevin Manahan	Sports director	*NJ.com*
Randy Miller	Beat reporter (New York Yankees)	*NJ.com*
Josh Moore*	Beat reporter (Kentucky football)	*Lexington Herald-Leader* (KY)
Tom Moore	Executive sports editor	*Southern California News Group*
Hunter Paniagua*	Digital sports coordinator	*Omaha World-Herald* (NE)
Matt Pepin	Sports editor	*The Boston Globe*
Michael Peters*	Sports editor	*Tulsa World*
Chloe Petersen	Trending sports reporter	*The Indianapolis Star*
Michael Phillips*	Sports editor	*Richmond Times-Dispatch*
Greg Pickel*	Beat reporter (Penn State football)	*Patriot-News* (Harrisburg, PA)
Ben Pope	Beat reporter (Chicago Blackhawks)	*Chicago Sun-Times*
Jay Posner**	Sports editor	*San Diego Union-Tribune*
Lori Riley	Reporter (high school sports)	*Hartford Courant*
Shannon Ryan*	Reporter (college sports)	*Chicago Tribune*
Mirjam Swanson	Sports columnist	Southern California News Group
John Talty*	Sports editor	*AL.com*

Name	Job title	News outlet
Jenny Vrentas	Reporter (enterprise/ investigations)	*The New York Times*
Mike Waters	Beat reporter (Syracuse basketball)	*Syracuse.com*

**No longer in his/her listed position
**Retired

Name, job title, and team affiliation of in-house media interviewees

Name	Job title	Team
Jill Beckman	Social media specialist	Tampa Bay Buccaneers
Jon Boyle	Senior reporter	Seattle Seahawks
Anthony DiComo	M.L.B.com beat writer	New York Mets
Jim Eichenhofer	Writer	New Orleans Pelicans
Michael Eisen	Senior writer/editor	New York Giants
David Helman*	Staff writer	Dallas Cowboys
Geoff Hobson	Senior writer	Cincinnati Bengals
Casey Holdahl	Digital reporter	Portland Trailblazers
Briana McDonald	Digital media coordinator	San Francisco 49ers
Couper Moorhead	Manager of content	Miami Heat
Jon Oehser	Senior writer	Jacksonville Jaguars
Mike Petriello	Writer/stats analyst	M.L.B.com
Myles Simmons	Senior writer	Carolina Panthers
Matthew Tabeek*	Digital managing editor	Atlanta Falcons
Darren Urban	Director of editorial content	Arizona Cardinals
Jim Wyatt	Senior writer/editor	Tennessee Titans
Lindsay Young	Staff writer/editor	Minnesota Vikings

**No longer in his/her listed position

Name, job title, and primary beat of Athletic interviewees

Name	Job title	Beat
Nicole Auerbach*	Senior writer	The Athletic CFB
Andrew Baggarly	Staff writer	San Francisco Giants
Dan Brown	Staff writer/editor	The Athletic M.L.B.
Zach Buchanan*	Staff writer	Arizona Diamondbacks
Scott Dochterman	Staff writer	University of Iowa
Seth Emerson	Senior writer	University of Georgia
James Fegan*	Staff writer	Chicago White Sox
Matt Gelb	Senior writer	Philadelphia Phillies
Jeff Howe	National insider	The Athletic N.F.L.
Chad Jennings	Staff writer	Boston Red Sox
Josh Kendall	Staff writer	Atlanta Falcons
Stewart Mandel	Editor-in-chief	The Athletic CFB
Brendan Marks	Staff writer	UNC/Duke basketball
Tori McElhaney*	Staff writer	Atlanta Falcons
Austin Meek	Staff writer	University of Michigan
Law Murray	Staff writer	Los Angeles Clippers
Fluto Shinzawa	Senior writer	Boston Bruins
Daniel Shirley	Senior editor	The Athletic CFB
Audrey Snyder	Staff writer	Penn State football
Bob Sturm*	Staff writer	Dallas Cowboys
Joe Vardon	Senior writer	The Athletic N.B.A.

*No longer in his/her listed position

Name and newsletter title/focus of Substack interviewees

Name	Newsletter	Focus
Matt Brown	Extra Points	Business of college sports
Craig Calcaterra	Cup of Coffee	Morning M.L.B. commentary
Kyle Devitte	Lacrocity	Professional lacrosse

Name	Newsletter	Focus
Jared Dubin	Last Night, in Basketball	N.B.A. coverage
Kelly Dwyer	The Second Arrangement	N.B.A. and pop culture
Justin Ferguson	Auburn Observer	Auburn football/basketball
Tim Haslam	Utah Lacrosse Report	Utah high school lacrosse news
Matthew Kory	Sox Outsider	Boston Red Sox analysis
Eric Nusbaum	Sports Stories	Sports culture
Jordan Sperber	Hoop Vision	Basketball film breakdown
Michael Weinreb	Throwbacks	Sports, history, and culture

Name, job title, and blog affiliation SB Nation *interviewees*

Name	Job title	Blog
James Atwood	Writer	AZ Snakepit
Kyle Barber	Managing editor	Baltimore Beatdown
Mark Brown	Manager/editor-in-chief	Camden Chat
John Butchko	Editor	Gang Green Nation
Eric Cole*	Deputy manager	Talking Chop
Matt Collins*	Managing editor	Over the Monster
Sean Corp	Managing editor	Detroit Bad Boys
Evan Dammarell*	Editor	Fear the Sword
Riley Feldman	Staff editor	Brew Hoops
Christopher Gates	Lead writer	The Daily Norseman
Andrew Mearns	Managing editor	Pinstripe Alley
Matthew Miranda*	Editor	Posting and Toasting
Joe Mullinax*	Site manager	Grizzly Bear Blues
R.J. Ochoa**	Manager	Blogging the Boys

Name	Job title	Blog
Max Reiper	Editor-in-chief	Royals Review
Evan Western	Managing editor	Acme Packing Company
Al Yellon**	Managing editor	Bleed Cubbie Blue

*No longer in his/her listed position
**Position with SB Nation constitute full-time, salaried work (all others are officially labeled as stipend-paid contractors)

Name, job title, and news outlet affiliation of misc. interviewees

Name	Job title	News outlet
Ross Dellenger*	National CFB writer	*Sports Illustrated*
Megan Flood	Associate producer	ESPN
Daniel Libit	Sports investigative reporter	Sportico
Jon Solomon	Editorial director (Sport & Society program)	The Aspen Institute

*No longer in his/her listed position

APPENDIX B
GLOSSARY OF TERMS

Agenda-setting: The process by which media outlets influence the importance and salience of issues by highlighting certain topics, thereby shaping public perception and discussion.

The Athletic: A subscription-based sports media platform offering in-depth and ad-free sports coverage.

Beat writer: A journalist assigned to cover a specific sports beat, such as a particular team, league, or type of sport.

Boosterism: The practice of excessively promoting or advocating for a team, athlete, or sport, often by media outlets with a vested interest in the success of the subject.

Box score: A statistical summary of a sports game, typically presented in a tabular format and providing details such as scores, player performances, and key statistics.

Byline: The name of the author credited for a particular article or piece of journalism, typically appearing at the beginning or end of the content.

Diffusion of innovations (DOI): A theory explaining how new ideas, practices, or technologies spread within a society or social group over time.

Digital media: Media content distributed and consumed through digital platforms, such as websites, social media, podcasts, and online publications.

Furlough: A temporary leave of absence from work, often without pay, due to economic challenges or other organizational reasons.

Game recap: A journalistic piece summarizing and analyzing the key events and highlights of a sports game.

In-house sports media: Media outlets directly affiliated with a sports team or organization, often providing coverage from a biased or promotional perspective.

The Institute for Diversity and Ethics in Sport (T.I.D.E.S.): A research arm of the University of Central Florida, founded by Dr. Richard Lapchick, that examines issues related to gender and race in sports media by publishing yearly report cards.

Interpretive communities: Groups of individuals who share similar interpretations and understandings of cultural texts, such as sports journalism.

Journalistic access: The level of permission granted by sports organizations or individuals to journalists for attending events, conducting interviews, and gathering information.

Journalistic boundary work: The process by which journalists define and maintain professional boundaries, often in relation to public relations and promotional activities.

Journalistic gatekeeping: The power and influence journalists have in deciding which stories are covered and how they are presented to the audience.

Live sports broadcast: Real-time broadcasting of sports events, often including commentary, analysis, and visual coverage.

Media availability: The designated times when athletes, coaches, or other sports figures are accessible to the media for interviews and interactions.

Media credential: Official permission granted to journalists, photographers, or other media personnel to access and cover a sports event.

Media pundit: An expert commentator or analyst in the media, providing opinions and insights on sports-related topics.

Media relations: The interaction between media professionals and sports organizations, often managed by dedicated personnel responsible for facilitating communication.

Multimedia: Content that incorporates a combination of different media forms, such as text, images, audio, and video.

News paywall: A barrier that restricts access to certain news content online, requiring payment or subscription to view.

Niche gratification theory (NGT): A theory explaining how media content caters to specific interests and preferences of niche audiences.

Nuts-and-bolts sportswriting: Detailed and factual sports journalism that focuses on the essential elements of a game or event.

Podcast: A digital audio or video file available for streaming or download, often featuring discussions, interviews, or storytelling related to sports.

Press conference: A formal gathering where sports figures address the media, answering questions and providing information.

Press release: An official statement or document issued by a sports organization or individual to communicate information to the media.

Qualitative research: Research methods focused on understanding the nuances and complexities of human experiences, often through interviews, observations, or content analysis.

Reporting scoop: Breaking news or exclusive information obtained by a journalist before other media outlets.

SB Nation: A sports blogging network and media company that covers various sports topics with a fan-centric approach.

Semi-structured interviewing: An interviewing technique that combines open-ended questions with a predetermined structure, allowing for flexibility and depth in responses.

Sports beat: The specific area or topic assigned to a journalist for coverage, such as a particular sport, team, or league.

Sports blogger: A writer who creates content, often in a personal and opinionated style, on a blog platform focusing on sports topics.

Sportscaster: A broadcaster or commentator who provides play-by-play or analysis during sports broadcasts.

Sports columnist: A journalist who writes regular opinion pieces or columns on sports topics.

Sports editor: An editor responsible for overseeing and managing sports coverage within a media organization.

Sports feature writing: Journalistic pieces that go beyond reporting facts to provide in-depth analysis, storytelling, and perspective on sports topics.

Sports notebook story: A brief, often collection of notes or observations compiled by a sports journalist covering various aspects of a game or event.

Sports play-by-play: A detailed, chronological description of the events happening in a sports game, typically delivered in real-time during a broadcast.

Subcontractor: An individual or organization hired by a media outlet to provide specific services or content, often on a freelance basis.

Subscription news: A model where users pay for access to news content, often in the form of digital subscriptions.

Substack: A platform that allows writers to create and distribute subscription-based newsletters.

"Toy department" moniker: A colloquial term referring to the sports section of a media outlet, often implying that sports coverage is less serious or important than other news.

Uses and gratification (U&G): A communication theory that explores how audiences actively choose media content based on their needs, desires, and gratifications

INDEX

Accel Partners 124

Acme Packing Company 130, 176

Advance Publications 62, 76

AL.com 91, 172

Amazon 153, 157

American Airlines Center 40

American City Business Journals 101

American Football Conference (A.F.C.) 30

American League (A.L.) 122

American University 136

Antetokounmpo, Giannis 128–129

AOL 123–124

Arizona Cardinals 30–31, 152, 173

Arizona Diamondbacks 60, 174

Athletics Nation 122–123, 125–126, 142

Atkin, Emily 85

Atlanta Falcons 41–42, 60–61, 155, 173–174

Atlantic Coast Conference (A.C.C.) 55

Auburn Observer 92, 151, 153, 175

Auburn University 91–93, 100, 151, 173

Auerbach, Nicole 54–55, 174

Axios 50

Baggarly, Andrew 1, 3, 63–66, 174

Baltimore Orioles 142

Bankoff, Jim 120, 123–124

Barber, Kyle 175

Barber, Phil 3

Baseball Prospectus 96

Beaver Stadium 67

Beckham, Odell, Jr. 39

Beckman, Jill 28, 44–45, 173

Bedard, Greg 88, 110

Beehiiv 101

Best, Chris 90, 94

Bleed Cubbie Blue 123, 176

Bleszinski, Tyler 119, 122–123, 125–126, 142

Blog Maverick 40

BlogSpot 88

Blogging the Boys 133–134, 138, 175

Boosterism 13, 66, 177

Boston Bruins 64, 174

Boston Herald 65, 71

Boston Red Sox 65–66, 96–100, 151, 174–175 88, 110

Bowden, Jim 55
Boyle, John 43–44, 155, 173
Braccia, Andrew 124
Brady, Tom 45
Brew Hoop 128–129, 175
Brisbee, Grant 66, 120
Brown, Dan 59–60, 174
Brown, Mark 142, 175
Brown, Matt 91, 101, 174
Brown, Mike 25–27
Brown, Paul 25
Butchko, John 126–130, 175
Buzzfeed 105

Cageside Seats 124
Calcaterra, Craig 88–91, 93–94, 96, 100,
    104, 152–153, 174
Camden Chat 142, 175
Carolina Panthers 34, 173
CBS 157
Chadwick, Henry 4
Charlotte Observer 58
Cheers 126, 128
Chicago Bears 123
Chicago Cubs 56, 122
Chicago Red Stars 163, 171
Chicago Sun-Times 67, 163, 171
Chicago Tribune 12, 172
Chicago White Sox 56, 67, 174
Cincinnati Bengals 25–27, 39, 162, 173
Cincinnati Enquirer 25–26, 172
Cincinnati Reds 57, 123
City Year 75
Clemson University 60
ClipperBlog 75
CollegeLax.US 106
Comcast Interactive Capital 124
Common Sense 85
Computer-assisted reporting 11
Corp, Sean 135–137, 175
Costabile, Annie 163–164, 171
COVID-19 7–8, 11, 35, 39, 61, 66, 68, 70,
    89, 91, 101, 105, 108, 111, 117, 124,
    139, 157

Cream City Central 129
Cuban, Mark 40–41
Cup of Coffee 88, 91, 96, 152, 174

Daily Kos 122
Daily Memphian 132
Daily Norseman 175
Dallas Cowboys 37–38, 73–74, 133–134,
    158–159, 173
Dallas Mavericks 40–41
Data journalism 11
Davis, Seth 55
Deadspin 141, 158
Deloitte Sports Fan Insight survey 153
Detroit Bad Boys 136–137, 175
Detroit Pistons 136–137
Devitte, Kyle 100–102, 106, 110, 159, 174
Devitte matrix 101
DiComo, Anthony 28, 43, 173
Diffusion of innovations (D.O.I.) 3, 10–11,
    85–86, 147, 177
Disney+ 71, 97
D.K. Pittsburgh Sports 88, 110
Dochterman, Scott 72–74, 174
Doyle, Jude Ellison Sady 85, 90
D Rays Bay 123
Dubin, Jared 104, 175
Duke University 57–58, 174

East Valley Tribune 31
Eichenhofer, Jim 42–43, 173
Eisen, Michael 26–28, 37, 39–41, 173
Emergent thematic analysis 17, 52
ESPN+ 70
ESPN 16, 29–30, 32, 54–55, 58, 70, 75, 89,
    120, 136, 156–157, 163–164, 176
ESPN.com 54–55
ESPN Insider 29, 120
ESPN The Magazine 54
Extra Points 91, 101, 174

Facebook 5, 99, 124, 133
FanNation 118
FanSided 118, 129–130, 155

Fegan, James 67, 174
Feldman, Bruce 54
Feldman, Riley 128–130, 175
Ferguson, Justin 91–94, 96, 100, 104, 151,
    153, 175
Fichtenbaum, Paul 54
Flood, Megan 16, 164, 176
Florio, Mike 34, 88
Fordham University 27
Fortuna, Matt 54
FOX Sports 38, 53–54, 58, 120, 157–158
Franklin, James 67
Front Office Sports 41, 141
Futurism 157

Game recap 4, 7, 27, 30, 41, 44, 65–66,
    106, 136–137, 155, 178
Gang Green Nation 126–127, 175
Gannett, 30, 62, 76, 120
Gates, Christopher 123, 175
Gen Z 71, 153
Georgian Tech 61
Geracie, Bud 1–3, 155, 171
Ghost (newsletter platform) 72, 101
Gibbs, Lindsey 15, 85
Golden age of sportswriting 42
Golden State Warriors 1
Google 5, 124, 135
Gretzky, Wayne 160
Grizzly Bear Blues 131–132, 140, 175
Gronkowski, Rob 45
GSPN 129

Halprin, David 133
Hansmann, Adam 1–2, 12, 49–51, 53–54,
    56, 63, 70, 72, 77
Hartford Courant 150, 172
Haslam, Tim 106–109, 120, 151, 159, 175
Heated 85
Helman, David 37–38, 173
Hobson, Geoff 25–28, 37, 39, 41, 162, 173
Holdahl, Casey 36, 173
Hoop Vision 92–94 159, 174
Horowitz, Jamie 54

Houston Astros 60
Howe, Jeff 71–72, 174
Hulu 71

Indianapolis Colts 2, 32–33
In-group 118
Inside Lacrosse 100–101
InTheCrease.com 125
I.R.B. 16

Jacksonville Inside Report 26
Jacksonville Jaguars 26, 32–33, 152, 173
Japers' Rink 125
Jennings, Chad 65–67, 174
Jennings, Chantel 54
Journalistic boundary work 3, 12–13, 28,
    44–45, 147, 151–152, 156, 163, 178
Journalistic gatekeeping 3, 8, 9, 14, 28, 99,
    103, 109, 125, 129, 137, 147, 149, 152–
    153, 163, 165, 178

Kansas City Royals 60
Kawakami, Tim 1–3, 60
Kelly, Craig 32
Ketchman, Vic 26
Khosla Ventures 124
Kory, Matthew 96–100, 110, 151, 175
Kovacevic, Dejan 88, 110
Kravitz, Bob 2

Lacrocity 100–102, 159, 174
Land of 10 72
Last Night, in Basketball 104, 175
Las Vegas Raiders 34
Las Vegas Review-Journal 34
Lee, Gregory 75
Lineback 84
Locked on Sports 118, 132
Lookout Landing 123
Los Angeles Clippers 75, 174
Los Angeles Rams 34

Mailchimp 89, 92, 106–107
Mandel, Stewart 53–56, 174

Manning, Eli 39
Manning, Peyton 32
MapQuest 123
Mara, John 26–27
Marks, Brendan 57–59, 174
Mather, Alex 1–3, 12, 49–54, 56, 63, 68,
    70, 72, 76
Max (HBO) 71, 97
McCaffrey, Jen 66
McCovey Chronicles 120, 123
McDonald, Briana 34, 173
McElhaney, Tori 60–62, 174
McKenzie, Hamish 84, 90, 94, 101, 105,
    156, 157
Mearns, Andrew 134–135, 139, 175
Media relations 7, 12, 26, 31, 36–37, 39–
    40, 162, 179
Media scrum 8
Medill School of Journalism 53
Mercury News 1–3, 11, 59, 63–64
Miami Heat 161, 173
Millennial 41, 153
Miller, Randy 162, 172
Milwaukee Brewers, 60
Milwaukee Bucks 128–129
Minnesota Vikings 36–37, 123, 173
Miranda, Matthew 138–140, 142, 158,
    175
M.L.B. Advance Media 28, 43
M.L.B. on FOX 158
M.L.S. 125
M.M.A. 124
Monda Center 36
Montgomery Advertiser (AL) 91
Moorhead, Couper 161, 173
Moulitsas, Markos 122–123
Moviefone 123
Mullinax, Joe 131–133, 135, 140–141, 175
Murphy v. N.C.A.A 162
Murray, Law 74–75, 174

Napster 71
National Association of Black Journalists
    (N.A.B.J.) 75

N.B.A. 1, 28–29, 40, 42–43, 52, 59, 71,
    75, 95, 104, 124–125, 128–129, 138–
    140, 175
N.B.C. 126, 157
N.B.C. Sports 34, 54, 58, 88–89, 90–91,
    152–153
N.C.A.A. 55, 106
N.C.A.A. Tournament 55
Netflix 57, 70–71, 97
New England Lacrosse Journal 100–101
New England Sports Net 71
New Orleans Jazz 42
New Orleans Pelicans 42, 173
New York Daily News 75
New York Giants 26–27, 39
New York Jets 126–127
New York Knicks 138–140, 158
New York Mets 28, 53, 173
New York Yankees 65, 134–135, 162, 172
N.F.L. Network 30
Niche gratification theory (N.G.T.) 3, 9–
    10, 52, 62, 68, 147–148, 151, 163, 179
NJ.com 162, 172
Northwestern University 53
Nusbaum, Eric 103–105, 108–109, 120, 175
N.W.S.L. 163

Oakland Athletics 2, 119, 122
Ochoa, R.J. 133–135, 138, 175
Oehser, John 32–33, 152, 173
Olson, Max 54
O'Neil, Dana 55
Opelika-Auburn News (AL) 91
Orange County Register (CA) 122

PandoDaily 84
Pasquarelli, Len 32
Patreon 89, 139
Paywall 11–12, 18, 49–50, 52–53, 54, 69–
    72, 75–77, 83, 85–90, 92–93, 95–105,
    107–111, 120, 127, 151, 154–157,
    161, 179
Penna, Elinor Kaine 84
Penn State University 45, 67, 172, 174

Perpich, David 51
Pew Research Center 148
Philadelphia 76ers 59
Philadelphia Eagles 27, 59
Philadelphia Flyers 59
Pinstripe Alley 134–135, 175
Podcast 38, 93, 118, 125, 132–133, 151, 178–179
Polian, Bill 32–33
Portland Trailblazers 36, 173
Posting and Toasting 138–140, 158, 175
Power Plays 15, 85
Print circulation 3, 150
Pro Football Talk 34, 88
Public relations 25, 27, 29, 37, 40, 53, 160, 162, 178

Reds Reporter 123
Reporting scoop 29, 148, 154, 179
Reuters Digital News Report 57, 69–70, 87
Riley, Lori 150, 172
Rosenthal, Ken 158
Rutgers University 26–27
Ryan, Shannon 12, 172

San Diego Padres 63
San Francisco 49ers 3, 34, 173
San Francisco Chronicle 2
San Francisco Giants 3, 63, 66, 120, 122–123, 174
San Jose Sharks 125
Sanserino, Michael 62
Santa Rosa Press Democrat 3
Schecter, B.J. 68
Schefter, Adam 29, 162
Schultz, Jeff 61
Seattle Seahawks 43–44, 155, 173
S.E.C. Country 60
Sethi, Jairaj 90
Sharkspage 125
Shinzawa, Fluto 64–65, 174
Shirley, Daniel 60–61, 174
Silicon Valley 1, 124
Simmons, Myles 34, 173

Simon, Bryce 136
Sirius XM 72
Slater, Anthony 1, 3
Slow Boring 90
Snyder, Audrey 67, 174
Sperber, Jordan 92–94, 96, 100, 104, 159, 175
Sports blogging 117, 121, 123, 133, 136–137, 139, 142, 155–156, 159, 179
SportsCenter 164
Sports gambling 124, 162
Sports Illustrated 16, 51, 53–55, 68, 70, 118, 120, 148, 157, 176
Sports Stories 103–104, 175
Stark, Jayson 55
Stein, Marc 95
Steinberg, Dan 3
Strava 1
Sturm, Bob 73–74, 158–161, 174
Substack Pro 90, 106

Tabeek, Matthew 41–42, 155, 173
Tampa Bay Buccaneers 28, 44–45, 173
Target 153
Tennessee Titans 30, 152, 162, 173
Tesla 84
Texas A&M University 133
The Arena Group 157
The Atlantic 108
The Bookings Institute 134
The Boston Globe 64–65, 172
The Commercial Appeal (Memphis, TN) 132
The Florida Times-Union 26, 32
The Gazette (Cedar Rapids, IA) 72
The Home Depot 153
The Institute for Diversity and Ethics in Sport (T.I.D.E.S.) 15, 178
The Journal News (Westchester, NY) 65
The long tail 149, 165
The Macon Telegraph (GA) 60
The New York Times 2–3, 18, 43, 50–52, 62, 67–68, 70, 77, 85, 95, 105, 124, 148, 161, 173

The Oregonian (Portland, OR) 36
The Ringer 108
The Star-Ledger (Newark, NJ) 26–27
The Strickland 139–140
The Wall Street Journal 11
The Washington Post 69, 120
Thompson, Marcus II 1, 3
Throwbacks 108, 175
TMZ 123
Toy department 6, 13, 66, 180
Tribune Publishing 62, 76
Trump, Donald 51
Twitter 88, 90–91, 118, 129

Uber 95
University of Georgia 60–61, 174
University of Iowa 72, 174
University of Michigan 57, 136, 174
University of North Carolina at Chapel
    Hill 57–58
University of Pittsburgh 56
University of South Carolina 60
University of Tennessee 30
University of Utah 106
Urban, Darren 30–31, 33, 152, 173
Uses and gratifications 2.0 121
Utah High School Activities
    Association 106
Utah Lacrosse Report 106–107, 151,
    159, 175
Uthman, Daniel 53–55

Vanity Fair 124
Vannini, Chris 54
Vardon, Joe 70–71, 174
Vice Sports 96
Vikings Territory 36
Villacin, Adam 103–104
Vox Media 18, 90, 105, 118–120, 122–125,
    127, 134–135, 141–142
Vrentas, Jenny 51–52, 148, 173

Wagner, Laura 141
Wal-Mart 153
WashingtonPost.com 3
Weinreb, Michael 107–109, 120, 175
Weiss, Bari 85
Western, Evan 130, 176
Whole Foods 153
Wilder, Charlotte 120
Windy City Gridiron 123
Wired 149
Wisenhunt, Ken 31
Wojnarowski, Adrian 29, 162
W.N.B.A. 12, 85, 163
Wyatt, Jim 30–31, 33, 152, 162, 173

Yellon, Al 122, 176
Yglesias, Matthew 90
Young, Lindsey 36–37, 173
YouTube 58, 133

Zoom 39, 91

COMMUNICATION, SPORT, AND SOCIETY

Lawrence A. Wenner, Andrew C. Billings, and Marie C. Hardin
General Editors

Books in the Communication, Sport, and Society series explore evolving themes and emerging issues in the study of communication, media, and sport, broadly defined. The series provides a venue for key concepts and theories across communication and media studies to be explored in relation to sport. The series features works building on burgeoning media studies engagement with sport, as well as works focusing on interpersonal, group, organizational, rhetorical, and other dynamics in the communication of sport. The series welcomes diverse theoretical standpoints and methodological tactics seen across the social sciences and humanities. While some works may examine the dynamics of institutions and producers, representations and content, reception and fandom, or entertain questions such as those about identities and/or commodification in the contexts of mediated sport, works that consider how communication about sport functions in diverse rhetorical and interpersonal settings, how groups, families, and teams use, adapt, and are affected by the communication of sport, and how the style, nature, and power relations in communication are wielded in sport and media organizations are particularly encouraged. Works examining the communication of sport in international and/or comparative contexts or new, digital, and/or social forms of sport communication are also welcome.

For additional information about this series or for the submission of manuscripts, please contact the series editors:

Lawrence A. Wenner I Andrew C. Billings I Marie C. Hardin
lwenner@lmu.edu I acbillings@ua.edu I mch208@psu.edu

To order other books in this series, please contact our Customer Service Department:

peterlang@presswarehouse.com (within the U.S.)
orders@peterlang.com (outside the U.S.)

Or browse online by series:

www.peterlang.com

www.ingramcontent.com/pod-product-compliance
Lightning Source LLC
Chambersburg PA
CBHW050652280326
41932CB00015B/2879